CW00828806

Medical style of a new generation

Something Old, Something New

Essays on the TCM Description of Western Herbs, Pharmaceuticals, Vitamins & Minerals

by

Bob Flaws

Blue Poppy Press

Published by:

BLUE POPPY PRESS
1775 LINDEN AVE.
BOULDER, CO 80304

FIRST EDITION
JANUARY, 1991

ISBN # 0-936185-21-X
Library of Congress Catalog card # 90-084989

Printed at Westview Press, Boulder, CO.

This book is printed on archive quality, acid free, recycled paper.

Blue Poppy Press neither suggests nor endorses medical self-care by lay persons. Readers wishing to avail themselves of the treatments contained herein should seek out qualified professional care.

PREFACE

Talking about Chinese medicine in America is not the same as talking about Chinese medicine in China. Chinese medicine in America is a relatively new, alternative health care profession. In China, it is a centuries old tradition. Although native Chinese practitioners have practiced in Chinatowns since the middle of the last century, the first American colleges of acupuncture and Chinese medicine only opened at the end of the 1970s. Therefore, amongst the non-Chinese community, Chinese medicine is a new health care option barely 10 years old.

During the last 10 years, above and beyond conducting our private practices, American practitioners of Chinese medicine have largely devoted our energies to legalizing our profession and creating a professional identity. At present, roughly half of the states of the Union have enacted laws legalizing acupuncture, thus insuring their citizens' right of access to this therapy. Many states have local professional associations and there are a number of national professional associations to which acupuncturists and Chinese medical practitioners may belong. However, it is ironic that just as we are on the verge of establishing our professional identity here in America, the winds of change are already asking us to evolve beyond our assumed boundaries and self-imposed limitations. These are interesting times and the zeitgeist is inexorably moving forward.

Personally, I see the introduction of Chinese medicine to the West as only an intermediary step or link in an evolutionary process. It seems to me that the entire planet is in the throes of developing a planetary economy and a planetary consciousness. It is interesting to watch how closely these two are linked. At the same time, modern Western medicine is more and more perceived by the American public as exorbitantly expensive and not entirely safe. Its therapies too often cause iatrogenesis and its therapists too often lack human vision and warmth. Whatever interest there is here in the United States in Traditional Chinese Medicine (TCM) largely stems from this lack of trust in modern Western medicine and a search for a more humane and holistic, though nonetheless professional approach to medicine.

There are some who would sound the death knell for modern Western medicine. But modern Western medicine is not going to fold its tent and disappear for all its short-comings and faults. Nor should it. Although as TCM practitioners we daily meet the walking wounded who have been hurt and abused by modern Western medicine, modern Western medicine does have good therapies and a lot of insight to offer on its own level. There are also some who would like to see TCM here in the United States gain the same status and support it enjoys in the People's Republic of China. This is also probably not going to happen. Rather, what I envision is a universal New Medicine being shaped out of a combination of modern Western medicine, TCM, and other healing traditions from around the world. These may include Western naturopathy and chiropractic, various bodywork systems, various psychotherapies, clinical nutrition and ecology, homeopathy and homotoxicology, Ayruvedic, Tibetan, and Unani medicines, and indigenous folk remedies and modalities from around the world.

It is possible that, as these alternatives each themselves gain their own professional identity and, in some cases, legal status in the United States, the American health care scene may become a pleuralistic marketplace. To some extent it is that way now. In such a marketplace, the health care consumer may pick and choose one system one time for one complaint and another system another time for another complaint. However, such pleuralism tends to breed competition rather than co-operation on the part of practitioners and confusion in patients. Such confusion, i.e. doubt, undermines the very real effects of faith and placebo. Therefore, I believe the evolution of a universal new orthodoxy is to be preferred to pleuralistic heterodoxy as long as this orthodoxy is enlightened.

I think TCM may play a pre-eminent role in such a universal New Medicine. I believe that it, perhaps more than any other alternative health care system in the world today, is able to supply the ground theory unifying all other medical theories and techniques. As I reiterate over and over again in the following essays, I believe the theory of TCM is both broad enough and wise enough to explain and encompass all other healing modalities. However, to fulfil this mission, American practitioners of TCM must be willing to push the envelope of this system.

I believe that using Chinese medical theory, one can describe any other therapy or medicinal as if it were "Chinese". I also believe that such TCM descriptions allow for more holistic prescribing with less iatrogenesis or side effects -- that such TCM descriptions allow for wiser, whole-person prescribing. Chinese medical theory is a rational system of logic which is ultimately founded on a direct perception of what Aldous Huxley called the perennial philosophy. Although the Marxist government of the People's Republic of China has attempted to expunge as much of this philosophy from TCM as possible, yet it is mystical insight which is the source of this system's vision and the foundation of its logic. And it is precisely a new rational exposition of such perennially valid mystical insight which medicine and indeed society at large so desperately need today.

Be this as it may, if TCM is to fulfil its potential destiny as the midwife to a universal New Medicine, it must itself evolve in four key areas. These are in the domains of theory, therapy, technology, and Spirit. This book is about expanding TCM's materia medica and, therefore, primarily has to do with evolution in therapy. In *Cervical Dysplasia & Prostate Cancer* and also in *Scatology & the Gate of Life*, I have written about possible evolutionary changes in theory and I hope to say more about this in the future. I have included in this volume as well one essay devoted to the theoretical expansion of the *Bu Nei Bu Wai Yin* category of etiological factors. In the future, I hope to have the opportunity of addressing at some length Spirit and TCM. As for technology, already there is work under way relating TCM Patterns (of Disharmony) to Western laboratory findings. Electronic pulse reading machines are being developed for didactic purposes. And there are various computer programs now being written and marketed to help with TCM diagnosis and therapy.

This book is a collection of essays on the methodology of adding new medicinals to the TCM pharmacopeia. As a rational *cum* empirical style of medicine, TCM methodology is based on a logical progression from diagnosis by *Bian Bing* and *Bian Zheng* to a statement of therapeutic principles to the erection of a treatment plan embodying those abstract principles. TCM medicinals are prescribed based both on logical analysis and on empirical efficacy. In a universal New Medicine, where a medicinal comes from is of relatively little importance, except perhaps in establishing that medicinal's TCM description. Whether a medicinal is Chinese or Hottentot is a provincial concern. As we move towards a global economy and consciousness, we are gaining greater and greater access to medicinal substances from around the world. The bottom line is which are the most effective medicinals for a given patient's complaints, not that they come from here or there. Therefore, in order to make rational use of non-Chinese medicinals of proven clinical efficacy, it is important that their "Chinese" descriptions be worked out. If not, the rationality of TCM, which is precisely the most precious thing I believe TCM has to offer to a universal New Medicine, will be lost.

Such new medicinals can come from various sources. They may be non-Chinese herbs from around the world. The TCM pharmacopeia as it presently exists is already made up of scores if not hundreds of herbs which originated in some non-Chinese locale. These include Betelnut from India, *Xi Yang Sheng* or American Ginseng, and a host of other medicinals introduced to Chinese doctors by missionaries Buddhist, Muslim, and Christian, traders from the four directions, soldiers, and tourists. New medicinals may also include Western pharmaceuticals, vitamins and minerals, and homeopathic preparations.

In our modern milieu, even those of us TCM practitioners who decide not to prescribe such non-Chinese medicinals must still develop TCM descriptions of such non-Chinese medicinals if only to better understand their synergism and antagonism with our remedies and their iatrogenic potential. Our modern Western patients are prescribed Western pharmaceuticals by their Western physicians. They buy Western pharmaceuticals over the counter. And they use Western herbs and orthomolecular supplements based on hearsay, the prescription of naturopaths and chiropractors, and the advice of health food store clerks. Although we may write a very classical Chinese prescription for our patients, as soon as these patients leave our office, they may also be prescribed or enticed to take who knows what else. It is incumbent upon us as practitioners of a rational system of medicine to have a rational explanation both for ourselves and our patients of these non-TCM medicinals' effects. Anything less, it seems to me, is like an ostrich with its head in the sand.

This book is not a *Ben Cao*. It is not a materia medica of either non-Chinese herbs or Western pharmaceuticals. Although it does include a small *Ben Cao* of orthomolecular supplements, even this is not categorically complete. The development of a *Ben Cao* of Western and non-Chinese herbs and medicinals is a necessarily slow process dependent on scholarly research, clinical experience, and much thought. Such a *Ben Cao*, when and if it is ever written, will perhaps best be compiled by a number of practitioners and theoreticians working together and there is some talk at the moment of such a combined effort. My intention in publishing this book, however, is to provide an example of the methodology with which we, as a profession, may together write TCM *Ben Cao* for Western pharmaceuticals, herbs, orthomoleculars, and homeopathics.

Busy practitioners may wish for the ease of simply going to a book and looking up the TCM description of Pygeum Africanum or hydrochlorothiazide. On the other hand, I personally have found that the process of working out such TCM descriptions of non-TCM medicinals has greatly honed and expanded my own understanding and ability to do TCM. Therefore, I encourage my readers not to be frustrated by the tantalizing tidbits contained in this meager collection of essays but rather to attempt themselves to generate their own TCM descriptions of non-TCM medicinals with which they come in contact in their own clinical practice. I find this a very useful exercise. Recently Michael Tierra, author of *Planetary Herbology,* wrote me about collaborating with a dozen other practitioners with an interest in this kind of description development. If only one or two scores of practitioners devoted their research and study time to this endeavor, in 20 years we could have these *Ben Cao.*

To do medicine means to be *in practice.* Developing TCM descriptions of non-TCM medicinals is a great way to practice one's TCM. TCM is a system of thought more than it is a collection of medicinals, and the more its practitioners practice thinking within this system, the better practitioners we become. Therefore, we all should take this evolutionary mandate as an opportunity to not only lay the foundations of a New Medicine for the future but to also become more skilful in our current system. Tomorrow is built upon today. I invite us all to put on our thinking caps and *think*.

CONTENTS

A Perennial Spring

The TCM Properties and Uses of St. Johnswort in the Possible Treatment of AIDS And the Universal Applicability of Chinese Medicine

Traditional Chinese Medicine is not valuable because it comes from China. That is completely incidental. Rather, it is valuable because it is a universally valid theory of health and disease. It is a rational and rigorously logical theory which has been developed over not less than 2,500 years during which time its theories and therapies have been validated and refined by empirical experience in clinical practice. Unlike many folk medicines which are equally holistic, Traditional Chinese Medicine is a literate, professional medicine which has proven to be effective in treating a widely diverse gene pool within a heterodox society dispersed over the full range of geographic environments. The universal validity and practicality of Traditional Chinese Medicine has been further proven in the last fifteen years as it has been adopted all over the world. Foreign practitioners studying in China have taken Chinese medicine back to Europe, Africa, India, the Mideast, and North, Central, and South America and have applied it successfully to their own patient populations.

As Traditional Chinese Medicine strives to become recognized as the universal medicine it is, it faces a challenge which it must surmount if it is to be recognized as something other than an exotic import. This challenge is TCM's ability to incorporate the indigenous substances and therapeutic techniques of its adopted homes into its panoply of modalities. If Chinese medicine can add to its materia medica such indigenous medicinals, potentially even including certain Western synthetic drugs, based on its own, intrinsic, rational methodology, then it stands poised to be the progenitor of a truly holistic, rational, planetary medicine. If, on the other hand, Chinese medicine cannot or will not broaden its scope to include all medicinal substances, no matter where or what their origin, it will consign itself to the radical fringes of world health care.

Happily, Chinese medicine has met this challenge before. During the Tang dynasty, many exotic medicinal substances where imported to China by Buddhist missionaries from Southwest Asia and from the Mideast over the Silk Road. Many of these ingredients are now standard "Chinese" medicinals, such as Acacia Catechu (*Er Cha*), Fructus Amomi Cardomomi (*Bai Dou Kou*), Semen Oroxyli Indici (*Mu Hu Die*), and Lignum Aquilariae Agallochae (*Chen Xiang*). This incorporation of foreign ingredients into the Chinese materia medica has continued up to today as evidenced by American Ginseng's being a major factor in the Clipper Ship trade of the eighteenth century and corn silk's being prescribed in Chinese clinics today. In addition, Vietnamese, Korean, and Japanese students of Chinese medicine returning home to their own countries in dynasties past added their indigenous herbs to those that they learned in and imported from China. Although herbal medicine in Japan is still called *Kanpo Yaku*, Han medicine, it is as much a part of Japanese culture as karate and the tea ceremony which also originated in China. Likewise, although Traditional Chinese or Oriental Medicine may always be identified as such in contradistinction to modern Western medicine, we practitioners of this medicine will be parochial if we limit ourselves to only what has been used before or currently in China. Ironically, it is contemporary Chinese practitioners in China who are willing and most engaged in pushing the envelope of so-called Chinese medicine, where the combination of traditional Chinese and modern Western medicine is often simply called *Xin Yi*, New medicine.

This challenge is fraught with difficulties and dangers, but it begins by attempting to describe indigenous medicinals according to the rubric of TCM. If a practitioner can describe a new or non-Chinese medicinal according to the categories of description used in Traditional Chinese Medicine, then that substance can be potentially used by a practitioner of TCM without violating the integrity or logic of our conceptual system. Without such a "traditional Chinese" description, incorporation of a substance into our materia medica is no more than empirical eclecticism. Although some many have no difficulty with this, to me the greatest benefit of Chinese medicine is its combination of proven empirical efficacy with its thoroughly rational, conceptual methodology. Empiricism may cure, but rationality explains and ultimately enlightens, thus educating both practitioner and patient how to live so as to prevent and avoid disease altogether.

Medicinal substances in Traditional Chinese Medicine are described according to several categories of information. A practitioner of TCM needs to know a substance's Taste and Temperature. We also need to know what Meridian Routes it enters. Next we need to know the medicinal's theoretical Functions as stated in the terminology of TCM therapeutic principles. Knowing those, we next need to know its symptomatic Indications. If possible, we should then know or describe its most common or effective Combinations since TCM is based on polypharmacy synergism. As professionals, we also need to know a substance's Contraindications. And finally, we need to know a substance's appropriate Dosage, Preparation, and Administration.

St. Johnswort

St. Johnswort is a medicinal herb which is currently attracting a lot of attention from PWAs (people with AIDS). It is currently being tested both in Europe and America for potentially controlling if not eliminating HIV in infected persons. Many HIV positives are already taking St. Johnswort even before conclusive documentation of its effectiveness. As a doctor of Oriental medicine in America, I regularly treat persons infected with HIV and am often asked if taking St. Johnswort is good or bad according to Chinese medicine. Since this issue is possibly a matter of life and death, I have had to educate myself on St. Johnswort even though it does not appear as an ingredient in any standard Chinese herbal formula of which I am aware. However, if and when I can satisfactorily describe this herb's "Chinese" properties according to the rubric of TCM, then I can advise my patients on its use and even, when appropriate, prescribe it.

First of all, Chinese medicine does recognize a Chinese species of this plant as a medicinal substance. G.A. Stuart in *Chinese Materia Medica, Vegetable Kingdom*, describes Hypericum Chinensis based on an entry in Li Shi-zhen's *Ben Cao Gang Mu*[1]. Its Chinese name is *Jin Zi Cao*. *A Barefoot Doctor's Manual* describes a Hypericum Sampsonii and gives sixteen different Chinese names, none of which is *Jin Zi Cao*[2]. It is listed under *Yuan Bao Cao*.

Although the pictures given for Hypericum Perforatum (St. Johnswort) in Western herbals and for Hypericum Sampsonii in *A Barefoot Doctor's Manual* are essentially identical, not being a botanist, I cannot say how closely these plants are related and, therefore, how likely they are to have the same medicinal properties. However, the indications for *Yuan Bao Cao* are very similar to those given in *Indian Herbology of North*

America for Hypericum Perforati[3]. Therefore, based on the Chinese description of *Yuan Bao Cao* in *A Barefoot Doctor's Manual* and exercising the logic of Chinese medical theory on Western descriptions of St. Johnswort, I think we can describe this herb's properties and actions well enough to pass some professional judgements upon it.

Western herbals, such as *Indian Herbology of North America* and *The Herb Book*[4], say that St. Johnswort is good for the treatment of bronchitis, bedwetting, dysentery and diarrhea, hemoptysis, worms, jaundice, dysuria, turbid urine, hysteria, nervous irritability, and insomnia, especially as menopausal complaints, coccydynia, sciatica, head complaints arising from "watery matters of obstruction of the phlegm of the head"[5], "gases rising to the head"[6], menstrual irregularity, stomach spasm, and phlegm on the chest and lungs. Professional practitioners of TCM know that there are a number of different potential etiologies for diarrhea, bronchitis, insomnia, menstrual irregularity, etc. and that no one herbal ingredient will successfully treat the same named disease due to different etiologies. However, if we look for the single *Bing Yin* or disease factor which might account for varieties of each of these complaints, Damp Heat is a common denominator covering many of these symptoms.

There are Damp Heat Patterns of enuresis, jaundice, dysuria, turbid urine, and coccydynia and sciatica. In addition, Damp Heat can play a part in Stomach disorders and menstrual complaints. Further, Dampness may be associated with bronchitis and phlegmatic Lungs and may also cause headaches. In most cases of Damp Heat, the Dampness is due initially to impaired Spleen Qi's not transporting and transforming Liquids. However, since Dampness is heavy and turbid, it tends to seep down and collect in the Lower Burner. Three *Zang* are responsible for Water metabolism: the Lungs, the Spleen, and the Kidneys. Failure of any one of these Organs' ability to transport and transform Liquids may eventually effect the functioning of the other two, thus giving rise to pulmonary and/or genito-urinary disorders.

The Heat associated with Damp Heat ultimately comes from the *Ming Men Zhi Huo*, but most often more specifically comes from or is due to Liver Heat. The Liver controls the patency of Qi flow which means the free flow of body warmth as well as functional activity. In particular, the Liver is responsible for circulating the Lower Burner. The Liver has an innate tendency towards Excess of Qi and, therefore, Yang. When the passage of this Qi, which is Yang, is occluded by Dampness in the Middle and Lower Burners, this Qi and Heat back up. As the Qi accumulates, it becomes warmer due to pressure and this Heat then is transferred to or becomes entangled with the Dampness, thus giving rise to Damp Heat. Therefore it is said in Chinese medicine that Heat and Dampness are mutually promoting. The fact that this Heat is largely derived from the Liver *vis a vis* the indications of St. Johnswort is evidenced by those other symptoms whose common denominator is Rebellious Qi, Liver Qi, or Ascension of Liver Yang. These include hemoptysis, hysteria, nervous irritability, insomnia, "gas rising to the head" possibly drafting with it Dampness and/or Phlegm thus causing headache and dizziness. Likewise, stomach spasm and menstrual irregularity, dysmenorrhea, menopausal syndrome, and sciatica all also suggest Liver Qi involvement. Alma R. Hutchens supports the opinion that St. Johnswort has a direct and special action on the Liver: "This tea with a small amount of aloe powder is of special influence on the liver..."[7]

Based on my study of St. Johnswort, I would like to advance the following TCM description of it.

Common English names: St. Johnswort, Johnswort, St. John's Grass, Klamath Weed, Tipton Weed

Botanical name: Hypericum Perforatum

Pharmacological name: Herba Hyperici Perforati

Part used medicinally: the aerial parts, i.e. the herb

Taste: Bitter and Sour

Temperature: Cold

Meridian Routes: Liver, Gallbladder, Stomach, Bladder, Intestines

Functions: Clears and eliminates Damp Heat in the Lower Burner
Regulates the Qi and induces downward movement of Blood
Drains downward and leads Stagnation out
Relieves Depression and calms the *Hun*
Benefits the lumbus and stops pain
Kills Worms

Indications: Enuresis, dysuria, turbid urine due to Damp Heat; Damp Heat dysentery and diarrhea; hemoptysis, hematemesis, and epistaxis due to Rebellious Liver Qi and/or Ascension of Liver Yang; jaundice due to Damp Heat; coccydynia, sacroiliac pain, sciatica, and knee pain due to Damp Heat, Stagnant Liver Qi, and Stagnant Blood; headache, dizziness, blurred vision, hysteria, nervous irritability, and insomnia due to Ascension of Liver Yang; menstrual pain, irregularity, and menopausal nervous problems due to Stagnant Heat and Ascension of Liver Yang; and worms. In addition, St. Johnswort activates the Blood and disperses Stagnation when applied topically in the treatment of sprains, strains, fractures, and dislocations.

Combinations: St. Johnswort appears to have similar properties to Radix Achyranthis (*Niu Xi*), Semen Arecae (*Bing Lang*), and Herba Patriniae Heterophyllae (*Bai Jiang Cao*). Like Achyranthes, Herba Hyperici Perforati clears Damp Heat from the Lower Burner, activates and destagnates the Blood, benefits the lumbus and legs, and induces Qi and Yang downwards. Therefore, Achyranthes and St. Johnswort might be advantageously combined in order to strengthen these functions. In particular, St. Johnswort might be added to *San Miao San* for the treatment of Damp Heat low back and leg pain, cystitis, and vaginitis.

Like Semen Arecae, St. Johnswort moves the Qi and promotes urination, drains downward and leads Stagnation out, and also kills Worms. Therefore, it might be profitably combined with Caulis Mutong (*Mu Tong*), Rhizoma Alismatis (*Ze Xie*), and Semen Arecae for the treatment of dysuria and edema due to Excess or with Fructus Immaturus Citri Seu Ponciri (*Zhi Shi*), Radix Saussureae Seu Vladimiriae (*Mu Xiang*), and Rhizoma Coptidis (*Huang Lian*) for the treatment of Damp Heat diarrhea, dysentery, and colitis.

St. Johnswort also shares some characteristics with Herba Patriniae Heterophyllae. These two might be favorably combined for Depressive Heat/Stagnant Blood dysmenorrhea accompanied by a tendency to either vaginitis or cystitis. Likewise, I can imagine combinations of Herba Hyperici Perforati with Cortex Ailanthi Altissimae (*Chun Bai Pi*), Rhizoma Smilacis Glabrae (*Tu Fu Ling*), and Radix Clematidis (*Wei Ling Xian*), to name but several other possibly efficacious combinations with already tried and established Chinese herbs.

Contraindications: Similar to Radix Achyranthis, I would suggest avoiding the use of Herba Hyperici Perforati during pregnancy, in persons suffering from Spleen Deficiency diarrhea or Collapse of Middle Qi, and in cases of loss of astringency due to Lower *Yuan* not consolidating, such as in Kidney

Deficiency spermatorrhea, leukorrhea, and menorrhagia.

Dosage: Michael Tierra in *Planetary Herbology* gives the dose in decoction of Herba Hyperici Perforati as from 3 to 9 grams[8]. *A Barefoot Doctor's Manual* gives the dose in decoction of Herba Hyperici Sampsonii as from 15 to 30 grams. For the remedial treatment of active disorders, I would suggest trying doses from 9 to 30 grams depending upon whether this ingredient were the ruler, minister, servant, or messenger.

St. Johnswort & AIDS

In terms of the treatment of AIDS, the use of St. Johnswort does make some sense. According to the diagnostic methodology of TCM, AIDS is a Latent Evil (*Fu Xie*) of the Warm Disease category. When it becomes active, it manifests as various sorts of Damp Heat Toxins. It may also be said to progress from the inside out, i.e. from the *Xue Fen* or Blood Phase to the *Wei*, although this is by no means absolute, and from below to above. In treating persons who are HIV positive but ARC and AIDS asymptomatic, I stress avoiding anything which might induce or engender the accumulation of Dampness or Heat within the body. Therefore, prophylactic doses of Herba Hyperici Perforati do make some sense as long as it is not taken by persons already Spleen Qi Deficient[9,10]. It has been reported in the AIDS network that overdoses of St. Johnswort cause fatigue and somnolence, possible symptoms of injury to the Spleen Qi. This side-effect can probably be mitigated by combining this ingredient with one or more Spleen-tonifying ingredients to off-set such injury.

Recently there has been a great deal of interest in Compound Qi or crystalline trichosanthin derived from Radix Trichosanthis (*Tian Hua Fen*) as a possible antidote to the AIDS virus.

Considering that AIDS is also a species of Wasting disease and is similar to diabetes in some ways, and considering Radix Trichosanthis' TCM properties, I believe Herba Hyperici Perforati and Radix Trichosanthis might also be profitably combined to create a patent medicine for the suppression or eradication of HIV in infected persons.

Radix Trichosanthis quells Heat and generates Fluids when Fluids have been injured by Heat. It also cools and transforms Hot Phlegm. It dissolves Toxins and expels pus. In addition, it regulates the Qi, moves the Qi downwards, broadens the chest, and soothes irritability. At present, there is a Chinese patent medicine called *Yue Quan Wan*, Jade Spring Pills, composed of one quarter Radix Trichosanthis. This pill is indicated for diabetes or Thirsting and Wasting Disease. Its other ingredients include Radix Puerariae (*Ge Gen*), Radix Rehmanniae (*Sheng Di*), Fructus Schizandrae (*Wu Wei Zi*), and Radix Glycyrrhizae (*Gan Cao*).

Radix Puerariae or Kudzu also nourishes Fluids and alleviates thirst. It stops diarrhea due to Pathogenic Heat but can also be used to treat diarrhea due to Spleen Deficiency when combined with Spleen-tonifying ingredients. Radix Rehmanniae or raw Rehmannia clears Heat and cools the Blood, nourishes the Yin and Blood and generates Fluids, and cools upward blazing of Heart Fire for the treatment of mouth sores, low-grade fevers, irritability, and insomnia. Fructus Schizandrae is an astringent. It helps to stop sweating due to *either* Yin or Yang Deficiency. It relieves chronic cough due to Lung and Kidney Deficiency. It stops diarrhea due to Spleen and Kidney Deficiency, remembering that when diarrhea persists for a long time, Lower *Yuan* becomes weak and loses its ability to consolidate even if the diarrhea was initially due to an Excess Evil. In addition, Schizandra calms the Spirit and treats insomnia and loss of memory. Ted Kaptchuk says Schizandra strengthens the mind's ability to be focused, clear, and determined[11]. It does this by tonifying the *Jing* Essence. Although Bensky and Gamble say Schizandra enters the Lungs and Kidneys, it, in fact, enters all Five *Zang*[12]. Its names translates as Five Flavored Seed meaning that it has all Five Phase energies. Radix Glycyrrhizae not only harmonizes all the other ingredients in this formula and diminishes the possibility of unwanted side-effects, but it also in its own right eliminates Evil Heat, distributing this energy to its proper Organs[13]. Licorice also benefits the Spleen and tonifies the Qi, thus mitigating the Cold effects of Pueraria and Trichosanthes.

For the treatment of AIDS in persons infected with HIV, I have recently begun using the ingredients in *Yue Quan Wan* modified by the inclusion of Herba Hyperici Perforati, Cortex Tabebuiae Impetiginosae (aka Pau D'Arco or Taheebo), Sclerotium Ganodermae, and Rhizoma Smilacis Glabrae.

Pau D'Arco comes from South America and is also currently popular as an immune system strengthener amongst Western herbal users. Although it is not a "Chinese" herb, it merits inclusion in a planetary materia medica and can be described according to the rubric of TCM. It is Sweet, Spicy, and Neutral. It enters the Stomach, Spleen, Bladder, and Liver. It drains Dampness from the Lower Burner. It facilitates the separation of Clear and Turbid, clears and eliminates Damp Heat from the skin, and possibly dissolves Damp Toxins. It has anti-tumor properties and activates the Qi and Blood. It is well combined with Rhizoma Dioscoreae Hypoglaucae (*Bi Xie*).

Sclerotium Ganodermae (*Ling Zhi*) is described in the *Shen Nong Ben Cao* as benefitting Heart Qi, tonifying the Middle Burner, and increasing the eyesight and intelligence. It enters all Five *Zang* and calms the Spirit. Because of the foregoing, I believe we can say that *Ling Zhi* also tonifies the *Jing* Essence. Nowadays in China, *Ling Zhi* is being promoted as having cancer-preventing properties and is used as a tonic for persons

undergoing radiation and chemotherapy. Traditionally it was
mostly used in single ingredient preparations but recently has
begun to show up in compound prescriptions formulated both
in China and in the U.S.

Rhizoma Smilacis Glabrae clears Damp Heat Toxins and also
clears Damp Heat from the skin. It is currently used in China
to treat both chronic and acute syphilis, but especially secondary
and tertiary syphilis. Harris L. Coulter, in *AIDS & Syphilis, The
Hidden Link*, suggests that the AIDS virus and syphilis
treponemes are mutually pathogenic[14]. In fact, there are many
similarities between the signs and symptoms of syphilis and
AIDS. Even if they are not both one and the same disease
mutated by time as Coulter suggests, yet their *Bing Yin* or
etiology and their *Bing Ji* or pathophysiology are, from the
point of view of TCM, remarkably similar. Therefore, I have
included this ingredient based on its specificity as an anti-
syphilitic as well as on its "Chinese" heteropathological
functions.

I call this combination *Fu Fang Yue Quan Ji* or Modified Jade
Spring Preparation. I am currently administering it to some of
my HIV patients as powder steeped in boiling water. Its
composition is as follows:

Radix Puerariae	30 grams
Radix Rehmanniae	30 grams
Radix Trichosanthis	30 grams
Herba Hyperici Perforati	30 grams
Cortex Tabebuiae Impetiginosae	30 grams
Sclerotium Ganodermae	30 grams
Rhizoma Smilacis Glabrae	30 grams
Radix Glycyrrhizae	15 grams
Fructus Schizandrae	10 grams

These herbs are ground separately into a fine powder and then mixed together. The dosage is between 5-10 grams each time, 3 times per day in warm water after meals. For HIV patients who are ARC or AIDS symptomatic, this formula may be modified based on the following suggestions:

For Damp Heat diarrhea, add Radix Pulsatillae (*Bai Tou Weng*), Cortex Fraxini (*Qin Pi*), Rhizoma Picrorhizae (*Hu Huang Lian*) or Rhizoma Coptidis (*Huang Lian*), and other modifications similar to *Bai Tou Weng Tang* (Pulsatilla Decoction).

For skin rash, add Cortex Dictamni Radicis (*Bia Xian Pi*), Semen Cnidii (*She Chuang Zi*), Fructus Tribuli (*Bai Ji Li*), raw Semen Coicis (*Yi Yi Ren*), etc.

For fatigue, add Radix Astragali Seu Hedysari (*Huang Qi*) and Radix Pseudostellariae (*Tai Zi Sheng*).

For weight loss and cachexia with thirst, add Tuber Ophiopogonis (*Mai Men Dong*) and Radix Glehniae (*Sha Shen*).

For nausea and vomiting, add Rhizoma Phragmitis (*Lu Gen*) and Folium Eriobotryae (*Pi Pa Ye*).

For glossitis and stomatitis, add Rhizoma Anemarrhenae (*Zhi Mu*) and Radix Achyranthis (*Niu Xi*).

For the treatment of acute symptoms, the dosages of the individual ingredients should be reduced to one third of the above powdered and encapsulated formula or should be adjusted based on understanding the therapeutic requirements of the presenting signs and symptoms. The prescription is then administered in decoction three times per day, one *Bao* or packet representing a one day dose.

TCM Polypharmacy

The therapeutic method of professional Chinese medicine is the prescription of heteropathic, polypharmacy prescriptions. Describing a single new ingredient is only the beginning of incorporating that ingredient into our materia medica. We must also be able to craft polypharmacy formulae with this ingredient in them. These may be entirely new prescriptions or may be modifications of ancient Chinese formulas. It is still too early to say just how effective the above prescription is for the treatment of HIV positive persons. Its composition is based on traditional Chinese concepts of etiology, disease mechanism, and diagnosis based on both *Bian Zheng* or discrimination of Patterns and *Bian Bing*, discrimination of named disease. Although its methodology is TCM, its ingredients come not only from China but from North and South America as well. By combining ingredients from around the world, we as practitioners begin to prove that Traditional Chinese Medicine is a universally applicable theory of etiology, diagnosis, and therapeutics not limited to a particular culture or dependent upon medicinals peculiar to one country or continent. Only if we non-Chinese practitioners can open our minds in this way, can Chinese medicine evolve to fulfil its potential destiny as the basis of a universally valid, professional holistic medicine, a New Medicine for new times with a two thousand year plus pedigree.

ENDNOTES

1 Stuart, G.A., *Chinese Materia Medica, Vegetable Kingdom*, Southern Materials Center, Inc. Taipei, 1979, p. 211

2 Revolutionary Health Committee of Hunan Province, *A Barefoot Doctor's Manual*, Cloudburst Press, Mayne Isle & Seattle, 1977, p. 223

3 Hutchens, Alma R., *Indian Herbology of North America*, Merco, Windsor, Ontario, 1974, p. 257-260

4 Lust, John, *The Herb Book*, Bantam Books, NY, 1974, p. 344-345

5 Hutchens, op.cit., p. 258

6 Ibid., p. 258

7 Ibid., p. 258

8 Tierra, Michael, *Planetary Herbology*, Lotus Press, Santa Fe, 1988, p. 200

9 *The San Francisco Bay Times*, Vol. 10, No. 8, May, 1989, p. 15

10 *AIDS Treatment News*, San Francisco, #74, Feb. 24, 1989, p. 3; #77, April 21, 1989, p. 3

11 Kaptchuk, Ted, *Product Guide*, Jade Pharmacy, Aptos, CA, 1988, p. 2-9

12 Bensky, Dan & Gamble, Andrew, *Chinese Herbal Medicine, Materia Medica*, Eastland Press, Seattle, 1986, p. 541

13 Sung Hyun Baek, course notes, Oriental Medical Research, Inc., Chicago

14   Coulter, Harris L., *AIDS & Syphilis, The Hidden Link*, North
       Atlantic Books, Berkeley/Wehawken Book Co., Washington,
       DC, 1987

VALIUM

ITS TCM FUNCTIONS, INDICATIONS, & CONTRAINDICATIONS

Diazepam, better known by its brand name Valium, is the most commonly prescribed medication in the United States.[1] It is a tranquilizer intended to relieve mild to moderate anxiety and nervous tension, yet without causing extreme sedation.[2] According to nationally known pharmacist Joe Graedon,

> Without any doubt, your doctor's most popular drug is Valium. This tranquilizer is prescribed as if it were candy. Valium is used to treat everything from stomach-aches and sinusitis to pulled muscles and hemorrhoids. Doctors like to pass this drug off as a muscle-relaxant even though it is probably no more capable of relaxing our muscles than a couple of stiff drinks. They are afraid that if they tell the patient that Valium is a tranquilizer he will be insulted by the implication that the trouble is in his head or that the doctor cannot really cure the problem... For an over-worked doctor, it is easier to prescribe Valium than it is to spend the time to locate the cause of the trouble.[3]

Because Valium is such a commonly prescribed medication, it is reasonable to think that many persons seeking treatment by TCM practitioners either are currently using this drug or resort to it occasionally. Therefore, I think it is important that Western practitioners of TCM have some idea concerning Valium's TCM functions and effects. Jeremy Ross, in *Zang Fu*, has written that, here in the West, we must pay special atten-

tion to iatrogenesis as a *Bing Yin* or disease causing factor due
to Western medication's tendency to cause so many side-
effects.[4] However, before we can adequately take such drug
induced iatrogenesis into account in both our diagnoses and
treatment plans, we must be able to describe, in a rational and
consistent manner, how such drugs do what they do according
to the theories of TCM.

In all the essays contained herein, I have tried to establish a
problem-solving methodology for ascertaining how non-Chinese
medicinals and stimuli work according to TCM theory. This
methodology is based on searching for the common TCM
mechanisms behind both the substance's desired effects and its
possible side effects. By looking for such a TCM common
denominator, I think we can, more often than not, find a
rational and pragmatic TCM explanation for such Western
drugs' action. However, when we attempt such an explanation,
it is extremely important that only information capable of being
gathered by the Four (Methods of) Diagnosis be used in our
logical equation. As a system of thought, TCM is a circle or
loop. Its internal logic is predicated on only certain types of
factual data. Many Westerners attempt to synthesize Chinese
and Western scientific data without realizing that often these
different data are apples and oranges. Western descriptions of
a drug's effects on the limbic system cannot be used in arriving
at a TCM explanation or theory since, in TCM, there is categorically no such concept of a limbic system. TCM is, as it were, a
computer language, and only by using the right commands and
codes can we make the TCM computer work. Attempting to
describe the TCM functions and effects of diazepam or Valium
is an example of this problem-solving methodology.

Because Valium relieves anxiety and nervous tension, we can
say that it has an *An Shen* or Spirit calming function in TCM.
That is fairly obvious and can be ascertained through questioning.

"Did you feel anxious and upset before taking Valium?"
"Yes."
"Do you feel calmer and more at ease now?"
"Yes."

That part is fairly easy. But in Chinese medicine, there are
three ways sedation may be achieved. The first is through
clearing Heat (*Qing Re*). Heat travels up and tends to accumulate in the Heart. Although the Heart needs Righteous Yang,
it should not be the repository of any Evil Heat or Fire.
Rather, this Yang should transform into Light or *Shen Ming*,
Spiritual Brilliance, consciousness. When Heat does accumulate
in the Heart, this disturbs the *Shen* just as if there were a fire
under the emperor's throne. The second method of achieving
sedation is through nourishing the Pure Substances that in turn
nourish the Heart *Shen*. These are Qi, Yang, Blood, and Yin.
Should any of these four become exhausted and, therefore, not
be supplied to the Heart, the Spirit likewise becomes *Bu An*,
similar to a starving person fretting about what will happen to
them. It becomes agitated, nervous, and jumpy. The third
method of calming the Spirit is to physically weigh down or
restrain it. When Yang energy perversely ascends upward, it
may invade the Heart and agitate the *Shen*. In such cases, so-
called heavy sedatives are employed to lower Yang and restrain
its perverse and excessive upward flow. Before we can understand how Valium calms the Shen, we must know whether it
clears Heat, nourishes Pure Substance, or lowers Yang. This
can be ascertained by looking at Valium's side effects.

The natural, expected, and unavoidable side effects of Valium
are drowsiness, lethargy, and unsteadiness of stance and gait.[5]
Drowsiness and lethargy suggest Qi Deficiency, but, in fact,
Valium does not disperse the Qi. Rather, it heavily depresses
Yang. The Clear Yang must arise for there to be *Shen Ming* or
consciousness. If Clear Yang is suppressed, this also causes
clouding or diminution of consciousness and function, remem-

bering that essentially Qi, energy, and *Yi*, awareness are two aspects of a single reality. This also accounts for unsteadiness of stance and gait. The persons feels as if they were going to "black out".

That Valium is a so-called heavy sedative according to TCM's rubric is confirmed by its unusual, unexpected, and less frequent but more serious side effects. These include dizziness, fainting, blurred vision, double vision, slurred speech, and nausea.[6] The first five all suggest lack of Qi Above. Because the Clear Yang is forcefully depressed, the Blood cannot nourish the Brain and sensory Orifices. Thus dizziness, fainting, blurred vision, and slurred speech occur. As for the nausea, this is due to the fact that heavy sedatives tend to injure the Spleen Qi. According to Hong-yen Hsu, "Because minerals, stones, and shells (i.e. heavy sedative medicinals) are detrimental to the spleen and stomach, strong tranquilizers should be used only temporarily."[7] Just as the Clear Yang must ascend to provide energy and nourishment to the Brain and sensory Orifices if there is to be *Shen Ming*, so the Spleen Yang must also ascend the Clear part of the digestate. If Spleen Yang is not permitted to rise unobstructedly, this can cause accumulation of Middle Qi first and then venting upwards of the Stomach Qi experienced as nausea. When something strong is forcefully push down, this pressure will have a tendency to vent itself wherever it can. Since the Stomach Qi is relatively replete in any case, it tends to rebel upwards fairly easily,

This likewise explains the other side effects of Valium: eye pain, glaucoma, susceptibility to infection causing fever and sore throat, and,, paradoxically, acute mental excitement, hallucinations, and rage. These all are due, in this case, to Yang Qi being suppressed. This Yang Qi then vents upwards under increased pressure any way it can. That this venting is associated with eye pain, rage, and throat irritation all suggest that Valium is not a very good choice as a sedative for persons suffering from Depressive Liver Fire Patterns. This is further corroborated by Valium's causing menstrual irregularity and depression in some patients, both of which are most often due to Liver imbalance.

It has been frequently reported to me by patients that Valium at first worked for them as a sedative. But as time went by, they found that the Valium itself produced irritation, excitation, and insomnia. These patients were all suffering from some form of Liver Qi, Depressive Liver Fire, or Liver Fire Entangled with Phlegm. In such persons, heavy sedation may be appropriate in the management of acute crises, but dredging and relaxing the Liver should be the Root principles of treatment, supplemented by clearing Heat when necessary. If, instead, we suppress and therefore compress a congested accumulation of Qi, we will turn it into Fire and Wind which will vent any way they can. Heavy sedation without activation and circulation of the pent-up energy will, over time, only complicate and exacerbate these conditions.

Therefore, taking Valium is somewhat similar to using very heavy quantities of Os Draconis (*Long Gu*), Concha Ostreae (*Mu Li*), or Cinnabaris (*Zhu Sha*) without any other complementary ingredients. In Traditional Chinese Medicine, heavy sedatives are never used alone. Professionally, they are always used in polypharmacy formulas which include other medicinals to clear Heat, dredge the Liver, and return True Yang to its Root, or to nourish Yin and Blood, or to transform Phlegm. One example of such a well crafted traditional Chinese *An Shen* formula incorporating heavy sedatives is *Chai Hu Long Gu Mu Li Tang* (Bupleurum, Dragon Bone, and Oyster Shell Decoction).

In this formula, Radix Bupleuri (*Chai Hu*) dredges and cools the Liver and Stomach. Cortex Cinnamomi (*Rou Gui*) returns True Yang to its Root. In other words, it redirects *Ming Men*

Zhi Huo from the Heart back to the Kidneys. Rhizoma Rhei (*Da Huang*) purges Heat from the *Yang Ming*. Radix Scutellariae (*Huang Qin*) clears Heat and Dampness. Rhizoma Pinelliae (*Ban Xia*) regulates the Qi, clears Heat, transforms Phlegm, and benefits the Spleen. Radix Codonopsis (*Dang Sheng*) or Radix Panacis Ginseng (*Ren Sheng*) support the Spleen so as to ward off incursion by the Liver across the *Ke* or Control cycle. They also protect the Middle Qi from damage by heavy sedatives. Fructus Zizyphi Jujubae (*Hong Zao* or *Da Zao*) likewise tonifies the Spleen and benefits the Qi but also calms the Spirit through nourishing the Heart. Sclerotium Pararadicis Poriae (*Fu Shen*) also benefits the Spleen, transforms Phlegm, harmonizes the Middle, and calms the Spirit through nourishing the Heart. Rhizoma Recens Zingiberis (*Sheng Jiang*) helps to harmonize the Middle, eliminates Dampness, and protects the Stomach from any injurious effect of the other ingredients upon the Stomach/Spleen. To these ingredients are added Dragon Bone and Oyster Shell which are the heavy sedatives. This is a very beautifully crafted formula which in small and moderate doses can be taken over fairly long periods of time without damage from the heavy sedatives.

Valium, on the other hand, has only the heavy property of Dragon Bone or Oyster Shell and cannot be considered, according to TCM theory, appropriate for long-term use. However, it may be usefully employed in conjunction with either acupuncture or Chinese herbal medicine, in which case, these two other therapies may help to round out the total treatment plan and mitigate the side effects of Valium. For instance, Valium might be taken along with the above mentioned *Chai Hu Long Gu Mu Li Tang* for a more immediate, stronger sedative effect during emotional crises. Or, acupuncture might be administered concurrent with the use of Valium to do those things which Valium cannot but which are necessary in order to achieve a harmonious and balanced therapeutic effects. Liver 2 (*Xing Jian*) and Liver 3 (*Tai Chong*) can be used in order to dredge the Liver and clear Liver Heat. Stomach 36 (*Zu San Li*) and Spleen (*San Yin Jiao*) can be used to support the Spleen, harmonize the Stomach, regulate Ascension and Descension, and to nourish the Blood and Yin. Pericardium 7 (*Da Ling*) or Pericardium 8 (*Lao Gong*) can be used to further clear Heat. And Stomach 40 (*Feng Long*) and Conception Vessel 12 (*Zhong Wan*) can be used to transform Phlegm when necessary. In this way, Valium would directly suppress ascendant and disturbing Yang, while the acupuncture would treat the Root causes for such Perverse Ascendancy. Then, as soon, as the emotional crisis was under control, only the acupuncture might be continued to consolidate the therapeutic effect. For persons with a long-term dependency on Valium, regulation of Ascension and Descension is a major therapeutic concern.

In terms of using Valium in a more discriminating way based on TCM theory, I think we can say that it is more appropriate for mental agitation due to Heart Fire without a substantial Liver Qi component. For instance, lowering Flaring of Deficiency Heart Fire in persons uncomplicated by Liver Qi Patterns should not create particular pressure from pent-up Yang. Whereas, in a person whose Pattern is Liver Fire and Phlegm, suppression of Yang only causes further implosive Transformative Heat. Also, Valium should be used with care in persons suffering from Stomach/Spleen Deficiency. Even more care should be exercised in persons suffering from Prolapse of Middle Qi or Collapse of Yang. Obviously, no one should take Valium who suffers from Heart Qi, Heart Yang, or Heart Blood Deficiency. All such persons do typically experience some degree of anxiety and nervousness, but these persons would be likely to experience further fatigue, lethargy, double vision, slurred speech, unsteady gait, and even syncope.

Western synthetic drugs are extremely empirically efficacious when compared to traditional "herbal" medicinals. Sometimes, such fast acting therapy is appropriate and Western drugs can fill this need. However, when Western MDs admit that the method of Valium's action is "not established... present thinking is that it *may* reduce the activity of certain parts of the limbic system,"[9] it becomes obvious that Western medicine itself lacks an adequate theoretical basis for the wise and humane discrimination of many of its medicinals. Traditional Chinese medical theory, on the other hand, can, in more instances than not, explain in both rational and pragmatic terms the function and properties of such Western medicinals in a way which makes their use all the more discriminating.

There is a story amongst Buddhist doctors about Jivaka, King of Physicians, who lived at the same time as Lord Buddha and was His doctor. One day when Jivaka was a student, his guru asked his assembled pupils to go out and bring back whatever they could find which had no conceivable medical use. Some students returned with full baskets; others with only a few items. But Jivaka returned at the end of the day empty handed. When his teacher chided him for failing to find even one thing which could never be used as medicine, Jivaka replied that when he questioned the properties and therefore the functions of each and every thing he met, he realized that everything might, in some certain circumstances potentially be used as medicine -- that there is nothing under the sun that can be eliminated *a priori* from a potential materia medica. Jivaka'a guru praised his student's insight and said that he alone had passed that day's test.

Likewise, if practitioners of Traditional Chinese Medicine defend our practice on the grounds that it is more "natural", we are eventually asking for an ontological argument we cannot win. Already, far-thinking MDs such as Larry Dossey have questioned the fallacy of this argument within holistic medicine.

In spite of a profound personal sympathy for many
of the leavening influences wrought by the holistic
health care movement, I must lovingly chastise it and
wish upon it a philosophical maturity it has yet to
attain. In many ways it has strained at a gnat and
swallowed a camel. Its opportunity as a truly transformative power will wither as long as it recreates
the same basic philosophical errors of the present
system.

The fundamental issues do not, after all, hinge on
pills, pesticides, x-rays, or who does what to whom.
I trust it is clear from earlier chapters that we all
have roots in the universe; that interpenetration of
all matter is the rule; and that the dividing line
between life and nonlife is illusory and arbitrary.
There is only one valid way, thus, to partake of the
universe -- whether the partaking is of food, water,
the love of another, or, indeed, a pill. That way is
characterized by reverence -- a reverence born of a
felt sense of participation in the universe, of a
kinship with all others and with all matter. Seen
against the scope of a universal interpenetration,
arguments over pills and herb teas, or about organic
versus artificial therapies, begin to sound like the
banter of children.[10]

If Nature equals the phenomenal world, then everything is co-
equally natural. Many traditional Chinese medicinals are
processed and manufactured substances, such as Massa Medica
Fermentata (*Shen Qu*) and powdered Pyritum (*Zi Ran Tong*)
which has to be soaked in vinegar and set to dry seven times
before it is ready to be used as a medicinal. *Secret Shaolin
Formulae for the Treatment of External Injury*[11] contains numerous prescriptions which require quite extensive and exacting
manufacturing processes that obviously are aimed at chemical
transformation of their constituents. The processing of Fructus
Praeparatus Zizyphi Jujubae (*Hei Zao*), aka Black Dates, and

the processing of Radix Praeparatus Aconiti Carmichaeli (*Fu Zi*) are further cases in point. And, in any case, we cannot turn back the hands of time. Synthetic and processed medicinals are a *fait accompli* in modern times.

The issue is, first, to use such potent medicinals only at the higher end of a hierarchy of increasingly more forceful and speedy interventions. In cases which truly do require such quick and forceful treatment, modern synthetic medicinals clearly do save lives and alleviate unnecessary suffering. Secondly, and perhaps even more importantly, we must develop a wiser theory for the administration of such heroic treatments. I believe the theory of Traditional Chinese Medicine can provide such a conceptual system and thus could be the foundation of a planetary medicine for the twenty-first century.

ENDNOTES

1   Graeden, Joe, *The People's Pharmacy*, Avon, NY, 1977, p. 4

2   Long, James W., M.D., *The Essential Guide to Prescription Drugs*, 4th Edition, Harper & Row Publications, NY, 1985, p. 253

3   Graeden, op. cit., p. 316

4   Ross, Jeremy, *Zang Fu, The Organ Systems of Traditional Chinese Medicine*, 2nd Edition, Churchill Livingstone, Edinburgh, 1988, p. 44

5   Long, op.cit., p. 254

6   Ibid., p. 254

7   Hsu, Hong-yen & Hsu Chan-shin, *Commonly Used Chinese Herb Formulas With Illustrations*, OHAI, LA, p. 339

8   Long, op.cit., p. 254

9   Ibid., p. 253

10   Dossey, Larry, M.D., *Space, Time, and Medicine*, Shambhala, Boulder, CO, 1982, p. 214-215

11   De Chan, *Secret Shaolin Formulae for the Treatment of External Injury*, trans. by Zhang Ting-liang & Bob Flaws, Blue Poppy Press, Boulder, CO, 1987

PREDNISONE

ITS TCM FUNCTIONS, INDICATIONS, AND CONTRAINDICATIONS

Harris L. Coulter, in *A Divided Legacy: A History of the Schism in Medical Thought*, categorizes all medicine into two fundamental methodologies: rational and empirical[1]. Rational medicine is based on theories and principles and is practiced according to logical concepts. Empirical medicine is based on the practical, clinical experience that certain remedies work in certain, seen before situations. Most medicines, in fact, are a combination of both rationally applied theories supported and tempered by empirical clinical experience. Some medicines are mostly or primarily empirical, such as classical homeopathy which grew out of a deliberate rejection of the rationality of Scholastic medicine. Other medicines are heavily rational, such as Galenic medicine, Ayurveda, Unani, Tibetan medicine, and Traditional Chinese Medicine. Although empiricism cures, rationality explains how and why. It is my opinion that the best medicine is one which has a profound and elaborate conceptual basis but whose theories and therapies have been proven by extensive empirical experience. Within the world today, I believe Traditional Chinese Medicine is the most mature, professional, and universally applicable, holistic medicine available.

Traditional Chinese Medicine is not just a collection of folk

remedies and empirical therapies. Although Chinese medicine
does have a vast panoply of well proven therapeutic modalities
and a large materia medica, the single most important part of
Chinese medicine is its universally applicable theories of
disease, diagnosis, and treatment. Even if not a single Chinese
herb were available here in the West, Chinese medicine could
still have a profound impact on the practice of Western
medicine through its theory alone. Although modern Western
medicine still holds sway as this century's most prominent
medicine, there is a growing sense that Western medicine lacks
the conceptual sophistication to wisely discriminate the application of its heroic modalities. Western synthetic medicines are
extremely empirically effective but often cause too many and
severe side effects. All too often in reading descriptions of
Western drugs, its practitioners themselves admit that they do
not know how or why these medicines work.

Chinese medicine, on the other hand, is based on such general
and universal concepts that its theories can, more often than
not, provide a clearer explanation and understanding of
Western pharmaceuticals than can Western science. Chinese
medicine's ability to more comprehensively and humanely
describe the functions of such a frequently prescribed Western
drug as Prednisone proves its universal applicability as a
conceptual system of thought and its superior clinical wisdom.
This system of thought can describe, in a rational and clinically
pragmatic manner, the impact of *any* substance, environment,
or even activity on any given individual regardless of whether
that stimulus comes from or is already known in China.

Prednisone

Prednisone, an adrenocortical steroid, is not a traditional
Chinese medicinal. However, by exercising the logic of

Traditional Chinese Medicine, we can describe its functions and impact on the human organism just as if it were Ginseng or Licorice. This takes a bit of sleuthing, but this Sherlockian endeavor is well worth the effort both in terms of clinically useful knowledge and in establishing a methodology for extending the applicability of Chinese medical concepts to potentially all stimuli encountered in all lands, climates, and cultures.

According to Dr. James W. Long, M.D., Western medical practitioners prescribe Prednisone for the symptomatic relief of inflammation in any tissue. It is used primarily in the management of serious dermatological problems, bronchial asthma, enteritis, ulcerative colitis, and various types of rheumatic disorders, such as arthritis, bursitis, and tendonitis. According to Western medical science, the method of this drug's action is not completely understood, and prolonged use of this drug causes a number of potentially very serious side-effects. The effect of this medication is purely symptomatic and it does not correct the underlying disease process[2].

In attempting to establish Prednisone's traditional Chinese functions, we can begin by looking for a common TCM *Bing Yin* or disease causing factor in the above conditions for which Prednisone is prescribed. The one *Bing Yin* that I find potentially common to varieties of each of the above mentioned pathological conditions is *Feng* or Wind, remembering that Wind can be either Internally or Externally generated and that ultimately Wind is nothing other than Qi. There are Wind-related *Zheng* or Patterns of various dermatological lesions; there are Wind complicated *Bi Zheng* or rheumatic complaints; there are Wind induced varieties of asthma; and there are Intestinal Wind species of colitis and enteritis. Therefore, I think we can say that Prednisone is similar in function to such Chinese medicinals as Herba Ephedrae (*Ma Huang*), Herba Seu Flos Schizonepetae (*Jing Jie*), and Radix Ledebouriellae

Sesloidis (*Fang Feng*).   These herbs are all Spicy Warm,
Surface-relieving medicinals.   They likewise can be used for
Lung problems, skin problems, musculoskeletal problems, and
Schizonepeta and Ledebouriella for Intestinal problems.

All the above three Chinese medicinals are dispersing in nature.
They cause the dispersion of Qi from the Inside of the body to
the Outside through the dispersing function of the Lungs. This
dispersing function is also related to the *Wei Qi* or *Wei Yang*
which is controlled by the Lung but whose production involves
the Intestines and Kidney Yang or the *Ming Men Zhi Huo*. All
three of these medicinals are Yang in nature and can cause
exhaustion and consumption of Yin as evidenced by their being
contraindicated in cases of Blood and Yin Deficiency. Ephe-
dra, in particular, catalyzes the release of *Jing Qi* which then is
liberated through the Surface as *Wei Yang*, ultimately leaving
the Kidneys depleted. Prednisone, likewise, has these same
characteristics and drawbacks which become clear if we look at
its Western medical contraindications and published side
effects.

Again according to Dr. James W. Long, the possible side effects
of Prednisone are edema, increased perspiration, increased
appetite and peptic ulcers, acid indigestion, muscle cramping
and weakness, irregular menstruation, acne, hirsutism, reactivation of tuberculosis, mental and emotional disturbances,
increased blood pressure, increased susceptibility to infection,
thrombophlebitis, pulmonary embolism, and worsening of
glaucoma, eye infections, and hyperthyroidism. Prednisone
should be used sparingly after sixty years of age and preferably
in everyone for only short periods of time. Moderate overdoses can cause edema, swelling of the extremities, facial flushing,
nervousness, skin irritation, and weakness. Large overdoses can
cause severe headaches, convulsions, heart failure, and emotional and behavioral disturbances. When taking Prednisone, a high
protein diet is advised and smoking may make the expected

actions of this drug all the more pronounced. Whereas, the following Western drugs may decrease the effects of Predni-sone: Inderal, Dilantin, Chloral Hydrate, and barbiturates. Other Western drugs, such as tricyclic antidepressants, aerosol asthma sprays such as Alupent, diuretics such as Lasix, and various vaccines, may cause serious complications and side effects by potentizing the negative effects of Prednisone[3]. All of the above can be well explained by Chinese medical theory.

Prednisone induced edema is due to its use dispersing Lung Qi and ultimately making the Lungs incapable of properly trans-porting and descending Water. This leads to moon-like swelling of the face, as in drug induced Cushing's Syndrome, and swelling of the extremities. Increased perspiration is due to Prednisone's dispersing the *Wei Qi* so that it is no longer able to close the *Qi Men* or pores. Increased appetite, acid indiges-tion, and peptic ulcers are due to Prednisone's exhausting the Yin, which in such cases means Stomach Yin. Muscle cramping and weakness have to do with Prednisone's exhaustion of the Qi and Blood. The Qi cannot provide the motive power for movement and the Blood fails to nourish the *Jin Mai* or Sinews and Vessels. This is a species of drug-induced *Wei Zheng* or Flaccidity Pattern. Irregular menstruation, likewise, has to do with exhaustion of the Blood and the creation of Deficiency Heat. If the period comes early, it is due to Heat. If it comes late, it is due to Insufficient Blood. If there us *Beng*, it is due to the Qi's being so weak that it is incapable of holding the Blood. If there is *Lou*, this is again due to Deficiency Heat and weak Qi. Acne is due to overstimulation of the *Ming Men Zhi Huo* leading to Stomach Heat rising to the Lungs accompanied by Yin Deficiency of the Lungs. Hirsutism has to do with Blood being dispersed upwards according to the *Nei Jing*. Reactivation of TB is due to Yin Deficiency of the Lungs. Mental and emotional disturbances have to due with parching of the Viscera leading to agitation of the *Shen*. Increased blood pressure is due to a generalized skewing of the Yin Yang balance with Yin becoming insufficient to hold Yang in check. Yang, therefore, rises up and outward. Increased susceptibility to infection specifically means increased susceptibility to *Wen Bing* or Warm infectious diseases as evidenced by the fact that vaccinations for Western-named *Wen Bing*, such as measles and yellow fever, may provoke fatal active cases of these in persons on Prednisone. Thrombophlebitis suggests the inability of the Lungs to descend the Qi and, therefore, control the Blood in the lower half of the body. The symptoms of pulmonary embolism are sudden shortness of breath, pain in the chest, coughing, and hemoptysis. These symptoms point to Chest *Bi* or Obstruction due to exhaustion of *Zong* or Chest Qi.

The fact that Prednisone should not be taken by persons over sixty is due to such persons already being Yin Deficient due to age. Likewise, smoking disperses Lung Qi and exhausts Lung Yin and, therefore, would naturally exacerbate the effects of Prednisone. A high protein diet, on the other hand, is nourishing to the Yin and would tend to offset Yin depletion due to Prednisone. Inderal, Dilantin, Chloral Hydrate, and barbiturates are all Western sedatives and so would naturally offset the Yang-exacerbating, Spirit- agitating effects of this drug. On the other hand, tricyclic antidepressants, aerosol asthma sprays, and diuretics all disperse the Qi and would synergistically potentize Prednisone's Qi dispersing function even more.

Cushing's Syndrome is "A constellation of clinical abnormalities due to chronic exposure to excess cortisol (the major adrenocorticoid) or related corticosteroids."[4] It is an often encountered iatrogenic complication of prolonged Prednisone administration. Its symptoms are the moon face mentioned above; truncal obesity with prominent supraclavicular and dorsal cervical fat pads, the so-called buffalo hump; slender distal extremities; muscle wasting and weakness; thin, atrophic skin with poor wound healing, easy bruising, and purple striae on the abdomen; hypertension; renal calculi; osteoporosis; glucose intolerance; psychiatric disturbances; cessation of linear growth in children; and menstrual irregularities in females. Most of these side effects we have discussed above. The buffalo hump is, in Chinese medicine, an accumulation of Dampness and Phlegm that the Lungs are not able to clear and descend. It is a species of Upper Swelling. Easy bruising and poor wound healing are due to Qi Deficiency, in this case Qi being unable to hold the Blood and consolidate the Surface. Purple abdominal veins suggest Stagnant Blood; while kidney stones (*Shi Lin*) are due to Stagnation and fulmination of Damp Heat Phlegm possibly complicated by Stagnant Blood. Cessation of linear growth in children is due to Kidney depletion and consumption of Yin, as is osteoporosis.

Chinese Descriptions of Prednisone

Prednisone is used in China by practitioners of Western medicine. Therefore, traditional Chinese doctors have been called upon to manage and treat its side-effects and the few references to Prednisone in the Chinese TCM literature confirm the above description and discussion of Prednisone. Dr. Ji Chuan Wong, writing in *Zhejiang Zhong Yi* (the TCM journal of Zhejiang Province), says that steriods may be tentatively classified in TCM as warming and tonifying the Kidney Yang. Further, Dr. Ji Chuan Wong goes on to say that long term usage leads to Yin Deficiency and Ascension of Yang followed by Yin Deficiency and Yang Collapse (*Yang Tuo*)[5]. Here I would only argue that Prednisone should not be thought of as a *Bu Yang* ingredient such as Cornu Cervi (*Lu Rong*). It has no true or Righteous tonifying effect. Rather it inflames or activates the Yang. This propels the Qi and thus opens up Obstruction and Stagnation which otherwise cause pain and inflammation. Dr. Ji Chuan Wong goes on to say that cessation of its use causes diminution of the *Ming Men Zhi Huo* and

Superior Floating of Deficient Yang. This then is followed by separation of Yin and Yang.

In an abstract appearing in *Shanghai Zhong Yi Yao Zha Zi*, 235 cases of intractable, recurrent nephrosis were treated with corticosteroids and a marked increase in Yin Deficiency was noted in these patients following steroid therapy[6]. Dr. Ma You Da treats steroid-induced Cushing's Syndrome with *Yi Guan Jian* (One Stack Decoction) which he prescribes for Liver Kidney Yin Deficiency/Stomach Yin Deficiency[7]. And Dr. Zou Yun Xiang says, "steroid induced Cushing's syndrome is the result of the dysfunction of 'ascension, descension, entering, and leaving'. The *Qi Fen* is injured first. Then *Xue Fen* is involved in the chronic stage, changing the Qi, Blood, and *Jing* into Wet Turbid Phlegm/ Stasis-ecchymosis, blocking the Organs, the *Luo Mai*, the Flesh and the Skin[8]."

In Chinese medicine it is said, *Bai Bing Jie Sheng Yu Qi*, hundreds of diseases arise from disorders of the Qi. If the Lungs are stimulated to over-disperse, eventually they become Qi exhausted as well as Yin Deficient. Descension is largely controlled by the Lungs and when Ascension and Descension become disordered, the Clear and the Turbid are not separated. This causes retention of Damp Turbidity and Phlegm. Rebellious Qi and accumulation of Evil Yin eventually lead to Qi and, therefore, Blood Stagnation. This then causes a complicated scenario which may be hard for any medicine to treat. In addition, since each patient has their own idiosyncratic, constitutional imbalances and predisposition, these explain why some patients experience more or less of certain side-effects.

Case History

The following case history exemplifies the negative side effects
of Prednisone and their correction with Traditional Chinese
Medicine. The patient was a 13 year old boy whose major
complaint was colitis. This had been diagnosed 9 months
previous to his first visit with me after another 3 months of
problems. The boy had been prescribed Prednisone which
initially had controlled his symptoms, but which now was not
working very well. When I saw the boy, he had been having
diarrhea 2-3 times per day with some bright red bleeding and
some tenesmus. The stools were chocolate brown and half-
formed but not mucousy. This current flare-up had begun six
weeks earlier precipitated by a bout of "stomach flu". He had
been hospitalized for 12 days because of blood and fluid loss
and he was currently anemic. His face was pale, he had the
typical Cushing's Syndrome moon face, and he was lethargic
and fatigued. His urine was darker than normal and a little less
in volume than normal. He was slightly photophobic, his
muscles were tight, and he experienced a little numbness in his
extremities. His tongue was dull red with a grayish yellow,
slightly excessive, turbid coating. It was not fluted or particularly swollen. His pulse was very fast and slippery. Fried foods,
oily foods, such as peanuts, spicy foods, and stress all made this
young man's condition worse.

My TCM diagnosis at that time was colitis due to Damp Heat
and Qi Congestion with some Blood Deficiency due to loss of
Blood and Body Fluids. Therefore, I prescribed *Bai Tou Weng
Tang Jia Jian*[9] (Modified Pulsatilla Decoction) with the addition
of Radix Angelicae Sinensis (*Dang Gui*) to tonify the Blood,
Radix Saussureae Seu Vladimiriae (*Mu Xiang*) to regulate the
Qi, and Radix Sanguisorbae (*Di Yu*) and Radix Rubiae (*Qian
Cao*) to stop the bleeding. After 7 days, the patient's father
reported that, although his son's stools were still loose, he was

doing better. In fact, the consistency of the stools was more watery, but there was no bleeding, urgency, or abdominal cramping. His bowel movements came twice per day and the boy was cheerful. Because the bleeding had stopped, I deleted Sanguisorba and Rubia. Instead, I added Semen Plantaginis (*Che Qian Zi*), popped Semen Coicis (*Yi Yi Ren*), and Rhizoma Atractylodis (*Cang Shu*) to seep Dampness from the Lower Burner. In addition, I added Radix Paeoniae Albae (*Bai Shao*) to more effectively tonify the Blood and relax the Liver and Radix Puerariae (*Ge Gen*) to strengthen the prescription's anti-diarrheal effect. One week later, the patient reported that he had not had diarrhea for a week. There was some "gas" pain in his abdomen, but otherwise he was feeling pretty good. I added Fructus Seu Semen Amomi (*Sha Ren*) to relieve the gas by helping Saussurea activate and regulate the Qi in the Intestines and represcribed the formula for another week. Sticking with this same prescription, I represcribed it again 2 more times for 1 week each time. During these 3 weeks, the boy had diarrhea only the day after he skipped his herbs. Also during these 3 weeks, his Western MDs reduced his Prednisone and postponed the surgery they had scheduled. Originally, recognizing the drug induced Cushing's Syndrome, they had decided it would be better to remove the colon than to keep the boy on Prednisone.

Approximately 2 months on Chinese herbal medicine, the boy experienced intense abdominal pain and hematuria. X-ray examination revealed kidney stones in his ureters. The MDs administered Demerol for the pain and suggested lots of liquids. As mentioned above, kidney stones are a potential side effect of Prednisone. At first, the Western doctors told the parents that the Chinese herbs had possibly caused the stones and advised that the boy discontinue them. Later, another doctor admitted the stones were steroid induced. While the boy was off his Chinese herbal medicine, his watery diarrhea returned. After consulting with me, I adjusted his formula by deleting Pueraria and Amomum and added Spora Lygodii (*Jin Sha Teng*), Herba Lysimachia (*Jin Qian Cao*), Rhizoma Imperatae (*Bai Mao Gen*), Herba Cirsii Japonici (*Da Ji*), and charred Fructus Gardeniae (*Zhi Zi*) to break the stones, promote urination, and stop the bleeding. As soon as the boy went back on the herbs, his diarrhea stopped, he felt much better, and there was no bleeding from either Yin orifice.

A few days later, the boy came in for me to look at his tongue and check his pulse. (He lived 30 miles away and was in school and, therefore, a lot of my up-dating of his formula had to be done over the phone.) His tongue was redder and wetter, although the coating was not as thick, nor was it grayish yellow. His pulse was quite fast but not as slippery and was also wiry down deep in the *Chi* positions. Feeling that at the moment Heat was more prominent than Dampness and that there was some Stagnation of Heat and Blood due to Damp Heat Entanglement, I took the standard *Bai Tou Weng Tang* formula and added to it Flos Lonicerae (*Jin Yin Hua*), Radix Paeoniae Rubrae (*Chi Shao*), Herba Patriniae (*Bai Jiang Cao*), and Rhizoma Imperatae (*Bai Mao Gen*). This eliminated any trace of bleeding and any abdominal pain. We continued with this prescription for 1 week. During this week, the boy experienced exacerbation of emotional stress due to family tensions which immediately precipitated some loose stools and a little bit of bleeding. The next time I represcribed herbs for this boy, I deleted the Lonicera and Red Peony, added back in the Sanguisorba, Rubia, Saussurea, Pueraria, Atractylodis, and Coix and also added fried Radix Dioscoreae (*Shan Yao*) and fried Semen Euryalis (*Qian Shi*). These last 2 ingredients were meant to strengthen the astringency of the Kidney Qi which I surmised had become weak due to both the Prednisone and the long duration of the disease.

For several weeks the boy and his family have continued to request this prescription. He feels quite good. There is no

bleeding, diarrhea, or cramps. He is having 1 bowel movement
per day. His Prednisone is down to 20 mg. per day from the 50
he was taking when he first came in to see me and his doctors
are hoping to reduce it further in the next week or eliminate it
entirely. In general, the boy is doing well, surgery has been
postponed indefinitely, and he has learned how to adjust his
diet and how to deal with stress more effectively. In the future,
I plan to change his guiding herbal formula from *Bai Tou Weng
Tang* to *Gui Zhi Tang* (Ramulus Cinnamomi Decoction)[10] with
the intention of strengthening the Spleen, harmonizing the
Stomach, facilitating the separation of Clear from Turbid, and
restoring the True Fire of the Kidneys to its Root. This may
have to be supplemented for a while with *Xiang Lian Wan*
(Saussurea and Coptis Pills) to ensure patency of Qi and to
clear persistent Evil Heat. However, I have full confidence that
Traditional Chinese Medicine can bring a happy conclusion to
this case.

Conclusion

Knowing how to categorize a drug such as Prednisone and
understanding its functions according to the theories of TCM, a
practitioner of Traditional Chinese Medicine has the potential
option of including this medicinal amongst their materia medica
(depending upon the law of the land and their knowledge of its
technical prescription). It makes no conceptual difference that
this medicinal is a synthetic drug discovered in the West.
Traditional Chinese Medicine is called herbal medicine, but, in
fact, it uses ingredients from all three kingdoms and has used
manufactured and processed medicinals for centuries[11]. Any
medicinal substance from any source may conceivably be added
to our materia medica without doing damage to our rational
methodology *if* we can describe it according to TCM's criteria
of categorization. In terms of Prednisone, it might be safely

and well employed in the treatment of Wind-induced dermatoses, rheumatic conditions, and Intestinal disorders but only short-term and only in patients with relatively robust Blood and Yin. This definitely would limit this drug's administration compared to its current, relatively indiscriminate prescription. By discriminating the use of Prednisone based on such a "Chinese" diagnosis, it might be more effective in those to whom it is given and doctors might avoid unnecessary side effects in contraindicated patients. Chinese medicine has always used certain very powerful, dispersing, potentially toxic ingredients, such as Radix Phytolaccae (*Shang Lu*), Semen Pharbitidis (*Qian Niu Zi*), and Radix Euphorbiae Kansui (*Gan Sui*). The key to the use of such potentially harmful medicinals' safe employ is their discriminating use based on differential diagnosis and a discrimination of Root and Branch.

Some Western practitioners of Traditional Chinese Medicine may refuse to even consider the incorporation of Western medicinals into "our" materia medica, and I am not saying that we should rush out and add Prednisone to our clinical repertoire even if we legally could. I am saying that Chinese medicine is not valuable because it is Chinese. It is valuable because its theory is so universally applicable that it can describe the medical impact of potentially anything on anybody. In China, the movement to create a synthesis between traditional Chinese and modern Western medicine is well afoot where this combination is often referred to simply as *Xin Yi* or New medicine. As we move into the twenty-first century, a new, global medicine must emerge transcending the cultural limitations of all previous medicines as we move towards a global community. Purists and converts may emotionally cling to parochial styles, but the larger community and the zeitgeist itself demands a synthesis and further medical evolution. Traditional Chinese Medicine has the theory which could be the foundation of a truly new and *superior* medicine utilizing both naturally occurring and synthetic medicinals from a planetary materia medica. We Western practitioners of TCM could be the progenitors of such a New Medicine in the West, but only if we open our minds and demonstrate Chinese medicine's ability to encompass the sum total of human medical experience. I believe Chinese medical theory has this ability, but it is up to us to prove it.

ENDNOTES

1   Coulter, Harris L., *A Divided Legacy: A History of the Schism in Medical Thought*, Weehawken Book Co., Washington, DC, 1975

2   Long, James W., *The Essential Guide to Prescription Drugs*, Harper & Row Publishers, NY, 4th Edition, 1985, p. 677

3   Ibid., p. 677-681

4   *The Merck Manual*, Robert Berkow, ed., Merck, Sharp, & Dohme Research Laboratories, Rahway, NJ, 13th Edition, p. 1273

5   *Ji Chuan Wong*, Zhejiang Zhong Yi, Hangzhou, #3, 1985, p. 105

6   *Shanghai Zhong Yi Yao Zha Zi*, Shanghai, #11, 1985, p. 11

7   Ma You Da, *Shanghai Zhong Yi Yao Zha Zi*, op. cit., p. 136

8   Zou Yun Xiang, *Yi An Xuan (Choice Medical Prescriptions)*, p. 37-41

9   Ingredients of *Bai Tou Weng Tang*:   Radix Pulsatillae, Rhizoma Coptidis, Cortex Phellodendri, Cortex Fraxini

10   Ingredients of *Gui Zhi Tang*: Ramulus Cinnamomi, Radix Paoniae Albae, Rhizoma Zingiberis Recentis, Radix Glycyrrhizae, Fructus Zizyphi Jujubae

11   Temple, Robert, *The Genius of China*, Simon & Schuster, NY, 1986, p. 127-131

BACTRIM/SEPTRA

ITS TCM PROPERTIES, FUNCTIONS, INDICATIONS, & CONTRAINDICATIONS

Septra is a compound drug manufactured by Burroughs Wellcome Ltd. It is composed of sulfamethoxazole and trimethoprim. This combination is also commonly marketed as Bactrim by Roche. Western MDs prescribe Septra or Bactrim for the treatment of otitis media, bronchitis and pneumonia, and infections of the intestinal and urinary tracts. Both sulfamethoxazole and trimethoprim are anti-microbial agents in Western medicine and this may lead some practitioners of Chinese medicine to assume that they are Cold in nature and clear Heat. However, based on my experience and the exercise of TCM logic, I do not think this is the case. In fact, attempting to describe the TCM functions and properties of this Western compound drug underscores the important fact that each such Western drug must be described individually in TCM. No blanket assumptions regarding classes of Western drugs can or should be made regarding their traditional Chinese functions and properties. Rather, the individual actions of each drug must be worked out through assessing that drug's intended action with its side effects and other idiosyncracies.

Both components of Septra are, in actuality, relatively benign as Western pharmaceuticals go. Neither is listed as having any particular natural, expected, or unavoidable side effects. It is not until we look at their unusual and unexpected side effects that a clear TCM understanding of their actions on the body

really arises. For sulfamethoxazole, its mild adverse reactions
include skin rashes, hives, itching, swelling of the face, and
redness of the eyes; reduced appetite, nausea, vomiting,
abdominal pain, diarrhea, and irritation of the mouth; and
headache, impaired balance, dizziness, ringing in the ears,
numbness and tingling of the extremities, and acute mental or
behavioural problems. Its serious side effects include anaphy-
lactic reaction, fever, swollen glands, and swollen, painful joints;
hemolytic anemia; fatigue, weakness, fever, sore throat, unusual
bleeding or bruising; hepatitis with or without jaundice; and
reduction in urine formation. Trimethoprim's mild side effects
include skin rashes, nausea, and vomiting. Its one serious side
effect is anemia.[1]

At first sight, sulfamethoxazole looks as if it is Cold in nature
similar to penicillin. This would explain its causing reduced
appetite, nausea, vomiting, diarrhea, and abdominal pain.
However, too many of its other side effects suggest Heat.
Therefore, it is necessary to look deeper for a common *Bing Ji*
or Disease Mechanism which might cause both Middle Burner
imbalance and Yang Ascension signs and symptoms. Essentially, I think Septra or Bactrim is very similar in nature and action
to Radix Bupleuri (*Chai Hu*). Otitis media, bronchitis, intestinal
tract infections, and urinary tract infections as a constellation
suggests the *Jue Yin/Shao Yang* as the effected Channels. Radix
Bupleuri is Bitter, slightly Acrid, and Cool and it enters the
Liver and Gallbladder Channels. It relieves *Shao Yang* stage
afflictions, such as types of bronchitis, pneumonia, and otitis
media. It dredges and disperses Liver Qi Congestion. Therefore, it can be used to treat disorders due to congestion
anywhere along the course of the *Jue Yin* or *Shao Yang*. But,
because it is Acrid, it tends to disperse the Qi and waste the
Yin. Likewsie, it has an Ascending energy, raising Yang
upwards. Therefore, Radix Bupleuri can cause nausea and
vomiting, both of which have to do with Upward Perversion of
Stomach Qi. In addition, because Bupleurum can easily over-

dredge the Liver in patients who are Blood Deficient, it can cause even more severe Blood Deficiency and generate signs and symptoms of Deficiency Heat.

Using these same descriptions of sulfamethoxazole, I think we can now make sense of its full constellation of side effects and idiosyncracies. Skin rashes, hives, itching, swelling of the face, and redness of the eyes all have to do with sulfamethoxazole's dispersing function. If, indeed, it is similar in nature to Bupleurum, it would be classified in TCM as a Cool, Acrid, Surface-relieving medicinal. It brings the Qi and Heat upward and to the Surface where it can congest (red eyes and dermal erythema) and also exhaust the Blood, thus giving rise to Internally generated stirring of Wind (itching, puffiness, and hives). Reduced appetite, nausea, vomiting, abdominal pain, and mouth irritation as a constellation suggest Stomach Yin Deficiency and Upward Perversion of Stomach Qi. This is all the more likely an explanation when we consider that sulfame-thoxazole is less likely to cause these side effects when taken with meals or on a full stomach. Headaches induced by sulfamethoxazole are due to Ascendant Liver Yang, which can also cause loss of balance, dizziness, tinnitus, and acute mental and behavioural disturbances. Numbness and tingling in the extremities are due to Liver Blood Deficiency due in turn to over-dredging of the Liver. Fever, sore throat, and swollen glands all suggest Ascension of Liver Heat entangles with Phlegm and the painful joints could be due to Malnourishment of the *Jin Mai*, the so-called Sinews and Vessels, with Stagna-tion of Blood and Obstruction by Heat, all again due to wasting of the Blood and Yin. Unusual bleeding or bruising could be due to Heat causing the Blood to run recklessly outside its Pathways. Whereas, hepatitis with or without jaundice definite-ly shows that the *Jue Yin/ Shao Yang* are effected directly. Reduction in urine formation could be due to either exhaustion of Yin Fluids by the Dry, Acrid nature of sulfamethoxazole and/or the Lung Qi's being over-dispersed by this drug.

Therefore, based on the above proposed description of
sulfamethoxazole the following TCM contraindications to its use
would be logical: Yin or Blood Deficiency with Deficiency Heat
or Upward Perversion of Yang. If its functions are, indeed,
similar to Bupleurum's, then this drug's TCM indications might
be: *Shao Yang Fen* otitis, *Shao Yang Fen* bronchitis and pneumonia, Liver Qi intestinal complaints, and *Qi Lin* urinary tract
disorders. These more discriminating indications and contraindications might make the use of this drug exact and free from
all side effects when prescribed correctly.

I believe trimethoprim in combination with sulfamethoxazole is
somewhat similar to combining Bupleurum with Herba Menthae
(*Bo He*). Herba Mentha is also a cool, Acrid, Surface-relieving
medicinal and is used to allow constrained Liver Qi to flow
more freely. Like Bupleurum, peppermint is also contraindicated in Yin Deficiency Patterns with Heat. Trimethoprim is even
more benign than sulfamethoxazole, as is peppermint compared
to Bupleurum. If trimethoprim is Cool, Acrid, Surface-relieving, and Qi-dredging but less potent than sulfemthoxazole and
therefore, tends to cause less side effects, then Bactrim/Septra
as a compound prescription has only a single set of properties
and functions. It contains no ingredients to moderate or
harmonize its effect on the total organism, nor is this basic
prescription tailored to the individual needs of specific patients
other than by adjusting its dose and course of treatment.

According to Pat Gourley, an RN working at Denver General
Hospital with HIV positives and PWAs, Bactrim is relatively
without side effects within the general population but can cause
increased side effects in persons infected with HIV. In fact, it
is one of the treatments of choice for PCP (pneumocystis carinii
pneumonia). However, again according to Mr. Gourley, as
many as 70% of HIV patients cannot tolerate this drug when
used to treat PCP. In my own experience, treatment of an
asymptomatic prostate infection, diagnosed by WBCs in one of

my HIV positive's urine, precipitated nightsweats and a loss of weight. This patient's TCM diagnosis before taking this medication was Liver Qi with some Dampness in the Spleen and Heat and Dryness in the Stomach and an underlying, constitutional Yin Deficiency. Given such a TCM diagnosis, Bactrim seems like a poor choice of treatment. Happily this man's nightsweats were immediately controlled by acupuncture. However, his weight loss has been more difficult to remedy and may not be remediable while he continues on Bactrim. According to his Western internist, he may be on Bactrim for three months or more with only a 30% chance of eliminating the prostrate infection. With this patient, there is the larger issue of whether such an asymptomatic (from the point of view of TCM) prostrate problem needs to be specifically addressed at all. But, begging that question, at least we can say that Bactrim/Septra is not an appropriate medication for this individual.[2]

This kind of TCM discrimination of Western medicinals is, I think, quite exciting. It opens the possibility for a combined Eastern-Western medicine in which Traditional Chinese Medicine provides the big picture, the general theories and guiding philosophy, and modern Western medicine provides the technical brilliance and quick-acting, potent medicinals. Such a medicine would not only give patients the best of both worlds, but the process of such a rapproachment would be healing to the profession of medicine itself. During the early and middle parts of this century, Chinese doctors attempted such a combined Eastern-Western medicine, but always from the other direction. They tried to explain how Chinese therapies and medicinals worked according to Western medical theory. This is exactly backwards. It is essentially the theory of TCM which is most valuable and which can provide a more humane, holistic, and wiser philosophy for the utilization of Western medicinals and procedures.

ENDNOTES

1   Long, James, W., M.D., *The Essential Guide to Prescriptions Drugs*, 4th Edition, Harper & Row, NY, 1985, p. 746-750 & 841-843

2   Since originally writing this essay, this patient's T cell count dropped dramatically from 195 to 125. This drop occurred after beginning Bactrim/Septra therapy. Because of this drop, the patient elected to begin AZT.   He had numerous side effects from the AZT and his T cell count has now dropped to 75. It seems to me that this patient's T cell count could have been predicted to decline due to Bactrim given the fact that, even according to Western medicine, this drug causes impairment to the hemopoietic function.

THE PILL & STAGNANT BLOOD

THE SIDE EFFECTS OF ORAL CONTRACEPTIVES ACCORDING TO TRADITIONAL CHINESE MEDICINE

Since 1960 when birth control pills were first introduced, they have become a fact of modern life. As an American practitioner of Traditional Chinese Medicine specializing in gynecology, I find use of the Pill at some point in my patients' lives is almost 100%. Because this is such a universal factor in my patients' medical histories, I have had, by necessity, to come to some conclusions regarding the Pill's TCM functions and effects. Although Dr. James W. Long lists 28 different kinds of combined estrogen/progestin oral contraceptives available in the United States manufactured by six different companies[1], I think it is possible to describe the TCM functions and effects of the Pill as if these were a single traditional Chinese, polypharmacy formula.

The intended therapeutic effect of combined oral contraceptives is to prevent pregnancy through the suppression of ovulation. Traditional Chinese Medicine, however, has no theory of ovulation *per se*. Traditional Chinese doctors are limited to information gathered only by our traditional Four Methods of Diagnosis (*Si Zhen*). These are Inspection (*Wang Zhen*), Olfaction/Auscultation (*Wen Zhen*), Palpation (*Qie Zhen*), and Interrogation (*Wen Zhen*). Inspection is limited to only that which can be seen with the unaided, naked eye. Since the ovum is not visible amidst the menstruate by the naked eye, traditional Chinese doctors have no concept of ovum in our medicine. Chinese doctors know that a man must ejaculate in a woman's vagina for conception to occur. We also know that a woman cannot become pregnant before menarche, a woman bleeds from her vagina monthly, and that this bleeding stops during pregnancy and at menopause when she becomes infertile. The only thing other than leukorrhea and babies which the Chinese doctor knows that comes from the vagina is Blood. Therefore, traditional doctors throughout Asia have believed, and pragmatically so, that conception takes place when the woman's Blood combines with the man's Reproductive Essence (*Sheng Zhi Zhi Jing* or sperm) within her *Xue She* or Blood Chamber.

The modern TCM practitioner knows that birth control pills make a woman infertile. This is common knowledge and can be ascertained through questioning. However, the Western medical explanation of how this is effected cannot be plugged into our conceptual methodology since we have no such concept as the ovum, nor can this concept be added to our system without rending its conceptual fabric. According to TCM theory, there are basically two broad categories of *Bing Ji* or Disease Mechanism accounting for infertility. These are 1) Insufficiency of Blood and 2) Stagnation of Blood. In the first case, there simply is not enough Blood in the Blood Chamber to unite with the man's Reproductive Essence. This can be due to hypofunction of the Spleen, Heart, or Kidneys, the three Chinese Organs which *Hua* or transform the Blood. In the second case, although there may be sufficient Blood, it is blocked and does not flow properly. Therefore, it cannot unite with the man's *Sheng Zhi Zhi Jing*. Factors causing Stagnation of Blood in a woman's Lower Burner include Cold, Liver Qi Congestion, Stagnant Heat, Phlegm Dampness, and trauma.

By looking at the total constellation of effects that the Pill has on women, I think it is possible to say that oral contraceptives induce iatrogenic infertility by causing Stagnation. This becomes apparent when we look for the common *Bing Ji* for the Pill's various side effects. These side effects include those which are considered "natural, expected, and unavoidable" and those which are "unusual, unexpected, and infrequent".[2] In the first category we find edema, weight gain, mid-cycle or break-through bleeding, change in menstrual flow (usually becoming scanter), absence of menstrual flow, and an increased tendency to yeast infections. In the second category are skin rashes, itching, and hives; headache, nervous tension, and irritability; accentuation of migraine headaches; nausea, vomiting, and bloating; breast enlargement, tenderness, and secretion; tannish pigmentation of the face; and reduced tolerance to contact lenses. More serious and even life-threatening adverse reactions include muscle and joint pains, thrombophlebitis, pulmonary embolism, stroke, high blood pressure, coronary embolism, retinal thrombosis, hepatitis with jaundice, emotional depression (which may be severe), formation of liver neoplasms, and gallbladder disease.

Although this litany of woes is long and seemingly diverse, all these may be explained in TCM terms as complications of Stagnation. Above I said that infertility is due to either Insufficient or Stagnant Blood. However, that was a bit of an over-simplification in my attempt to clarify the Blood's pivotal role in the TCM theory of fertility. There are Six Stagnations in Chinese medicine and all six are mutually promoting. They are Stagnant Qi, Stagnant Blood, Stagnant Food, Stagnant Heat, Stagnant Dampness, and Stagnant Phlegm. But, within these six, the first two are the two most discussed vis a vis menstruation and conception. Qi controls the Blood. In particular, this means that Qi transports, circulates, or moves the Blood. The Blood is the mother of the Qi. That means the Blood is the Root of the Qi, its substrate and foundation. Therefore, Qi Stagnation may lead to Blood Stagnation and Blood Stagnation may lead to Qi Stagnation. Since they both flow together, if one gets stuck, so will the other over time.

In the case of birth control pills, I believe this Stagnation begins with Liver Qi Congestion. It is the Liver which stores the Blood. The *Chong Mai*, the Vessel which controls menstruation and conception, is called the Sea of Blood and the Liver plays an important role in regulating this Vessel. The Liver's job is to store sufficient Blood so that menstruation and conception can occur *and* also to ensure this Blood's unhindered circulation. The Liver maintains the patency of Qi flow and, therefore, Blood flow of the entire organism, but it especially is responsible for the patency of circulation within the Lower Burner. All of the side effects of birth control pills can be explained as stemming from Liver Qi Congestion.

Nausea, vomiting, and bloating as a syndrome suggest Liver Qi invading the Stomach. Breast enlargement and tenderness are also primarily due to Liver Qi according to TCM.[3] Migraine headaches are usually a combination in women of Ascending Liver Yang and Blood Deficiency. First, the Liver Qi congests. This repletion of Qi causes exhaustion or evaporation of the Blood. When this Qi accumulates sufficiently, it vents upward coming apart from its foundation, the Blood, usually along the course of the *Shao Yang*. This causes headaches and neck tension in general and migraines in particular. Irritability is a well-known and common symptom of all Liver Qi originating or complicated scenarios. Since the eyes are the aperture of the Liver and since Liver Qi typically transforms into Heat which rises upward, eye irritation is easily understood. Retention of fluid and weight gain have to do with Liver Qi invading the Spleen and effecting that Organ's ability to *Yun* and *Hua* Fluids. Breakthrough bleeding is usually due to Depressive Heat causing the Blood to run recklessly out of its Channels, remembering the Chinese character for Channel (*Jing*) is the same as for menstruation. Scant periods are due to this Heat's evaporating the Blood. Amenorrhea may occur if either the Blood is wasted to the point where there is insufficient Blood to have a period or if the Qi Congestion leads to Blood

Stagnation with Blood Deficiency. Skin rashes are mostly due to Liver Heat, while itching is a species of Internal stirring of Wind due to Blood Deficiency. Increased tendency to vaginitis is also due to Transformative Depressive Heat in the Liver, remembering that it is the Liver Channel which irrigates the genitalia. Depression is another classic Liver symptom and even tannish pigmentation of the face has a Liver connection. In Chinese medicine, this is called *Huang E Ban*. Its Disease Mechanism is Spleen Deficiency causing Blood Deficiency complicated by Liver Wind and Heat[4]. This then causes Stagnation in the *Sun Luo* Above which gives the face a darker than normal color.

The more serious adverse effects of the Pill likewise participate in this Liver Qi/Blood Stagnation connection. Muscle and joint pain in women with a history of using the Pill is often either/or a combination of Stagnant Blood and Blood Insufficiency failing to nourish the *Jin* Sinews and *Mai* Vessels.[5] Thrombophlebitis, pulmonary embolism, and coronary thrombosis all are indicative of Stagnant Blood. In these cases, Stagnant Qi over time has resulted in Stagnant Blood. Stroke or CVA, on the other hand, is due to Liver Qi or Transformative Fire engendering Wind which gives rise to *Zhong Feng* or Windstroke. In women, there is a *Bing Ji* for high blood pressure due to Stagnant Blood injuring the *Chong*.[6] Retinal thrombosis suggests Stagnant Blood if there is pain and visible hemorrhage or exhaustion of Liver Blood if there is only sudden loss or impairment of vision. Hepatitis with jaundice is due to Depressive Liver Qi when due in turn to oral contraceptives. Whereas, abdominal tumors in the hypochondrium are a classic symptom of Stagnant Blood due to Stagnant Liver Qi. And cholecystitis/cholelithiasis also may be due not only to Damp Heat in the Gallbladder but also to Stagnant Liver Qi and Stagnant Blood.[7]

Because women who begin taking oral contraceptives have

various already pre-existing conditions, how any given woman will react to the Pill will also vary. For instance, some women with dysmenorrhea before taking the Pill experience its cessation when on the Pill. Typically, these women also experience a diminution in menstrual flow when on the Pill. When they go off the Pill, if the oral contraceptives have not caused a permanent worsening of their condition, they usually will also experience a resumption of their period pain. In such cases, the Pill causes more Stagnation of Blood and so less flow. It must be remembered that Stagnation of Blood impairs the creation of fresh or new Blood. On the Pill, there is not enough volume of flow with the period to experience the pressure of dysmenorrhea. When the Pill is suspended, the circulation is relatively freed and the Blood, therefore, may become more in volume. Since there is still Stagnation, this increased flow and volume causes the return of dysmenorrhea.

Other women may not experience any period pain before taking the Pill but have intense dysmenorrhea while on it. In this case, the woman usually does not have significant, pre-existing Stagnation. When she begins oral contraceptives, this causes Stagnation. If her volume of Qi and Blood is relatively full, this Stagnation may be experienced during menstruation as dysmenorrhea. Yet other women may experience the complete cessation of menstruation when taking oral contraceptives with failure to resume menstruating even after discontinuing the Pill. These women usually already have Blood Deficiency which is then severely complicated by Stagnation. In effect, these women are rendered permanently sterile unless treated by Traditional Chinese Medicine in order to disperse Stagnation and tonify the Blood.

Some women are put on the Pill not in order to cause tempo-rary infertility but in order to regulate their period. These women are suffering from what in Chinese medicine is called *Yue Jing Bu Tiao*, Irregular Menstruation. These women may get their periods either early or late or on no fixed schedule. Because the Pill does make the period come precisely on time, I think that we can also theorize that so-called combined oral contraceptives have a two cycle function. First they Stagnate the Qi (and Blood) to prevent conception. Then they activate the Qi and Blood to promote menstruation. Although they also seem to have their own internal Qi-activating effect, essentially, this artificial stagnation and activation of the Qi and Blood results in Stagnation and Exhaustion of the Blood.

Case History

The following case history is a typical report from a young American woman. The patient was a 22 year old college student. Her major complaint was intense intravaginal burning in response to the presence of semen. There were no sores or inflammation on her external genitalia and internal gynecological examination had likewise revealed no internal sores or inflammation. This burning had begun at 19 years of age. During this same time, she had recurrent yeast infections after each period. These a Western gynecologist had diagnosed as a pH imbalance one year before seeing me. The patient was able to control these infections by douching with distilled water after each period. This young woman had taken the Pill from 14 to 18 years of age and then again from 19 to 1 month before seeing me. During the time she was on the Pill, she also experienced lack of vaginal lubrication during sex which was improving since discontinuing the Pill. When on the Pill, her menstrual cramps were relatively intense every month. She experienced both cramping and stabbing pain and she needed to take a Western painkiller. When she stopped the Pill, her period pain diminished. Also when on the Pill, her periods were excessive in volume and bright red. Premenstrually, she experienced irritability, lower abdominal bloating, and craving for chocolate. Her tongue was redder than normal with a yellowish fur. Her pulse was slippery and full in the *Cun* and *Guan* positions and wiry in the *Chi*.

My diagnosis was Liver Heat and Stagnation of Qi and Blood. Her Blood was relatively full. The oral contraceptives (in this case Norinyl) had caused intensification of the Stagnation. Because she was young and robust, this Stagnation led to Transformative Heat. Therefore I prescribed *Long Dan Xie Gan Tang* (Dragon Gall Purge Liver Decoction) in its Jade Pharmacy form of Quell Fire, 2 tablets 3 times per day. This was to specifically address her major complaint of vaginal burning with intercourse and ejaculation. I also counselled this young woman that her condition would not be completely rectified until we also subsequently eradicated her dysmenorrhea and PMS. This woman is still undergoing TCM treatment as we work to the Root of her condition.

Conclusion

Happily this woman, although she began the use of oral contraceptives at a very young age, is dealing with the iatrogenic consequences of the Pill also at a relatively very young age. Most of my patients are women in their thirties whose conditions are typically complicated by at least one or more abortions and various venereal and lower abdominal infections treated by various antibiotics, all of which also tend to cause Stagnation of Blood in the Lower Burner.[8] In my opinion, use of oral contraceptives are at least partially responsible for the apparent rise in PMS and endometriosis and infertility in modern women. It is my firm clinical impression and it is also logical according to TCM theory that use of the Pill does predispose a woman to breast, uterine, thyroid, and liver neoplasms. I am afraid that we are going to see an epidemic of these in ten years in the same women who are experiencing PMS and endometriosis today. Chinese medicine has both the theory and therapy to stop such an epidemic.

Beyond that, Western practitioners of Traditional Chinese Medicine, it seems to me, have an ethical obligation both to perfect our traditional Chinese diagnostic and therapeutic skills and to also extend our theory to cover the full gamut of stimuli which our patients experience. That means describing Western foods, Western drugs, Western herbs, vitamins, minerals, amino acids, etc. all according to the rubric of Chinese medicine. Only if we do that will our medicine truly speak to and address the needs of our patient population. As Jeremy Ross has written in *Zang Fu*,

> The incorrect use, or the side effects of the correct use, of Western medicines and treatments may result in deep and lasting disharmonies of the mind, the emotions, and the physical body. The signs of these drug-induced disharmonies are very common in the West, and can greatly confuse diagnosis. The practitioner must be aware of treatment as a common disease factor, and must assess this possibility in every case.[9]

Chinese medical theory is general enough that it can provide universally valid and pragmatic conclusions about any stimuli from any source if that stimuli creates effects which register according to our Four (Methods of) Diagnosis. Attempting to describe disease factors and stimuli which have not already been described by TCM is a complicated and time-consuming task which requires a high degree of proficiency in Chinese medical theory. It is a task somewhat analogous to Li Shi-zhen's monumental expansion of the *Ben Cao* in the sixteenth century. But, whether difficult or not, it is a task mandated by historical imperative, and a journey of a thousand *Li* begins with the first step.

ENDNOTES

1   Long, James W., *The Essential Guide to Prescription Drugs*,
        Fourth Edition, Harper & Row, NY, 1985, p. 571

2   Ibid., p. 573-574

3   See Wolfe, Honora Lee, *The Breast Connection, A Laywom-
        an's Guide to the Treatment of Breast Disease by Chinese
        Medicine*, Blue Poppy Press, Boulder, CO, 1989, for a full
        discussion of this scenario.

4   Liang Jian-hui, *A Handbook of Traditional Chinese Dermatol-
        ogy*, trans. by Zhang Ting-liang & Bob Flaws, Blue Poppy
        Press, Boulder, CO, 1988, p. 118-120

5   Ou Yang-yi, *Handbook (of) Differential Diagnosis (&) Treat-
        ment*, trans. by C.S. Cheung, Harmonious Sunshine Cultural
        Center, SF, 1987, p. 77

6   Lu, Henry, *Doctor's Manual of Chinese Medical Diet (2)*,
        Chinese Foundation of Natural Health, Vancouver, 1981, p.
        14

7   Chace, Charles, "Between a Rock and a Hard Place, Treat-
        ment of Gall Bladder Disease Using Chinese Herbal Medi-
        cine," *Journal of the American College of TCM*, San Fancisco,
        #3, 1987, p. 18-27

8   Flaws, Bob, "Pelvic Inflammatory Disease (PID)" *Free & Easy,
        Traditional Chinese Gynecology for American Women*, Blue
        Poppy Press, Boulder, CO, 1986, p. 37-46

9   Ross, Jeremy, *Zang Fu, The Organ Systems of Traditional
        Chinese Medicine*, Second Edition, Churchill Livingstone,
        Edinburgh, 1985, p. 44

The Best of Both Worlds

Herbal Formulas For American Women Combining Chinese & Western Herbs

An herbal formula crafted according to the diagnostic and prescriptive theory of Traditional Chinese Medicine is not just a collection of ingredients each of which has similar symptomatic indications. The hallmark of a true formula is its multi-faceted synergism based on a deep understanding of the disease mechanism to be treated. In a sense, a formula is one half of an equation. When each ingredient is analyzed both individually and as a whole, it should be apparent that it will neutralize either directly or indirectly either the main or a contributory disease mechanism in the patient at hand. This is why, often truly elegant, classical Chinese formulas include ingredients that on first sight appear incongruous or irrelevant, such as Moutan in Rehmannia Six Flavor Pills (*Liu Wei Di Huang Wan*).

Especially when it comes to crafting an herbal prescription for administration as a tableted proprietary medicine, it is no easy task to formulate a prescription which will be both general enough to be useful to a large number of slightly differing individuals yet specific enough to achieve a definite therapeutic effect. And, this must be accomplished in as many cases as possible without causing *any* side effectss.

In the last 10 years, Traditional Chinese Medicine has been a rising star on the American alternative health care scene. Perched on the check-out counters of almost every American health food store are various herbal patent medicines based on or incorporating Chinese herbal medicinals. I think it is safe to say that Chinese medicine is the most likely professional alternative medicine to have a large and profound impact on modern Western medicine. In fact, I believe Traditional Chinese Medicine stands poised to provide the theoretical foundation for a global New Medicine for the 21st century.

If this is to transpire, both practitioners of Chinese medicine and the public at large must come to recognize that so-called Chinese medicine is not an exotic and outlandish cultural import. Although the therapies and medicines of Traditional Chinese Medicine have been empirically proven in clinical practice over as much as 2000 years, still, the most important thing about Chinese medicine is its universally valid theories of diagnosis, disease mechanism, and therapeutics. These equally time-tested theories are general enough to be applicable in any country or climate and by any race or gene pool. However, for Chinese medical theory to be accepted as the universally valid and generally applicable system it is, it must also transcend its historically accidental cultural limitations. That means it must prove that it can incorporate medicinal substances from all over the world all according to its own theoretical rationale and rubric.

Chinese medicine has, in fact, met this challenge before. On the one hand, it succeeded in the Tang dynasty in China in incorporating medicinals brought to China by Indian and Central Asian missionaries and by Arab traders from the Mideast and the Spice Islands. On the other hand, Vietnamese, Tibetans, Mongolians, Koreans, and Japanese who studied Chinese medicine in China all succeeded upon returning to their home countries in developing pharmacopeias including indigenous medicinals described according to Chinese theory.

Already, American practitioners trained in Chinese medicine, such as Michael Tierra, David Frawley, and Peter Holmes, have begun attempting to identify the "Chinese" flavors, temperatures, meridian routes, categories, functions, and indications for indigenous American herbs. Likewise, others, such as Ted Kaptchuk, have tried to design formulas using all Chinese medicinals but prescribed specifically to treat the peculiar way Americans tend to get sick. Both of these endeavors are necessary if Chinese medicine is to truly live up to its potential in the coming century. As Michael Tierra correctly points out, we need to develop a new "planetary medicine"[1] -- a medicine perhaps based on traditional Chinese theory but incorporating all potential medicinals in the world, including even synthetic pharmaceuticals. And, this medicine needs to address the causes and mechanisms of disease in modern, post-industrial society. As Zhang Yuan-su of the Jin-Yuan dynasties said, we need new formulas for new times.

As an American clinician trained in China but practicing for the last 10 years here in America, I am acutely aware that Chinese people and Americans are not constitutionally the same, nor do we get ill in the same way. When I returned from China full of very neat and precise Chinese treatments, I quickly found that they did not always work the way they did in China. Therefore, over the years, I have had to tailor my practice to the precise needs of my patient population. Marvelously, Chinese medical theory is both general enough and complex enough to fit any and all situations.

One aspect of being a TCM practitioner in the United States is that a much greater proportion of my case-load is comprised of chronically ill individuals rather than the acutely ill. Such chronic complaints are characterized by their complexity, their shifting and variable signs and symptoms, and their nagging and recalcitrant natures. Such chronically ill individuals often do not have the time, patience, perseverance, or money to take

Chinese medicine as freshly decocted teas. Also, Americans are conditioned to think of tablets and capsules when we think of medicine. Therefore, when Health Concerns of Alameda, CA approached me to formulate several women's prescriptions which were suitable for manufacture as tablets, I was quite happy to be given this opportunity.

For the last 10 years, I have specialized in the treatment of American women. At first this was accidental; but I quickly made a conscious decision to devote myself to going deeply into TCM gynecology. Therefore, the following women's formulas are based on the experience I have gained in treating American women in America with Chinese medicine. Following TCM methodology, each formula is my own modification of a standard or classical Chinese formula. By beginning with such a guiding formula, one takes advantage of the time-tested, empirical experience of literally 100 generations of previous professional practitioners. Likewise, each formula is an indicated remedy for a specific Chinese Pattern (of Dishar-mony) or *Zheng*. Such *Zheng* or Patterns are differentiated in clinical practice according to standard, professionally agreed upon constellations of signs and symptoms, pulse, and tongue. Each formula's introduction includes a discussion of the disease mechanism it seeks to remedy, the properties of its individual ingredients, and its synergistic rationale.

Gotu Kola Heavenly Water 15

The onset of menstruation, both at menarche and every month, is called the arrival of *Tian Kui* in Chinese. *Tian Kui* means heavenly water. This term suggests many meanings, one of which alludes to the fact that the menstrual Blood is sent down to the Liver for storage in the *Bao Gong* or Uterus by the Heart. When enough Blood has collected in the *Bao Gong* and if conception has not taken place, this Blood is discharged primarily by the Liver Qi. In general, the menstrual cycle as a whole can be characterized as a rise and fall of Qi in the body vertically and the growth and decline of Blood in volume. Therefore, the menstrual cycle can also be described as a series of interactions and inter-relationships between the Qi and Blood.

The Qi is the commander of the Blood, but the Blood is the mother of the Qi. Qi's commanding of the Blood means the Qi transports or moves the Blood and also transforms or creates it. The Blood's being the Qi's mother means the Blood is the material root or basis of the Qi. Therefore, the relationship between the Qi and Blood is basically a Yin Yang relationship, the Qi being Yang and the Blood, Yin.

Many modern women experience PMS. Premenstrual dis-ease seems to have increased in frequency in the last generation and it typically increases in American women as they move from their late twenties into their thirties. Although there is more than a single scenario for the production of PMS, the most common disease mechanisms involve Stagnation of Qi and Blood Deficiency.

At mid-cycle, the Qi, which has travelled up to the upper body after the period, begins to move back down because of being magnetized by the Blood which has been being replenished. The Blood grows in the Heart from the transformation of Food and Liquids by the Spleen. When the Blood becomes replete, it is sent down for storage in the Liver. The Liver then stores the Blood in the Uterus. If insufficient Blood has been produced, Qi will tend not to descend into the lower body, but rather will flush back upwards since Qi is Yang. Likewise, if the Liver is tight due to stress, the flow of Qi and Blood may be impeded, in which case also the Qi may detach itself and flow back upwards. If the Qi flushes back upwards, it may cause breast distention, stuffy chest, Plum Seed Qi, and headache.

If the Qi merely becomes stuck in the pelvis due to impatency of the Liver, it may cause constipation, premenstrual cramping, flatulence, lower abdominal bloating, delayed or irregular periods, infertility, dysmenorrhea, and irritability. If the stuck Qi gathers to such an extent it implodes and transforms into Depressive Heat, this Heat may vent upward causing pain in the breasts, bitter taste, flank pain, irascibility, more serious headache, including migraine, and depression punctuated by erratic and explosive anger. If the Heat merely congests in the Lower Burner, it may cause vaginal inflammation, outbreaks of herpes, and urinary tract infections.

Because, when the Qi gets stuck, the Liver becomes Excess, the Spleen likewise, according to Five Phase Control theory, becomes Deficient. Deficient Spleen Qi leads to both Qi Deficiency characterized by fatigue and loose stools and diarrhea and also to Blood Deficiency, since the Spleen Qi is not able to transform the Blood. This then leads to Heart Blood Deficiency and palpitations, anxiety, and general hypoglycemic feelings. This also leads to the Spleen's craving sweets in an attempt to tonify Spleen Qi and Heart Blood. Also because of Spleen Qi Deficiency, Liquids or Body Fluids are not transported and transformed properly. This leads to water retention, leukorrhea, and chronic digestive difficulties characterized by loose stools or diarrhea, sticky stools, or stools which begin hard but end loose. Spleen Dampness is an almost inevitable end product of Spleen Deficiency and Liver Congestion in Americans aggravated by an endemic dietary imbalance of too much sugar, dairy, cold and raw foods, fats and greases, and too much cold liquids consumed at meals.

Paradoxically, when the Liver gets Hot, although the Spleen is Deficient and Damp, very often the Stomach also gets over-heated. This is experienced as increased appetite and facial acne along the course of the *Yang Ming*. This also contributes to premenstrual breast distention and painful inflammation.

Therefore, it is very common to find American women suffering from PMS due to a combination of Liver Qi, Depressive Liver Fire, Heart Blood Deficiency, Spleen Qi Deficiency and Dampness, and Stomach Heat. Liver and Stomach Heat generally tend to rise together and may also affect the Lungs, thus contributing to the tendency to premenstrual acne and even monthly bouts of upper respiratory "flu". Because of this complicated scenario, my experience is that Minor Bupleurum Decoction (*Xiao Chai Hu Tang*) plus Four Ingredients Decoction (*Si Wu Tang*) is a good basis for a premenstrual formula since it is based on "harmonizing" the Liver and Spleen, the Spleen and Stomach, the Qi and the Blood, and Ascension and Descension.

The standard ingredients in Minor Bupleurum Decoction are Bupleurum (Radix Bupleuri Falcati), Codonopsis (Radix Codonopsis Pilosulae), Scutellaria (Radix Scutellariae Baicalensis), Pinellia (Rhizoma Pinelliae Ternatae), Honey-baked Licorice (Radix Praeparatus Cum Mel Glycyrrhizae Uralensis), Fresh Ginger (Rhizoma Recens Zingiberis), and Red Dates (Fructus Zizyphi Jujubae). The standard ingredients in Four Ingredient Decoction are Rehmannia (Radix Conquita Rehmanniae Glutinosae), *Dang Gui* (Radix Angelicae Sinensis), Peony (Radix Alba Paeoniae Lactiflorae), and Cnidium (Rhizoma Ligustici Wallichii). However, Bupleurum is often too drying, and causes too much Heat, and exhausts the Blood in American women. This is because, even though its temperature is Cool, because of its Acrid, dispersing nature it tends to exhaust Yin. Likewise, its Ascending nature can exacerbate PMS if a woman tends to Yin Deficiency and therefore Floating Yang. Rehmannia, on the other hand, is often too greasy for Americans with Spleen Dampness and Dampness accumulating in the Lower Burner. In such persons it tends to cause diarrhea which can be difficult to stop. Such diarrhea may occur immediately or only after taking Rehmannia as part of a formula for some time. And Cnidium should not be given unless there is definite Stagnation of the Qi *and* Blood causing menstrual and not just premenstrual blockage. I have also deleted Fresh Ginger since this ingredient is impossible to include in a dry tablet. Its function is replaced in this formula by other additions.

Therefore, in modifying this formula for American women, I have eliminated these four ingredients. Such modification is called *Jia Jian* in Chinese. *Jia* means to add; *Jian* means to subtract. Therefore, in order to make this formula more effective, I have added a number of other ingredients. These are Gotu Kola (Radix Hydrocotylis Asiaticae), Passion Flower (Herba Passiflorae Incarnatae), Chaste Tree Berries (Fructus Viticis Agnus-casti), Poria (Sclerotium Poriae Cocoris), Cyperus (Rhizoma Cyperi Rotundi), Trichosanthis (Radix Trichosanthis Kirlowii), Orange Peel (Pericarpium Citri Reticulatae), and Green Orange Peel (Pericarpium Viridis Citri Reticulatae). In addition, I have substituted Pseudostellaria (Radix Pseudostel-lariae Heterophyllae) for Codonopsis. The final formula thus reads:

Gotu Kola	9 parts
Passion Flower	9 "
Pseudostellaria	9 "
Scutellaria	9 "
Pinellia	9 "
Poria	9 "
Peony	9 "
Dang Gui	9 "
Cyperus	9 "
Trichosanthis	9 "
Red Dates	9 "

Honey-baked Licorice	6 "
Orange Peel	6 "
Green Orange Peel	6 "
Chaste Tree Berries	6 "

Gotu Kola (Radix Hydrocotylis Asiaticae) is the ruler of this prescription. In many ways it is quite similar to Bupleurum. Both are Umbelliferates. Gotu Kola is likewise Cool and Acrid. Also like Bupleurum, Gotu Kola enters the Liver and Gallbladder Channels. It clears Heat, dissolves Toxins, stimulates the production of Body Fluids, and transforms Phlegm. However, it also relaxes constrained Liver Qi and relieves Depression. It is especially useful for promoting mental calm and it relieves nervousness. Michael Tierra goes so far as to say that Gotu Kola possesses Yin tonic properties[2]; however, I would simply say it possesses all the Qi-regulating properties of Bupleurum without Bupleurum's drawbacks. In Indian Ayurvedic medicine, Gotu Kola is the most important nervine.

Passion Flower (Herba Passiflorae Incarnatae) is not a traditional Chinese herb but we can say that it is a *Li Qi* or Qi-regulating medicinal. It is Bitter and Cool and enters the Heart and Liver Channels. It extinguishes Wind and alleviates spasms, clears Heat and pacifies the Liver, and releases the Exterior. It treats depression, muscular tension, insomnia, restlessness, headache due to Hyperactive Yang, and is especially good for the long-term treatment of menstrual complaints, including PMS and dysmenorrhea.

Pseudostellaria (Radix Pseudostellariae Heterophyllae) is a *Bu Qi* or Qi-tonifying medicinal. It is Sweet and Neutral and enters the Spleen, Lung, and Heart. It strengthens the Spleen and benefits the Qi, while at the same time it generates Fluids. Shaolin Patriarch De Chan felt it was better to use Pseudostellaria rather than Ginseng or Codonopsis for women because it also cultivates the Blood.[3] Like American Ginseng, Pseudostellaria nourishes the Yin, but Pseudostellaria tonifies the Spleen more; whereas American Ginseng works primarily on the Lungs.

Scutellaria (Radix Scutellariae Baicalensis) is categorized as a medicinal which clears Heat and dries Dampness. It is Bitter and Cold and enters the Heart, Lungs, Gall Bladder, and Large Intestine. It clears Heat and quells Fire, especially in the Upper Burner. This Heat typically arises from the Liver and Stomach below. Most adults have some chronic Evil Heat trapped in their Lungs and as long as this Heat remains, Lung function is somewhat weakened. Therefore, the Lungs fail to control the Liver, on the one hand, and house the *Po* or animal vitality on the other. When the *Po* is weak, the *Hun* and *Shen* both also become *Bu An* or agitated and restless. Therefore, clearing Heat from the Lungs and Heart is often one of the most effective ways of indirectly treating Liver Qi and Heat. Although not traditionally described as entering the Liver Channel, I think the fact that Scutellaria clears Damp Heat in the Middle and Lower Burners associated with such Liver diseases as Yang jaundice and *Re Lin* or Damp Heat Urinary Disturbance; because it clears Heat to *An Tai* or calm the fetus in the Uterus which is primarily controlled by the Liver; and also because it treats the *Shao Yang* phase of a *Shang Han*, strongly suggests that Scutellaria does, indeed, enter the *Jue Yin*.

Pinellia (Rhizoma Pinelliae Ternatae) is Acrid and Warm. It enters the Stomach and Spleen Channels. Pinellia dries Dampness, transforms Phlegm, and descends Rebellious Qi. It harmonizes the Stomach to reverse Upward Perversion and also dissipates Nodules and reduces distention. Pinellia is used in this formula to help regulate Ascension and Descension and eliminate Dampness, thus promoting harmonious Stomach/-Spleen function. Although Pinellia is categorized as a Cold

Phlegm transformer, it has definite Qi-regulating properties as well.

Poria (Sclerotium Poriae Cocoris) is Sweet, Bland, and Neutral. It enters the Heart, Spleen, and Lung Channels. It is a Dampness seeping medicinal which promotes urination and leeches out Dampness. Therefore, it supports Pinellia by ridding Dampness by another avenue. It strengthens the Spleen and harmonizes the Middle. It transforms Phlegm, especially Phlegm which has been drafted up by Liver Qi to the Heart, Lungs, or chest (and therefore the breasts). Poria also calms the Spirit and quiets the Heart. In this formula it assists Orange Peel in eliminating Congested Fluids in the Middle which block Ascension and Descension.

Peony (Radix Alba Paeoniae Lactiflorae) is a Blood-tonifying ingredient. It is Bitter, Sour, and Cool. It enters the Liver and Spleen. Peony nourishes the Blood and pacifies the Liver. Liver Qi Congestion can be dredged with Qi-regulating medicinals and relaxed from within by Blood-tonifying medicinals. Peony does the latter, and when combined with Qi-regulators, achieves a fuller, rounder, gentler effect. Peony also restrains Yang from floating upward and to the Surface and such flushing upward of Yang Qi accounts for a number of premenstrual symptoms, such as headache, insomnia, and breast distention.

Dang Gui (Radix Angelicae Sinensis) also tonifies the Blood. It is Sweet, Acrid, Bitter, and Warm and enters the Heart, Liver, and Spleen. It tonifies the Blood and regulates the menses, while it also invigorates and harmonizes the Blood. Dang Gui moistens the Intestines and promotes bowel movements which likewise tend to move the Qi down and decongest the Liver. Dang Gui is used to treat irregular menstruation and dysmenorrhea and works synergistically with Peony to relax the Liver by nourishing the Blood.

Cyperus (Rhizoma Cyperi Rotundi) regulates the Qi. It is Acrid, slightly Bitter, Sweet, and slightly Warm. It enters the Liver and Triple Heater Channels and it activates the Qi and resolves constrained Liver Qi. In this respect, it helps to harmonize the Liver and Spleen. It regulates menstruation and alleviates pain, such as dysmenorrhea. Cyperus unblocks Qi in the chest and the lower abdomen. When coupled with Dang Gui, it treats irregular menstruation and dysmenorrhea due to Stagnation of Qi and Blood. However, it will not tend to cause problems as Cnidium will in women without Blood Stagnation or menoxenia.

Trichosanthis (Radix Trichosanthis Kirlowii) is a Heat-clearing, Hot Phlegm-transforming ingredient according to most materia medica. However, its use is larger than that categorization would tend to infer. According to Bensky and Gamble, early *Ben Cao*, such as the *Shen Nong Ben Cao Jing*, made no distinction between Pericarpium, Semen, Fructus, and Radix Trichosanthis medicinally.[4] Radix Trichosanthis is Bitter, slightly Sweet, Sour, and Cool. It enters the Lungs and the Stomach. It clears Heat and generates Fluids. It also dissolves Toxins and expels pus. But it also broadens the chest by unbinding the Qi and moistens the Intestines and moves the stool. In terms of PMS, Trichosanthis helps treat the hunger, acne, thirst, constipation, and irritability which all occur as complex manifestations of Stomach/Lung/Liver Heat.

Red Dates (Fructus Zizyphi Jujubae) are commonly added to complex prescription to moderate and harmonize any harsh effects or side effects the other herbs might have, especially on the Stomach/Spleen. However, Red Dates are quite important in their own right. They are a *Bu Qi* or Qi-tonifying ingredient which are Sweet and Neutral and enter the Stomach, Spleen, and Heart. They tonify the Spleen and benefit the Stomach while calming the Heart Spirit. This is because they nourish the *Ying* or Nutritive Qi and the Blood and moisten Dryness, therefore nourishing Heart Blood. Symptomatically, they are used in the treatment of hysteria, restlessness, and anxiety due to Heart Blood/Spleen Qi Dual Deficiency.

Honey-baked Licorice (Radix Praeparatus Cum Mel Glycyrrhizae Uralensis) is Sweet and Warm and enters all twelve Regular Channels and especially the Spleen and Lungs. It is a Qi-tonifying medicinal which tonifies the Spleen and benefits the Qi. It also moistens the Lungs, soothes spasms, and moderates and harmonizes the properties of the other herbs in this formula. Because it is used here in its honey-baked form, it helps generate Fluids in the Stomach and protects the Stomach from any tendency for Cool and Bitter herbs to harm the digestion. When combined with Peony, as it is in this prescription, it relieves abdominal pain, intestinal spasm, and spasms in the calves and other muscles.

Orange Peel (Pericarpium Citri Reticulatae) is from the Qi-regulating category of traditional Chinese medicinals. It is Acrid, Bitter, Warm, and Aromatic. It enters the Spleen, Stomach, and Lungs. It activates the Qi and strengthens the Spleen. It dries Dampness and transforms Phlegm. In terms of PMS, Orange Peel directs the Qi downward and facilitates Ascension of the Pure and Descension the Turbid. In this formula, it works synergistically with Pinellia and Poria to eliminate Spleen Dampness, and with Cyperus and Trichosanthis to unbind Chest Qi so as to reduce breast distention.

Green Orange Peel (Pericarpium Viridis Citri Reticulatae) is an unripe form of orange or tangerine peel. It is Bitter, Acrid, and slightly Warm. It enters the Liver and Gallbladder Channels. It expedites the free flow of Liver Qi, breaks up and reduces Qi Accumulations, and eliminates Dampness and transforms Phlegm. It is stronger than regular Orange Peel in its Qi-regulating function, more strongly removing Stagnation. When coupled with Cyperus, it treats pain in the flanks or breasts due to Liver Qi. When both Orange Peel and Green Orange Peel are combined, they even more reduce breast swelling and distention, Orange Peel along the course of the *Yang Ming* and Green Orange Peel along the course of the *Shao Yang* and *Jue Yin*.

Chaste Tree Berries (Fructus Viticis Agnus-casti) are Sweet, Bitter, and Neutral and enter the Liver and Spleen. They are not a traditional Chinese medicinal but probably should be considered a Qi-regulating ingredient. They dredge the Qi, activate the Blood, and regulate the menses. Because they relieve pent-up Qi which can transform into Depressive Fire, they can restore normal sexual desire. A woman can be frigid due to *Ming Men* Fire being depressed inside. This is the same mechanism that gives rise to cold hands due to stress. Also a woman can be hyperactive sexually because of Depressive Liver Fire inflaming Stomach and Heart Fires giving rise to Flaring of the *Ming Men*. Chaste Tree Berries regulate towards normalcy both these tendencies. Therefore we can say that they regulate the *Ming Men* Fire and its relation to the other *Zang Fu*. In particular, Chaste Tree Berries relieve premenstrual tension and dysmenorrhea. David Hoffman is also of the opinion that they help restore balance to a woman's internal environment after the use of oral contraceptives.[5]

When taken as a whole, this formula is intended to dredge and relax congested Liver Qi, to relieve depression and lower Rebellious Qi, to eliminate Dampness and transform Phlegm, to clear Heat from the Stomach and Liver, to generate Fluids and nourish the Blood, to activate the Qi and destagnate the Blood, and to harmonize the Liver and Spleen, the Spleen and Stomach, the Stomach and Intestines, and the Qi and Blood. It is indicated for the treatment of PMS due to Liver Qi, Spleen Deficiency and Dampness, Blood Deficiency, and transformative Heat disturbing the *Shen* arising from the Liver and Stomach. In addition, this formula also treats irregular menstruation, delayed menstruation, painful menstruation, and fibrocystic disease when due to the above same constellation of disease mechanisms.

Modified Heart-clearing Lotus Seed Tablets

Another problem many American women are prone to in their thirties is chronic and recurrent vaginitis. Because so many women have an element of Spleen Dampness and simultaneous Yin Deficiency as part of the complex disease mechanism responsible for such chronic vaginal and urethral irritation and inflammation, many of the various standard Chinese patent medicines for this condition are not quite right. Dragon Gall Liver-purging Decoction (*Long Dan Xie Gan Tang*) is usually the first prescription in TCM dermatology texts for vaginitis. Yet it is too Cold and drying for the type of mixed Yin Deficiency, Spleen Damp, Hot Liver vaginitis I am referring to. Its ingredients are all purging, clearing, and reducing based on a diagnosis of simple Excess. However, most chronic vaginal inflammation is a mixed Excess/Deficiency scenario.

Moutan and Gardenia Free and Easy Powder (*Dan Zhi Xiao Yao San*) is also often also recommended for chronic leukor-rhea and vaginitis. But it also is not quite right in many cases. It does treat a mixed Excess/Deficiency Pattern but the Excess is Depressive Liver Heat and the Deficiency is Spleen Qi and Blood. Its ability to resolve Dampness having percolated down into the Lower Burner is not marked. And, not only does it not address any element of Yin Deficiency in a marked way, but the Bupleurum it contain may actually aggravate this condition. In addition, Bupleurm is a Surface-relieving ingredi-ent and in most cases of chronic skin irritation consolidation of the Surface and tonification of the *Ying* is one of the necessary therapeutic principles.

On the other hand, Anemarrhena-Phellodendron with Rehmannia Pills (*Zhi Bai Di Huang Wan*) address Flaring Fire due to Yin Deficiency but do not address the Spleen which is the root of any Dampness percolating downwards. In fact, Rehmannia is often not tolerated by persons with Spleen and therefore Intestinal Dampness. Likewise, these pills do not directly address the Liver as the Heat-aggravating factor within the disease mechanism. And, it is my experience that this formula works better for Heat flaring upwards rather than capped and trapped by Dampness below.

In such a case, I find a formula based on Heart-clearing Lotus Seed Drink (*Qing Xin Lian Zi Yin*) to be very effective. When additions are made to this classical formula based on targeting female urogenital inflammations, it can be called Modified Heart-clearing Lotus Seed Tablets (*Fu Fang Qing Xin Lian Zi Pian*). The composition of this modified prescription is:

Lotus Seed	12 parts
Ophiopogon	12 "
Poria	12 "
White Ginseng	9 "
Plantaginis	9 "
Scutellaria	9 "
Marshmallow	9 "
Smilax	9 "
Raw Astragalus	6 "
Lycium Bark	6 "
Moutan	6 "
Red Peony	6 "
Raw Licorice	3 "

This formula treats all five *Zang* directly and the Stomach and Bladder amongst the *Fu*. It clears Heat from the Heart, Lungs, Liver, Stomach, and Bladder. It tonifies the Qi and benefits the Spleen. It eliminates Dampness both by improving the Spleen's

transportation and transformation of Liquids and by seeping
Dampness below. By promoting unimpeded Spleen function,
this formula strengthens the Root of Postnatal production. By
clearing Heat, it ensures that the surplus from this production
bolsters the Prenatal Root. In addition, this formula also
ensures nourishment of the Blood and its unimpeded circulation. Although this prescription does not appear to be aimed
directly at the Liver, since the healthy and optimal functioning
of all four other *Zang* is promoted, the Liver is automatically
kept both nourished and checked.

Lotus Seed (Semen Nelumbinis) is from the astringent category
of traditional Chinese medicinals. It is Sweet, Astringent, and
Neutral and enters the Heart, Spleen, and Kidney Channels.
Lotus Seed clears Heart Fire and nourishes the Kidneys.
According to the great eighteenth century gynecologist, Fu
Qing-zhu, by dispersing the Heart/Son and nourishing the
Kidneys/Mother, Liver/Wood is automatically benefitted. In
addition, Lotus Seed strengthens the Spleen and stops diarrhea
and chronically loose stools. It is used in the treatment of
Heart/Kidney Not Communicating with symptoms of irritability,
restlessness, insomnia, palpitations, dry mouth, and either
spermatorrhea or leukorrhea.

Ophiopogon (Tuber Ophiopogonis Japonicae) tonifies Yin. Its
characteristics are that it is Sweet, slightly Bitter, and slightly
Cold. It enters the Lungs, Stomach, and Heart. Ophiopogon
nourishes Yin and clears Heat from all three of the Organs it
enters. Typically, when anyone of these is over-heated, all
three of them eventually become so. Although most commonly
found in formulas designed to moisten the Lungs, Ophiopogon
also moistens the Intestines and therefore promotes bowel
movements. Since the Intestines are the largest viscera in the
Lower Burner, their Yin affects all other Yin below. Ophiopogon treats irritability, thirst, and constipation as well as dry
cough with hard to expel mucous.

Poria has already been described above under Gotu Kola Heavenly Water 15.

White Ginseng (Radix Alba Panacis Ginseng) specifically refers to Jilin Ginseng produced in Heilongjiang, PRC. Ginseng is the premier Qi-tonifying herb in the traditional Chinese materia medica. It is Sweet, slightly Bitter, and Warm. It enters the Lung, Spleen, Stomach, and Kidneys. Unlike some other Qi-tonifying ingredients, such as Atractylodes, Ginseng first goes to the *Dan Tian* to tonify the Root and then its effects spread from there. That is one reason for its Chinese name, "man root". It powerfully tonifies the Original Qi, meaning the True or Postnatal Qi as defined by Li Dong-yuan. In addition, it strengthens the Spleen and tonifies the Stomach; it benefits Yin and generates Fluids; and it benefits the Heart Qi and calms the Spirit. Although Codonopsis tonifies the Lungs and Spleen, because Ginseng also strengthens the Kidneys, it supports the entire relationship between the Pre and Postnatal. Therefore, in this formula, it is important that Ginseng be used and not substituted by Codonopsis. Also it is important that only White Ginseng be used. If Red Ginseng were used, it could inflame the Heat or Fire in the Liver, Stomach, Heart, and Lungs.

Plantaginis (Semen Plantaginis) is a Damp-draining medicinal. It is Sweet, Bland, and Cold. It enters the Kidney, Bladder, and Liver Channels. It promotes urination and thereby clears Heat. It especially eliminates Damp Heat. However, Plantaginis also brightens the eyes when there is either dry eyes or obstructed vision in turn due to either Liver Blood/Kidney Yin Deficiency or Liver Heat. Kidney Yin Deficiency always implies some element of Kidney Qi Deficiency. If Kidney Qi is Deficient, the Kidneys will not be able to transport and transform Liquids and so Dampness will develop. This in turn further hinders Kidney Qi and thus the replenishment of Kidney Yin. Although Plantaginis does not directly *Bu Yin* or tonify Yin, still its net effect is to allow for the promotion of True Yin.

Scutellaria (Radix Scutellariae Baicalensis) clears Heat and dries Dampness. It is Bitter and Cold and enters the Heart, Lung, Gallbladder, and Large Intestine Channels. Scutellaria clears Heat and quells Fire, especially in the Upper Burner. However, it clears and eliminates Damp Heat from the Middle and Lower Burners. It promotes both Lung and Stomach function by clearing the Evil Heat which typically accumulates in these Organs and impedes their function. Thus it indirectly aids in regulating Ascension and Descension. In this formula, Scutellaria is present to clear Heat from the Lungs, Heart, Stomach, and Liver and also to eliminate Damp Heat from the Lower Burner.

Marshmallow (Radix Althaeae Officinalis) is a hemostatic medicinal which is Sweet, Bitter, and Cool and enters the Lungs, Stomach, Liver, Large Intestine, and Bladder. Its functions are that it cools the Blood and stops bleeding. It is most effective for Heat causing the Blood to run recklessly outside its Pathways and can be used for hemoptysis, hematuria, hemafecia, and epistaxis, all due to Liver Heat. Because it clears Heat from the Liver, Marshmallow is used to treat dry mouth, nose, throat, and a dry, ticklish cough due to Liver Heat ascending to disturb the Lungs. Likewise, it is Liver Heat causing upward perversion of the Blood and rebellion of the Lungs and Stomach which causes this hemoptysis and epistaxis respectively. Marshmallow, like Cacumen Biotae Orientalis, also liquifies Dry Phlegm and therefore treats persistent cough due to injury of Fluids. In addition, it promotes circulation of Blood and expels Congealed Blood. It therefore treats chest and flank pain, as in pleurisy, hiatal hernia, and kidney stones, and epigastric pain, as in gastric and duodenal ulcers. Because of its Liver Heat-clearing capacity, Marshmallow can clear Damp Heat from the Lower Burner when the Heat is due to the Liver. In such cases, Marshmallow can be used to treat cystitis, urethritis, and diarrhea or dysentery with blood and pus. Because Marshmallow treats breast lumps, mastitis, and insufficient lactation due to Liver Qi Congestion and also because it treats other signs and symptoms arising along the course of the *Jue Yin*, I think it must be said this herb enters the Liver. Like Comfrey, another styptic medicinal, Marshmallow also has lenifying, moistening, and demulcent properties as well. In Western herbalism, Marshmallow is a famous emollient. Therefore, in this formula, it is used specifically to soothe and promote the healing of the abraded pudendal tissues which are irritated due to chronic Fluid injury along the course of the Liver Channel irrigating the so-called Lower Yin.

Smilax (Rhizoma Smilacis Glabrae) is categorized as a medicinal which clears Heat and dissolves Toxins in Traditional Chinese Medicine. It is Sweet, Bland, and Neutral and enters the Liver and Stomach. Its functions are that it clears Damp Heat Toxins and clears Damp Heat from the Skin. It is used for the treatment of recurrent Hot Skin lesions, especially surrounding the genitalia. Smilax is closely related, if not identical, to Sasparilla. It is used to treat all manner of venereal diseases, including syphilis, gonorrhea, and herpes genitalia.

Astragalus (Radix Astragali Seu Hedysari) is, like Ginseng, a famous Qi-tonifying medicinal. It is Sweet and slightly Warm and enters the Spleen, Lungs, Kidney, Large Intestine, and Triple Heater channels. Because it enters both Yin and Yang Channels, it can be used for both the Upper *and* Lower Warmers. Astragalus supports the Stomach and Spleen and tonifies the Lungs. It stimulates the Heart, but clears Heart Fire. When used raw, as in this formula, it drains Dampness by promoting urination and also clears Flaring of Deficiency Fire from the Heart. In addition, Astragalus removes Heat which has floated to the Surface and is lingering in the Skin.

Lycium Bark (Cortex Radicis Lycii Chinesis) is a Blood-cooling ingredient. It is Sweet and Cold and enters the Lungs, Liver, and Kidneys. It clears Yin Deficiency Fire and clears Lung Heat. In addition, it also cools the Blood. Lycium Bark is often combined with Moutan to treat skin inflammations due to Heat entering the *Xue Fen* or Blood Phase. These two ingredients are also used to stop early, breakthrough, or protracted menstrual bleeding due to Heat causing the Blood to run recklessly outside its Pathways. In this formula, Lycium Bark is included in part because the Lungs rule the Skin and also because the Lungs control the descension of Fluids.

Moutan (Cortex Radicis Moutan) is also classified in Traditional Chinese Medicine as a Blood-cooling medicinal. It is Acrid, Bitter, and Cool and enters the Heart, Liver, and Kidneys. It, like Lycium Bark, clears Heat and cools the Blood and clears Deficiency Fire. However, it also invigorates the Blood and dispels Congealed Blood, clears Ascending Liver Fire, and drains pus and reduces swelling. Therefore, Moutan is useful not only in treating skin inflammation due to Hot Blood but also is commonly used to treat various menstrual disorders due to Stagnant Blood. Based on Liu Wan-su's Principle of Similar Transformation, when Heat becomes Stagnant, so may the Blood; and when Blood becomes Stagnant, it often generates Heat.

Red Peony (Radix Rubra Paeoniae Lactiflorae) is categorized as a Blood-invigorating ingredient. In Chinese, this class of herb is called *Li Xue* or Blood-regulating. It is Sour, Bitter, and slightly Cold and enters the Liver and Spleen. Red Peony invigorates the Blood and dispels Congealed Blood. It clears Heat and cools the Blood, and it also clears Liver Fire. Therefore, in combination with Moutan, Red Peony promotes normal menstruation and treats any tendency to early or painful menstruation. Because it clears Liver Fire as well as cools the Blood, Red Peony also clears Heat specifically from the genitalia which are irrigated principally by the Liver *Luo*. By adding Moutan and Red Peony to this formula, it extends this formula's effect to treat not only vaginitis but also the menstrual dysfunction which often accompanies chronic vaginitis.

Raw Licorice (Radix Glycyrrhizae Uralensis) has also been described above under Gotu Kola Heavenly Water 15. However, in this formula, Raw Licorice is used instead of Honey-baked Licorice. When used raw, Licorice clears Heat from the Heart. It also clears Heat and dissolves Fire Toxins causing various types of sores and inflammations. In addition, Raw Licorice helps distribute Hot and Cold energies to their appropriate Organs.

Many American women in their thirties and forties suffer from a combination of Damp Spleen, Hot Liver, Deficiency Heat, Damp Heat, and Stagnant Blood. Modified Heart-clearing Lotus Seed Tablets are designed to remedy this situation when it causes chronic or recurrent vaginal inflammation or sores with or without accompanying menstrual dysfunction. Its composition is grounded in the theories of Zhu Dan-xi, Li Dong-yuan, and Fu Qing-zhu and treats all Five Phases. Therefore, it can be used throughout the seasons and for a long time. It can also be used by women who suffer from infertility, early or painful periods, or dysfunctional uterine bleeding all from this same scenario. Both men and women can use this formula for the treatment of chronic bladder infections, gonorrhea, diabetes, stomatitis, kidney stones, and, in men, prostatitis when due to this same complex Pattern of Disharmony. In other words, its range of application is large.

Modified One Stack Fertility-promoting Tablets

According to Chinese medical theory, conception is the result of the union of Reproductive Essence (*Sheng Zhi Zhi Jing*) from the man and Blood from the woman in the woman's *Bao Gong* or Uterus. Although there are several reasons why a woman's Blood may not be able to unite with the man's Reproductive Essence in her Uterus, in my experience, the most common reason in American women in their later thirties is a combination of Insufficient Blood and Liver Qi Congestion.

It is said in the *Nei Jing* that the *Yang Ming* begins to decline by 35. Since the *Yang Ming* is the Root of Postnatal production of Qi *and Blood*, a woman's Blood production tends to be reduced after her mid-thirties. The *Nei Jing* also says that one's Yin, i.e. Kidney Yin, is reduced by half by the time one is 40. Since Kidney Yin or *Jing* Essence also is a necessary factor in the creation of Blood, it is easy to see that in many women in their mid and late thirties and early forties Insufficient Blood is a major contributing factor to their difficulty in getting pregnant. In some cases, such women with Blood and *Jing* Deficiency may get pregnant only to suffer a miscarriage. In Chinese medicine, the *Tai* or Fetus is nourished by maternal Blood and *Jing* and Insufficient Blood is the most common cause of spontaneous abortion.

However, even if there is sufficient Blood and *Jing*, its flow must be patent and unimpeded for it to be able to circulate to the Uterus there to unite with the man's Reproductive Essence. Because of the endemic high levels of stress within modern, post-industrial society, Liver Qi Congestion is almost universal in adult Westerners. Because the Liver stores the Blood, regulates the menstruation, and maintains the free flow of Qi and therefore Blood, some element of Liver Qi Congestion almost always complicates American women's infertility.

Women with *Jing Xue* (Essence Blood) Deficiency and Liver Qi Congestion infertility also often have a certain amount of Deficiency Heat within their systems. Liver Qi itself, because it is a Yang accumulation, tends to waste or exhaust the Blood stored in the Liver/Uterus/*Chong Mai*. When Yin Blood becomes exhausted, this gives rise to Deficiency Heat. In some cases, this scenario includes *both* Deficiency and Depressive Heat, Deficiency Heat after the period and Depressive Heat before.

The signs and symptoms of this complex Pattern include early, scant periods, often coming at 22-24 day intervals, premenstrual breast distention, emotional hypersensitivity and lability, possible dysmenorrhea, fatigue, low back pain, possible tinnitus, numbness in the hands and feet or stiffness in the joints, dry skin and hair, depression, sighing and chest oppression, lower abdominal bloating, night blindness or blurred vision, insomnia, and a fine, possibly fast, wiry pulse. The period is early because of Heat but scant because of Essence Blood Deficiency. The premenstrual breast distention, emotional lability and depression, dysmenorrhea, sighing and chest oppression, lower abdominal distention, and wiry pulse all are due to Liver Qi. Whereas, the scanty period, numbness and stiffness, dry skin and hair, night blindness or blurred vision, and fine pulse are all indicative of Blood Deficiency. And the low back pain, fatigue, tinnitus, and insomnia all suggest Kidney Deficiency, in which case, the fine, *rapid* pulse further indicates Kidney Yin Deficiency.

According to the great Jin-Yuan master of Internal medicine, Zhu Dan-xi, the first thing to accomplish in the treatment of female infertility is to regulate the menses. "In order to cure infertility, the first important thing is to adjust the menstruation." In ten years of specialization as a TCM gynecologist, I have only seen one woman suffering from infertility whose menstruation was normal according to TCM parameters. Menstruation is the expression of sufficient and unblocked Blood. Therefore, when the menstruation is regulated, meaning that it comes at 28 days, is sufficient in volume, is of a good, red color, without pain, and not clotty, conception should naturally occur. In addition, it is very important to also eliminate any premenstrual breast distention which, classically, is associated in Chinese medicine with female infertility.

Based on my experience in treating American women in their thirties and forties for infertility, I have found a modification of One Stack Decoction (*Yi Guan Jian*) to be a very useful and effective guiding formula. The standard composition of One Stack Decoction is: Raw Rehmannia (Radix Rehmanniae Glutinosae), Glehnia (Radix Glehniae Littoralis), Ophiopogon (Tuber Ophiopogonis Japonicae), *Dang Gui* (Radix Angelicae Sinensis), Lycium Fruit (Fructus Lycii Chinensis), and Melia (Fructus Meliae Toosendan). The purpose of this formula is to replenish the Yin of the Liver and Kidneys and to regulate the flow of Liver Qi.

Based on this standard prescription, I have made several additions and subtractions. First, Rehmannia is greasy and cloying and often is not tolerated well by Westerners with Damp Spleens and Intestines. In China, Rehmannia is cheap, easily obtainable, and well established by habit and consequently is easy to use. However, it is not the only ingredient that tonifies Kidney Yin and Blood. Therefore, I have deleted it and replaced it with a combination of Loranthus (Ramus Loranthi Seu Visci), Ligustrum (Fructus Ligustri Lucidi), and Ashwagandha (Radix Withaniae Somniferae). I have also replaced Ophiopogon in this formula with Shatavari (Tuber Asparagi Racemosi). In addition, I have added Cuscuta (Semen Cuscutae Chinensis) and Placenta (Placenta Hominis) to further tonify Kidney *Jing* and Blood, and False Unicorn (Radix Helionadis Dioicae) to further regulate the Qi and Blood. Peony (Radix Alba Paeoniae Lactiflorae) is added to nourish the Blood and relax the Liver by softening and comforting it. Then, by adding Pseudostellaria (Radix Pseudostellariae Heterophyllae), Poria (Sclerotium Poriae Cocoris), and

Honey-baked Licorice (Radix Praeparatus Cum Melem Glycyr-rhizae Uralensis), the Spleen is tonified, the Middle harmonized, and the Stomach protected. Therefore, the final composition of this formula, Modified One Stack Fertility-promoting Tablets (*Fu Fang Yi Guan Yun Sheng Pian*) is:

Loranthus	12 parts
Ligustrum	12 "
Glehnia	12 "
Shatavari	12 "
Cuscuta	9 "
Pseudostellaria	9 "
Ashwagandha	9 "
Dang Gui	9 "
Peony	9 "
Lycium Fruit	9 "
Poria	9 "
False Unicorn	9 "
Melia	6 "
Honey-baked Licorice	3 "
Placenta	1.5 "

Loranthus (Ramus Loranthi Seu Visci) is a Yin-tonifying medicinal in Traditional Chinese Medicine. It is a parasite similar to mistletoe which grows on mulberry trees. It is Bitter, Sweet, and Neutral and enters the Liver and Kidneys. Loranthus tonifies the Liver and Kidneys; nourishes the Blood and benefits the Uterus; and expels Wind Dampness. Because this ingredient expels Wind Dampness, it has a Qi-activating property which keeps it from being cloying or stagnating. Likewise, although it tonifies Yin and Blood, it is not Damp or greasy. Symptomatically, it has a definite beneficial effect on the Uterus. Because it treats Restless Fetus and Fetal Leakage (threatened abortion and bleeding during pregnancy), Loranthus used beforehand can help prevent these occurrences after conception has taken place. This is a very useful herb for replacing Rehmannia in a number of instances.

Ligustrum (Fructus Ligustri Lucidi) is described below under Damiana & Gotu Kola Modified Two Immortals Tablets.

Glehnia (Radix Glehniae Littoralis) is a *Bu Yin* ingredient which is Sweet, Bitter, Bland, and Cool. It enters the Lungs and Stomach. Glehnia moistens the Lungs and nourishes the Stomach. It generates Fluids and clears Heat. Like Ophiopogon, Glehnia's Heat-clearing function is often over-looked. By clearing Heat from the Lungs and Stomach, Glehnia helps to control the Liver indirectly by way of the *Ke* or Control cycle. As mentioned above, commonly the Lungs are the repository of a certain amount of lingering Deficiency Heat. When this is cleared, the Lungs can flourish. When the Lungs flourish, the Liver is kept automatically in check. In addition, by tonifying the Yin of the Lungs and Stomach, the Yin of the entire organism is benefitted since Kidney Yin Deficiency often develops from Lung/Stomach Yin Deficiency.

Shatavari (Tuber Asparagi Racemosi) is the Ayurvedic species of asparagus. It is the single most important female tonic in Ayurveda and specifically promotes regeneration of the substance of the reproductive organs. Its taste is Sweet and Bitter and its temperature is Cold. It enters the Lungs and Kidneys, although, like Ophiopogon with which it is closely related, it also has an effect on the Stomach and Heart. It nourishes Yin and clears Heat and moistens the Lungs and nourishes the Kidneys. In Ayurvedic medicine, Shatavari specifically nourishes the ovum and increases female fertility. Therefore, in this formula, its symptomatic action is more germane than Ophiopogon's. Also, even in TCM, Asparagus is better for nourishing the Kidneys, the repository of *Jing* Essence, than Ophiopogon. Shatavari means "she with a hundred husbands" which gives a clear idea of the fecundity this herb imparts.

Cuscuta (Semen Cuscutae Chinensis) is a *Bu Yang* ingredient. However, it can be used to tonify either Deficient Yin or Deficient Yang. That is because it benefits the *Jing* Essence which itself can be either Yin or Yang. Essence can be used to build substance or it can be transformed into *Jing Qi* to create function. Cuscuta is Acrid, Sweet, and Neutral. It enters the Liver and Kidneys. Besides tonifying the Liver and Kidneys, Cuscuta also calms the Fetus and prevents threatened or habitual miscarriage. In addition, it benefits the Spleen and Kidneys and treats diarrhea or loose stools due to Spleen/Kidney Dual Deficiency. Cuscuta is Warm but not Dry. Therefore, it does not waste or exhaust Yin. Neither is it cloying or greasy.

Pseudostellaria (Radix Pseudostellariae Heterophyllae) has been described above.

Ashwagandha (Radix Withaniae Somniferae) is another important Ayurvedic medicinal. Michael Tierra says that it is Bitter, Sweet, and Warm and enters the Lung and Kidney Channels.[6] In many respects, it is very similar to Schizandra. It contains leakage of Lung Qi and facilitates the grasping of Lung Qi by the Kidneys. It restrains the Essence and calms the Spirit. It probably should be classified as an astringent, remembering that astringency (*Gu*) is one of the five basic functions of Qi which is Yang. Tierra classifies this medicinal as a *Bu Yang* ingredient, but this is more a matter of interpretation. By astringing Essence, the Kidneys are benefitted, both Yin and Yang. Clear Yang arises supported by True Yin, and therefore, there is both mental clarity and calm. Because the Kidneys are firm, the low back is strong and supple and the joints are healthy and nourished. And because the Lungs and Kidneys work together, Postnatal Qi and Blood flourish. Ashwagandha is sometimes thought of as a man's tonic, but, in fact, it also benefits the woman's Uterus. In this regard, it improves function as opposed to substance. David Frawley says it stabilizes the Fetus in Deficient women.[7] This again has to do with astringency.

Dang Gui (Radix Angelicae Sinensis) has been described above.

Peony (Radix Alba Paeoniae Lactiflorae) has been described above.

Lycium Fruit (Fructus Lycii Chinensis) is classified as a Blood-tonifying ingredient. It is Sweet and Neutral and enters the Liver and Kidneys. Like a number of other ingredients which enter both the Liver and Kidneys, Lycium Fruit has the capability of tonifying Liver Blood and Kidney Yin and Yang. It nourishes Liver Blood and tonifies Kidney Yin; benefits the Essence and brightens the eyes. When combined with *Dang Gui*, Glehnia, and Melia, Lycium Fruit treats epigastric and flank pain with dry mouth and throat, a bitter taste, and acid regurgitation, i.e. heartburn, due to a combination of Deficiency and Depressive Heat.

Poria (Sclerotium Poriae Cocoris) has been described above.

False Unicorn (Radix Helionadis Dioicae) should be categorized as a Blood-activating medicinal. It is Acrid, Bitter, and Warm and enters the Heart, Spleen, and Liver. It activates the Blood and transforms Stagnation, primarily in the Lower Burner. In addition, it clears and eliminates Damp Heat in the Lower Burner manifesting as leukorrhea. Like many other activating ingredients, False Unicorn not only activates the Blood but also the Qi. In Chinese medicine, some conditions are described as primarily Qi Stagnations complicated by Blood or Blood Stagnations complicated by Qi. False Unicorn is best for the latter. But because it also activates the Qi and dredges the Liver, it also harmonizes the Liver and Spleen/Liver and Stomach, similar to Albizzia and Saussurea. Therefore, it treats dyspepsia, lack of appetite, and morning sickness. Because it courses the Liver Channel, it has an especial effect on the genito-urinary tract. Therefore, it treats dysmenorrhea, delayed menstruation, amenorrhea, infertility, sacroiliac pain, and *Lin Bing*, all due to Liver Qi Stagnation. False Unicorn activates the Qi and harmonizes the Blood; consequently, it harmonizes the *Chong* and *Ren*. In addition, like Melia below, it also kills Worms.

Melia (Fructus Meliae Toosendan) is a Qi-regulator which is Bitter and Cold. It enters the Liver, Stomach, and Small Intestine Channels. It clears Heat and dries Dampness, regulates the Qi and stops pain. Like False Unicorn above, it also kills Worms. It is used to treat Damp Heat Qi Stagnation manifesting as pain in the epigastrium, flank, hypogastrium, and groin. In this formula, Melia is used to specifically course the Liver Channel in the Lower Burner and thus regulate the flow of Qi and Blood in the Uterus. Because Melia is Cold, although it activates the Qi, it in no way heats or exhausts Yin Blood.

Honey-baked Licorice (Radix Praeparatus Cum Mel Glycyrrhizae Uralensis) has been described above. In this formula, it specifically protects the Stomach from any harmful influence from Melia while at the same time aiding Glehnia, Shatavari, and Pseudostellaria in generating Fluids in the Stomach and promoting Lung Yin.

Placenta (Placenta Hominis) is a Yang tonic. It powerfully tonifies the Qi, Blood, Yang, and *Jing*. It is Sweet, Salty, and Warm and enters the Lungs, Liver, and Kidneys. Although Placenta is often used in cases of consumption (*Lao*) and convalescence, it is also used in gynecology to treat infertility, habitual miscarriage, and insufficient lactation. Whether Placenta tonifies the Qi, Blood, Yang, or *Jing* in a given individual depends upon the other ingredients with which it is

combined. In this formula, it is meant to tonify Lung Yin and
Qi, Spleen and Kidney Qi, Blood, and *Jing*. Placenta lends
itself well to administration by pill and has an obvious relationship with the Uterus. In TCM, the *Bao Gong* in a woman is
functionally analogous to the *Dan Tian* in a man. It is the place
where Blood is stored. Men store *Jing*; women, Blood. For
the same reason, the Liver is called the Prenatal Organ in
women.

This formula is designed to treat infertility in women suffering
from Blood and Yin Deficiency with a combination of Deficiency and Depressive Heat arising from Liver Qi. Such women
typically experience early, scant periods, breast distention, and
emotional lability and depression. In some cases where Yin
Deficiency mainly manifests after the period and where Liver
Qi and/or Depressive Fire is more pronounced before the
period, this formula can be used in rotation with a more
powerful Qi-regulating, dredging prescription, such as Bupleurum Entangled Qi Tablets, Relaxed Wanderer, or *Xiao Yao
Wan*. In such cases, Modified One Stack Fertility-promoting
Tablets should be given from the end of menstruation to mid-
cycle. Then from mid-cycle to the onset of the period, a
stronger Qi-regulating formula may be given as appropriate.
During the period itself, it is best not to take any medication
unless there is pronounced dysmenorrhea, which should be
treated at that point according to a discrimination of Patterns
(*Bian Zheng*).

Damiana & Gotu Kola Modified Two Immortals Tablets

Just as the onset of menstruation is called the arrival of *Tian
Kui*, menopause is called in Chinese the cessation of *Tian Kui*.
The *Tian Kui* or *Yue Jing*, moon flow, is the product of a
relative monthly repletion of Blood in women. Blood is created

out of the Pure Essence of Food and Liquids transformed by the Stomach/Spleen and the *Jing* Essence stored in the Kidneys. *Jing* Essence is necessary for the creation of Blood in the same way that *Yuan Qi* from the Kidneys is necessary for the creation of Postnatal Qi. Therefore, until Stomach/Spleen function matures and enters a dynamic relationship with the Kidneys at classically 7 x 2 or 14 years of age in females, there is not the replete production of Blood sufficient to flow over monthly as the period. However, the process of living is the consumption of *Jing* which is a Yin substance. Life itself can be seen as the evaporation and transformation of Yin by Yang, and by the age of 7 x 7 or 49, a woman's Kidney Yin or *Jing* is depleted to the point where her internal economy can no longer support a monthly discharge of Blood. There is no longer a relative Excess to be spared.

Therefore, the body in its wisdom shuts off this monthly discharge as one way of slowing the consumption of Yin and *Jing*. This is called a woman's change in life or her climacteric and it represents a definite reorganization of energies and priorities within the woman. When this change proceeds smoothly, there are minimal complaints associated . But some women seem to get hung up in mid-process. For whatever reason, their Blood and/or Yin have become so weak that even after the crisis triggering the shutting off of the menstruation, they cannot replenish their Blood and Yin as quickly and as easily as other women. So they experience prolonged Yin and Blood Deficiency symptoms and Floating Upward of Yang: hot flashes, night sweats, irritability, hysteria, insomnia, palpitations, vertigo, tinnitus, Heat in the Five Centers, forgetfulness, hypertension, low back pain, possible migraines, and depression.

Modern TCM gynecology texts differentiate menopausal syndrome into four different *Zheng* or Patterns. They are Liver Kidney Yin Deficiency, Kidney Yang Deficiency, Dual Kidney Yin & Yang Deficiency, and Heart Spleen Dual Deficiency.

Liver Kidney Yin Deficiency is shorthand for saying Liver
Blood/Kidney Yin Deficiency and Heart Spleen Dual Deficiency
means specifically Heart Blood/Spleen Qi Deficiency. However,
in clinical practice, one does not see such discrete Patterns in
individual patients and especially not in American women.
Rather, most menopausal American women tend to have some
element of Liver Blood, Kidney Yin *and* Yang , Heart Blood,
and Spleen Qi Deficiency with Floating Yang in the upper body
and Fluid Dryness in the lower.

Traditional Chinese gynecologists working at the Shu Gang
Hospital in Shanghai have developed a very effective formula
called Two Immortal Decoction (*Er Xian Tang*) to treat Liver
Kidney Yin & Yang Deficiency with Flaring of Deficiency Fire
Above. It consists of Curculigo (Rhizoma Curculiginis Or-
choidis), Epimedium (Herba Epimedii), Morinda (Radix
Morindae Officinalis), *Dang Gui* (Radix Angelicae Sinensis),
Phellodendron (Cortex Phellodendri), and Anemarrhena
(Rhizoma Anemarrhenae Asphodeloidis). However, in clinical
practice, this formula is seldom used unmodified. The following
formula is for the typically complicated menopausal syndrome
I see amongst American women. It is composed of Two
Immortal Decoction plus Two Extremes Pills (*Er Zhi Wan*) plus
Licorice, Wheat, & Red Dates Decoction (*Gan Mai Da Zao
Tang*) *Jia Jian*, i.e. with additions and subtractions.

Schizandra	9 parts
Oyster Shell	9 "
Epimedium	9 "
Morinda	9 "
Dang Gui	9 "
Ligustrum	9 "
Eclipta	9 "
Damiana	9 "
Gotu Kola	9 "
Pseudostellaria	9 "

Red Dates	9	"
Anemarrhena	9	"
Phellodendron	6	"
Honey-baked Licorice	6	"
Scrophularia	6	"
Eight Moon Fruit	6	"
Aloe	3	"

Curculigo has been deleted from the standard Two Immortals Decoction since this formula is often too Hot for American women with all three Kidney Yang tonics. Without Curculigo, it is less likely to cause a build-up of Evil Heat within. Curculigo has been replaced by Damiana which is described below.

The ingredients of Two Extremes Pills, Eclipta and Ligusticum, have been added to increase the tonification of Yin and Blood, but without greasy, cloying ingredients like Rehmannia. Also, two of the three ingredients of Licorice, Wheat, & Red Date Decoction have been added to address Heart/Spleen Deficiency. Wheat (Fructus Tritici Aestivi Levis) has been deleted because it does not lend itself to incorporation in tablets. It has been replaced by Schizandra.

In addition, Pseudostellaria has been added to increase the Qi-tonifying effect of this prescription. Oyster Shell is meant to suppress Floating Yang and astringe Yin, thus eliminating hot flashes and night sweats. Gotu Kola and Eight Moon Fruit are meant to dredge any Stagnant Liver Qi which often predates and complicates menopause. Neither of these two ingredients exhaust Yin and both are specifically indicated during the climacteric. Scrophularia is meant to not only clear Deficiency Heat but aid Eclipta in preventing avalanche or breakthrough bleeding. And Aloe is meant to promote bowel movements and to purge Liver Heat downwards just a bit.

Schizandra (Fructus Schizandrae Chinensis) is called Five Taste

Seed in Chinese. Although its flavor is usually described as Sweet, Sour, and slightly Salty, it fact, it contains all five flavors. Its skin is Sweet, its flesh is Sour and Salty, and its core is Acrid and Bitter. Therefore, although it is also usually said Schizandra enters the Liver, Lungs, and Kidneys, in fact, it also enters the Spleen and Heart as well. In this regard, its energy first descends from the Spleen to the Kidneys and Liver from whence if then ascends to the Heart and Lungs. This is similar to how Ginseng works. Schizandra's temperature is Warm.

Schizandra is categorized in TCM as an astringent, but it is also a tonic. It tonifies both Yin and Yang and both Pre and Postnatal Qi. Schizandra stops energy from leaking from the body, whether from the Lungs, the Skin, or the Two Yin (anus & urethra/vagina). It also promotes strong muscles, soft skin, and high density bones. In addition, Dr. Sung Baek says that Schizandra warms the Uterus and enhances hormone production, especially in older women. In the present formula, it is used to replace Wheat (Fructus Tritici Aestivi Levis) since Wheat is too inert an ingredient for tableting and because Schizandra both stops spontaneous and night sweating and calms the Spirit in the treatment of anxiety and insomnia.

Oyster Shell (Concha Ostreae) is a so-called heavy sedative in Chinese medicine. It is Salty, Astringent, and Cool and it enters the Liver and Kidneys. Its functions are to calm the Spirit by restraining Floating Yang. It prevents leakage of Fluids, including perspiration, leukorrhea, and uterine bleeding in women. Therefore, it benefits the Yin. Its functions of softening Hardness and dissipating Nodules are germane to this formula in that they help to prevent any tendency to breast malignancies. Oyster Shell is used herein mostly to Lower Yang and to stop sweating, but obviously it has several other subsidiary benefits for menopausal women. In some cases, its ability to also astringe the Blood is useful in terms of breakthrough and dysfunctional uterine bleeding.

Epimedium (Herba Epimedii) is a Yang tonic herb. It is Acrid, Sweet, and Warm. Epimedium also enters the Liver and Kidneys. It tonifies the Kidneys and fortifies the Yang. However, it also tonifies both Yin and Yang and actually harnesses Ascendant Liver Yang. In addition, it expels Wind, Cold, and Dampness in cases of *Bi* Obstruction with symptoms such as numbness and cramping in the hands and feet. Unlike some Yang tonics, the energy of Epimedium tends to promote its own easy circulation. It does not tend to accumulate, but disperses throughout the system. This prevents it from causing pathologic Heat to accumulate.

Morinda (Radix Morindae Officinalis) is also a *Bu Yang* herb. It is similarly Acrid, Sweet, and Warm and enters the Liver and Kidneys. It tonifies the Kidneys and fortifies the Yang and strengthens the *Jin* Sinews and the Bones. Because it disperses Wind and expels Cold in cases of *Bi* Obstruction, Morinda, like Epimedium, tends to circulate itself without pathologic accumulation of Heat. Morinda and Epimedium work together to Yangize the woman who, energetically in some ways, at menopause becomes more like a man. (Likewise, at their climacteric, men become energetically more like women.)

Damiana (Folium Turnerae Aphrodisiacae) is another Yang tonic, though not a traditional Chinese one. It is Acrid and Warm and enters the Liver and Kidneys. It tonifies the Kidneys and fortifies the Yang. However, it aids in the smooth flow of Qi and Blood, moistens the Intestines, and promotes bowel movements. It strengthens the *Jin* Sinews and the Bones. Therefore, it would seem to have some Blood-tonifying or *Jing*-tonifying effect as well. Besides alleviating recurrent genito-urinary complaints due to emotional causes, Damiana also relieves anxiety and depression. Some people say it has a salutary effect on the dreams; therefore, we might say it calms the *Hun*.

Dang Gui (Radix Angelicae Sinensis) has been described above under Gotu Kola Heavenly Water 15.

Ligustrum (Fructus Ligustri Lucidi) is a *Bu Yin* herb. It is Sweet, Sour, and Cool and enters the Liver and Kidneys. It nourishes Liver Blood and tonifies Kidney Yin. Symptomatically, Ligusticum is indicated for the treatment of dizziness, spots in front of the eyes, tinnitus, and premature greying of the hair.

Eclipta (Herba Ecliptae Prostratae) is often prescribed together with Ligustrum. They are very similar in properties and functions. Eclipta is a *Bu Yin* ingredient which is Sweet, Sour, and Cool and enters the Liver and Kidneys. It likewise nourishes Liver Blood and tonifies Kidney Yin. However, it also cools the Blood and stops bleeding, breakthrough and dysfunctional uterine bleeding not being an uncommon part of many women's menopause.

Pseudostellaria (Radix Pseudostellariae Heterophyllae) has been discussed under Gotu Kola Heavenly Water 15 above. In this formula, Pseudostellaria is meant to tonify the Qi and benefit the Spleen in order to ensure the Spleen is generating and sending up enough Blood to the Heart.

Red Dates (Fructus Zizyphi Jujubae) have been discussed above as well. Here it should be remembered that Red Dates tonify the Qi *and* nourish the Blood while at the same time calming the Spirit.

Gotu Kola (Radix Hydrocotylis Asiaticae) has been described above. In this formula, it is meant to decongest Liver Qi and relieve depression while at the same time not evaporating or wasting Yin Blood.

Anemarrhena (Rhizoma Anemarrhenae Asphodeloidis) is a Heat-clearing medicinal. It is Bitter and Cold and enters the

Lung, Stomach, and Kidneys. It clears Heat and quells Fire.
But it also nurtures Yin, moistens Dryness, and generates
Fluids. It is used to treat night sweats, Heat in the Five
Centers, and bleeding gums as well as nervous excitability and
irritability. Anemarrhena is commonly matched with either
Phellodendron or Scrophularia, both of which are in this
formula.

Scrophularia (Radix Scrophulariae Ningpoensis) cools the
Blood. It is Salty, slightly Bitter, and Cool. It enters the Lung,
Stomach, and Kidney Channels. Scrophularia clears Heat and
cools the Blood; nourishes Yin; and quells Heat and dissolves
Fire Toxins. In addition, it softens Hardness and dissipates
Nodules. In this formula, it is meant to assist Anemarrhena in
controlling Deficiency Fire and nourishing Yin and Eclipta in
cooling the Blood and stopping erratic bleeding.

Eight Moon Fruit (Fructus Akebiae Trifoliatae) is a somewhat
lesser used Qi-regulating herb. It is Bitter and Cold and enters
the Liver and Stomach Channels. It promotes the free flow of
Qi and activates the Blood. It kills Worms and dissolves
Toxins. Eight Moon Fruit is indicated for the treatment of
Chest *Bi* or Obstruction and for relieving pain due to congestion of the Liver and Stomach. It also treats period pain.
Eight Moon Fruit is considered especially appropriate for
dredging the Qi during menopause.

Phellodendron (Cortex Phellodendri Amurensis) clears Heat
and dries Dampness. Its taste is Bitter and its temperature is
Cold. It enters the Kidney and Bladder Channels. Although
this herb drains Damp Heat, particularly from the Lower
Burner, it also clears Ascension of Deficiency Fire due to
Kidney Yin Deficiency. In addition, Phellodendron drains Fire
and dissolves Fire Toxins. When coupled with Anemarrhena,
it treats night sweats and hot flashes due to Floating Yang.

Honey-baked Licorice (Radix Praeparatus Cum Melem Glycyr-rhizae Uralensis) has been described above under Gotu Kola Heavenly Water 15.

Aloe (Herba Aloes) is categorized as a purgative in Traditional Chinese Medicine. It is Sweet, Bitter, and Cold and enters the Large Intestine. It purges Fire and moves the stool and clears Heat and cools the Liver. Therefore, it is used to treat chronic constipation, dizziness, irritability, tinnitus, headache, and red eyes. Michael Tierra says that Aloe is useful for the treatment of PMS and menopause and this is correct.[8] He also says it enters the Liver and functions as a Yin tonic. However, because of the close inter-relationship between the Liver and Large Intestine, it is possible for Aloe to purge Heat from the Liver without "entering" the Liver directly. Likewise, because of the Large Intestine's relationship to the generation of Yin in the Lower Burner via the Internal Duct, purgation of the Bowel may result in improved generation of Yin without going so far as to say it is a Yin tonic. In any case, Aloe's inclusion in this formula helps to alleviate the chronic constipation which often accompanies menopause, helps to check the Liver and benefits the Yin, and is appropriate in small amounts especially in pill form.

This formula is meant as a whole to treat a wide range of menopausal signs and symptoms. These include hot flashes and night sweats, depression, anxiety, irritability, palpitations, low back pain, tinnitus, insomnia, constipation, breakthrough and dysfunctional uterine bleeding, bleeding gums, and even greying of the hair. It can also prevent the occurrence of menopausal migraines and hypertension and can help to prevent breast malignancies.

Once women go through their change in life, their consumption of Yin slows down drastically. No longer losing Blood on a monthly basis they cannot really afford to lose, they retrench and consolidate their Yin. If menopause proceeds smoothly and is not allowed to drag itself out, most women can live another twenty years before beginning again to feel marked symptoms of decline. Damiana & Gotu Kola Modified Two Immortals Tablets are designed to make that transition as smooth and as quick as possible.

All four of these formulas are available from Health Concerns, 2236 Mariner Square Dr. #103, Alameda, CA 94501 1-800-233-9355.

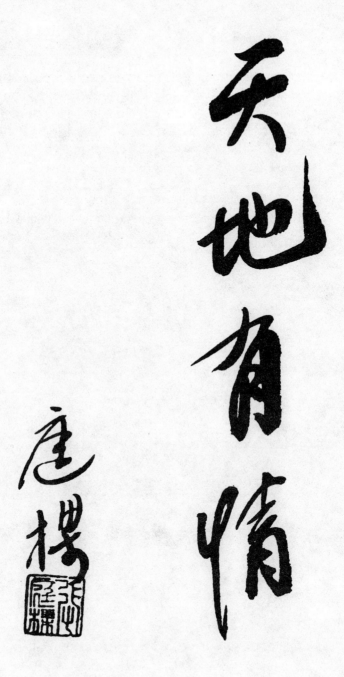

Heaven and Earth are compassionate

FAR-REACHING ASPIRATION TABLETS

FOR RELIEF OF DEPRESSION

Many American women suffer from depression due to frustration and pent-up emotions. Chinese medicine describes depression as being mostly due to Stagnant Qi and Liver Congestion. In Chinese medicine, the Qi and the mind are essentially identical. Objectively, the Chinese doctor describes the flow of Qi. Subjectively, we experience this flow as our mind, emotions, and sensations. At root, every emotion is a felt physical sensation which has been given an abstract name, such as anger and grief. Many practitioners learn that anger makes the Qi rise, but that is a somewhat one-sided understanding based on Western linear concepts of causality. Anger makes the Qi rise, but also *is* rising Qi. Likewise, fright scatters the Qi but simultaneously fright is scattered Qi. This goes for all the Seven Passions of Chinese medicine. Depression is stuck Qi, Qi which simply is not flowing freely. It is the Liver's job to maintain the free flow and patency of the Qi and Blood. Frustration or impedance of the free flow of Qi causes Liver Qi Congestion and Liver Qi Congestion is experienced by many people as depression.

Our modern Western society is, compared to most traditional cultures, very frustrating for all of us. And for women these days life seems especially frustrating. Therefore, the incidence of Liver Qi and depression amongst American women is higher than in, say, a traditional culture like rural China. Although Traditional Chinese Medicine describes the mechanism of depression quite well, I have found that there are more and perhaps even better Western herbal medicines than Chinese for the treatment of depression. In Asia, the notions that life is inherently unsatisfactory and that suffering is endemic to the human condition have possibly mitigated against Chinese doctors paying as much attention to the herbal treatment of mental/emotional problems in general. Whereas, in the West, we have a long tradition of internal medicine treating tempera-mental disequilibrium. For instance, in Galenic medicine, choleric, melancholic, sanguine, and phlegmatic tendencies were seen as much character traits as humoral imbalances and traditional Western herbs have always been used to treat overtly psychological complaints. By crafting a formula based on Chinese medical disease mechanism theory and using a combination of both Chinese and Western herbal medicines, we can create a very precise and effective treatment for the kind of depression so commonly encountered amongst American female patients.

The Chinese treatment principles for treating depression due to Liver Qi Congestion are to dredge the Qi, relax the Liver, and relieve depression. However, because of the interdependence of the Six Stagnations, a good prescription for depression should also ensure transformation of Phlegm, seepage of Water, clearing of Transformative or Stagnant Heat, activation of the Blood, and regulation of Ascension and Descension. The ingredients in Far-reaching Aspiration Tablets do all these things and also each has been selected because of its special, symptomatic effectiveness in the treatment of depression. In other words, not only does each ingredient fulfill one or more of the above treatment principles, but each one also has a known, definite, and pronounced traditional effect on the human affect as an anti-depressant. This is the selection and composition of herbal ingredients based both on abstract principles and symptomatic empiricism.

Polygala	9 parts
Vervain	9 "
Gambir	9 "
Gardenia	9 "
Albizzia Flowers	9 "
Damiana	9 "
Peony	9 "
Dang Gui	9 "
Pinellia	9 "
Poria	9 "
Aquilaria	3 "

Polygala (Radix Polygalae Tenuifoliae) is categorized as a Heart-nourishing, Spirit-calming medicinal in Chinese medicine. Heart nourishment in Chinese medicine implies nourishment by Blood. However, besides nourishing the Heart, Polygala also facilitates the flow of Heart Qi and relieves constrained Qi flow in the chest due to pent-up emotions and excessive brooding. *Xiong Men* in Chinese means chest oppression or a tight, heavy, constricted chest. This is a common symptom of stress and depression and is caused by both flushing up of accumulated Qi from the Liver under the Diaphragm and the stagnation of Qi flowing through the *Jue Yin* and *Shao Yang* Collaterals of the chest. In addition, Polygala expels Phlegm and opens the Orifices, thus improving both Heart and Lung function. Therefore, Polygala has a salutary effect on the *Shen* which resides in the Heart, the *Hun* which resides in the Liver, and the *Po* which resides in the Lungs. When Qi becomes stuck, often Phlegm accumulates and it is this accumulation of Phlegm which contributes to depressed persons' inability to contact and interact with the outside world. Polygala's taste is Bitter and Acrid and its temperature is Warm. It enters the Heart, Lung, and Kidney Channels. Its Chinese name, *Yuan Zhi*, Profound

Will or Far-reaching Aspiration, attests to this medicinal's ability to catalyze renewed vim, vigor, and zest for life.

Vervain (Herba Verbenae Officinalis) is also Acrid and Bitter, but its temperature is Cool. It enters the Liver and Gall Bladder Channels and would probably be classified as an Acrid, Cool Surface-relieving medicinal similar in many respects to Bupleurum in Chinese medicine. Like Bupleurum, Vervain has pronounced Qi-activating and Qi-regulating properties. Vervain resolves *Shao Yang Fen* diseases, but more importantly, it dredges the Liver and relieves constraint. For this purpose, it can be used to treat such symptoms as dizziness, vertigo, tinnitus, chest, breast, and flank pain, headache, *Qi Lin* or urinary strangury due to emotional constraint, loss of appetite and epigastric pain, menstrual complaints, especially delayed and painful periods, and mastitis and agalactia. Like Bupleurum, Vervain also raises the Clear Yang. However, it is my opinion that Vervain has more pronounced regulating function on the mind and emotions than Bupleurum and that it is more effective for relieving nervous tension and depression than that classical Chinese herb. Western herbalists have traditionally used Vervain to treat depression, melancholia, and hysteria.

Gambir (Ramulus Uncariae Cum Uncem) is categorized in Chinese medicine as Wind-extinguishing, tremor-stopping medicinal. It is Sweet and Cool and enters the Liver and the Heart. This ingredient extinguishes internally generated Wind due to hyperactivity of the Liver and alleviates spasms. It also quells Heat and pacifies the Liver. It is often used in Chinese medicine for treating emotional states caused by Constrained Liver Qi transforming under pressure into Fire and Wind manifesting as anger, irritability, a tendency to fly off the handle, and emotional shakiness. In Chinese medicine, Gambir is used to *Jiang Ya* or reduce upsurging pressure due to frustration.

Gardenia (Fructus Gardeniae Jasminoidis) is a Heat-clearing medicinal. It is Bitter and Cold and enters the Liver, Lungs, and Stomach. It clears Heat and alleviates irritability. It drains Damp Heat from any of the Three Burners and treats Damp Heat entangled with Constrained Liver Qi as in Yang hepatitis. In addition, Gardenia cools the Blood and stops bleeding but also reduces swelling and activates Congealed Blood due to trauma. Gardenia is especially effective for clearing Transformative or Stagnant Heat arising out of Liver Qi Congestion and is well known in Asia as an anti-depressant.

Albizzia Flowers (Flos Albizziae Julibrissinis) are a somewhat lesser known but very effective Heart-nourishing, Spirit-calming Chinese medicinal. They are Sweet and Neutral and enter the Heart and Liver. They promote the free flow of Constrained Liver Qi, activate the Blood, and calm the Spirit. They are especially useful for treating depression, irritability, chest oppression, and epigastric pain due to frustration and pent-up emotions. In this formula, Albizzia Flowers assist Polygala in nourishing the Heart, calming the Spirit, and broadening the Chest, and Vervain and Gambir in dredging the Liver and relieving depression.

Damiana (Folium Turnerae Aphrodisiaciae) is a Yang tonic which is Acrid and Warm and enters the Liver and Kidneys. It tonifies the Kidneys and fortifies the Yang. However, it promotes the flow of Qi and Blood, moistens the Intestines, and promotes bowel movements. It strengthens the *Jin* Sinews and the Bones and, therefore, it would seem to have some Blood-tonifying effect as well. Some might question Damiana's inclusion in a formula for depression since depression is so often complicated by Stagnant Heat. However, like Epimedium, Damiana circulates the Yang it restores and thus activates pent-up and over-heated Qi. Therefore, in this formula, it assists Vervain in elevating the Clear Yang and thus elevating the Spirit. Damiana is a well-known traditional Western anti-depressant.

Dang Gui (Radix Angelicae Sinensis) is a *Bu Xue* or Blood-tonifying medicinal in Traditional Chinese Medicine. It is Sweet, Acrid, Bitter, and Warm and enters the Heart, Liver and Spleen, the three Organs which control the Blood. It tonifies the Blood and regulates the menses; activates and harmonizes the Blood; and moistens the Intestines and moves the stools. In this formula, it is meant primarily to relax the Liver by nourishing Liver Blood. However, by regulating the menses and activating the Blood which is the mother of the Qi, Dang Gui also helps discharge pent-up Qi with the menstrual discharge.

Peony (Radix Alba Paeoniae Lactiflorae) is also a *Bu Xue* herb. It is Bitter and Sour and Cool. Peony enters the Liver and Spleen and nourishes the Blood. It harmonizes the Liver and stops pain by softening and smoothing the Liver. Peony also consolidates the Yin and harmonizes the *Ying* and *Wei*. Here it is used to assist Dang Gui in nourishing Liver Blood, activating the Blood so as to prevent Blood Stagnation, and regulating the menstrual discharge.

Pinellia (Rhizoma Praeparata Cum Zingiberem Pinelliae Ternatae) is a Cold Phlegm-transformer. It is Acrid and Warm and enters the Spleen and Stomach. This medicinal is considered somewhat Toxic in Chinese medicine if used in too high a dose or for too long. However, this toxicity is allayed when the herb is processed with Ginger as in this formula. Pinellia dries Dampness, transforms Phlegm, and descends Rebellious or Counterflow Qi. It harmonizes the Stomach and stops vomiting and dissipates nodules and reduces swelling. In this formula, Pinellia assists Polygala in transforming Phlegm. However, it also helps insure proper Ascension and Descension and thus helps to lower Stomach/Liver Qi and move food downwards. Thus it also benefits the Spleen and helps the

Spleen keep the Liver in check. Although this is the one Chinese herb in this formula not considered a specific anti-depressant, because of its Qi-regulating properties as well as the tendency of Phlegm to complicate Liver Qi Patterns, Pinellia is commonly encountered in Chinese formulas specifically designed to treat depression, such as *Si Qi Tang* and *Wen Dan Tang*. In particular, Pinellia is useful for relieving pressure, constraint, and pent-up feelings in the chest and pit of the stomach.

Poria (Sclerotium Poriae Cocoris) drains Dampness or seeps Water, however one chooses to say this in English. It is Sweet, Bland, and Neutral and enters the Heart, Spleen, and Lungs. It promotes urination and leeches out Dampness, strengthens the Spleen and harmonizes the Middle, transforms Phlegm, and quiets the Heart and calms the Spirit. Dampness is one of the Six Stagnations. When Liver Qi impedes Spleen *Qi Hua* or *Yun Hua*, Dampness tends to accumulate. This Yin Evil thus further impedes the transportation and transformation of Qi and this creates a vicious cycle. By seeping Dampness, this Yin impediment to free Qi flow is removed. Poria assists Pinellia in eliminating Dampness by addressing that issue from a different angle. It also assists Pinellia in harmonizing the Middle. *He Zhong* means ascending the Pure and descending the Turbid which is accomplished by regulating the Qi flow of the Stomach and Spleen. The Stomach Qi should flow down and the Spleen Qi should flow up. Also, Poria assists both Pinellia and Polygala in transforming Phlegm. In its own right, Poria is an *An Shen* or Spirit-calming medicinal with definite nervine effects.

Aquilaria (Lignum Aquilariae Agallochae) is a very precious herbal medicine much valued and used in Ayurvedic, Tibetan, and Chinese medicines. In TCM, it is classified as a *Li Qi* or Qi-regulating ingredient. It is Acrid, Bitter, Warm, and Aromatic. It enters the Kidney, Spleen, and Stomach Channels. Aquilaria

activates the Qi and stops pain; it reverses Rebellion or
Counterflow Qi; and it aids the Kidneys in grasping or consolidating the Qi. In Tibetan medicine, this is perhaps the main
medicinal for treating mental/emotional problems. There are
many qualities or grades of this medicinal sold and the higher
the quality, the greater the *Xiang* or aroma. Likewise, the more
the aroma, the more pronounced and profound this herb's
effect on the mind and the less needs to be used in the
formula. Like Polygala, Aquilaria can be considered a pectoral,
for it broadens the chest and relieves chest oppression due to
Qi accumulation and ascension. In this regard, Aquilaria not
only activates the Qi but holds the Qi down at its Root in the
Lower Burner, thus providing a sense of stability and grounded-
ness.

Taken as a whole, this formula addresses all the major aspects
and complications of depression: Stagnant Qi, Stagnant Blood,
Heat, Dampness, and Food, and Phlegm Entanglement. It
treats feelings of chest oppression and constriction, lack of
appetite, irritability, anger, and frustration, flank pain, bitter
taste in the mouth, burping, belching, and epigastric pain, and
a tendency towards constipation or sluggish stools. It is my
experience that mental/emotional disturbances often respond
better to smaller doses taken over long periods of time.
Therefore, this formula lends itself to administration by tablet.
For successful treatment, its use should be accompanied by
regular aerobic exercise, daily programmed deep relaxation, a
diet conducive to the Liver and Spleen, regular laughter
provoked by comedies, and involvement in public service or
charitable activities.

This formula is available from Health Concerns, 2236 Mariner
Square Dr. #103, Alameda, CA, 94501, 1-800-233-9355.

Milk Thistle & Aloe 11 Tablets

For the Relief of Chronic Constipation

Chronic constipation can be both bothersome and difficult to treat. Many Chinese formulas do not address well the chronic constipation often met in American women. Either they are too strong and cause diarrhea, such as *Da Chai Hu Tang, Da Cheng Qi Tang,* and *Xiao Cheng Qi Tang,* or their laxative effect is too weak, such as *Ji Chuan Tang,* and they don't work. This is because most Chinese laxative formulas are designed to treat either Heat in the *Yang Ming* or Intestinal Dryness/Kidney Yang Deficiency due to old age. However, in my experience, many American women with chronic constipation suffer from Liver Qi Congestion affecting the Lungs, Spleen, Stomach, and the Intestinal *Luo.*

In such cases, the Liver fails to maintain the patency of peristalsis. This it does by releasing bile into the Intestines. When there is Liver Qi Congestion, this bile tends not to be released and thus the Intestines become sluggish. This can be described according to Five Phase theory as Liver insulting the Large Intestine. At the same time, the Liver also tends to affect the Lungs' function as well similarly due to insult. It is the Lung Qi which must disperse and descend and which supplies the downward descending, motivating force for the Large Intestine. In such cases, constipation is accompanied by chest distress or oppression, a full feeling in the chest which many people associate with stress.

Likewise, when the Liver becomes congested and, therefore, Excess, the Stomach/Spleen are both also effected. Most typically the Spleen becomes Deficient and the Stomach becomes Excess. When the Spleen becomes Deficient, it has trouble transporting and transforming Foods and Liquids and thus Dampness tends to accumulate in the Spleen. The presence of this Dampness compromises even further the function of the Spleen and causes soft, sticky, incomplete stools. The Stomach, on the other hand, tends to become Excess, which also means Hot. Liver Qi and Stomach Qi tend to flush up together towards the Lungs and Heart and also tend to transform into Heat. This Heat can exhaust Body Fluids causing dry stools and even heartburn. When the Stomach and Spleen come out of balance in this way, ascension of the Pure and descension of the Turbid becomes impaired making defecation difficult.

When such a scenario exists over time, the Blood in the *Luo Mai* or secondary Collaterals in the Lower Burner in general but Intestines in particular becomes Stagnant. Since Stagnant Blood impedes the Qi, Qi-regulating medicinals alone are not enough to overcome this long-term, chronic blockage. Often this blockage and stagnation of the Blood also manifests as hemorrhoids, varicose veins, and/or various menstrual complaints.

In addition, when Liver and Stomach Heat draft upward, the *Ming Men Zhi Huo* or Lifegate Fire declines in the Lower Burner. The body is Hot above but Cold below. Since the Kidneys rule the Intestines according to the *Nei Jing*, it is also beneficial to return this Yang Qi to its source in the Kidneys/Lower Burner to provide strong motivation for the Intestines.

This complicated scenario underscores the close physiological interdependence of the Liver, Gall Bladder, Stomach, Spleen,

Lungs, Large Intestine, and the Kidneys. To treat this kind of chronic and recalcitrant constipation, the requisite therapeutic principles are to: 1) dredge the Liver; 2) benefit the Spleen; 3) eliminate Dampness but at the same time moisten Dryness and clear Heat as necessary; 4) return Yang to its Source; and 5) destagnate the Blood in the *Luo Mai*. For these purposes I have formulated Milk Thistle & Aloe 11 Constipation Tablets. These tablets consist of:

Milk Thistle Seeds	9 parts
Cascara Sagrada	9 "
Barberry	9 "
Dang Gui	9 "
Persica	9 "
Atractylodes	9 "
Trichosanthes	9 "
Aurantium Immaturus	6 "
Cinnamon	6 "
Saussurea	6 "
Amomum	3 "
Licorice	3 "
Aloe	1/2 "

Milk Thistle Seeds (Semen Silybi Mariani) are Sweet, Bitter, slightly Acrid, and slightly Cool. They enter the Liver and Large Intestine Channels. They are a Blood de-stagnating medicinal which also lubricates the Intestines promoting bowel movements. Because they are slightly Acrid they also activate the Qi and dredge the Liver. However, I believe their main effect is on the Blood. In Western Naturopathy, Milk Thistle Seeds are used to treat both gall and Kidney stones. Typically, acute episodes of cholelithiasis and nephrolithiasis are accompanied by sharp, stabbing pain. This type of pain is due to Blood Stagnation. Milk Thistle Seeds are also used to treat chronic hepatitis, hepatomegaly, and cirrhosis of the liver. In all three of these diseases, Blood Stagnation typically plays a part.   Likewise, Milk Thistle Seeds are used to treat dysmenorrhea, delayed menstruation, and amenorrhea and a species of each of these menstrual disorders are due to Stagnant Blood. And finally, Milk Thistle Seeds are also used as a lactagogue. Milk is made from Blood and the breasts are connected to the *Chong Mai* which has its root in the Uterus/*Bao Gong*. Stagnant Blood in the Uterus impedes the creation of fresh Blood and thus affects the abundance of milk. In addition, because Silybum is Bitter and slightly Cool, it has some Heat-clearing effect on the Liver. But because it is also Sweet it also benefits Yin. Like Semen Cassiae Torae, Milk Thistle Seeds are appropriate for treating chronic constipation due to Liver Blood Deficiency. Like Semen Pruni Persicae, they are also appropriate for treating constipation complicated by Stagnant Blood.

Cascara Sagrada (Cortex Rhamni Purshianae) should be categorized as a purgative medicinal according to Chinese medicine. It is Bitter and Cold and enters the Spleen, Stomach, Liver, and Large Intestine. It drains Heat and moves the stools while also clearing Heat and cooling the Liver. It is an excellent medicinal specifically for the treatment of chronic constipation due to Liver Qi Stagnation. In this formula, Cascara Sagrada assists Milk Thistle Seeds in both dredging the Liver and promoting bowel movements.

Barberry (Cortex Radicis Berberis Vulgaris) is categorized as a purgative in Western herbalism, but in Chinese medicine it should probably be classified as an Acrid, Cool, Surface-relieving medicinal similar to Bupleurum and Cimicifuga. In addition to being Acrid and Cool, it is also Bitter and Astringent as well. It enters the Liver, Gall Bladder, Spleen, Stomach, and Large Intestine Channels. Barberry relieves the Surface and encourages the eruption of rashes. It dredges the Liver and promotes bowel movements. Barberry also raises the Yang to rescue prolapse and at the same time dissolves Fire

Poison affecting the Stomach Channel.

Because Barberry harmonizes the Liver/Spleen and Stomach/Intestines, it treats poor appetite, stuffy chest, abdominal distention, and chronic problems of the stools including both diarrhea and constipation. At the same time, it clears and eliminates Damp Heat from the Lower Burner and therefore treats venereal infections with yellow discharge, burning, bloody stools, and hemorrhoids. In addition, it both clears Heat from the upper reaches of the Liver Channel, the gums, throat, and head, but also raises prolapsed Qi from the pelvis causing hemorrhoids and dysmenorrhea. And finally, it also harmonizes the *Shao Yang Fen* or level of a *Shang Han* or acute, Externally invading disease. Therefore, Barberry has a wide range of salutary effects and not only assists Milk Thistle and Cascara Sagrada in dredging the Liver and promoting bowel movements, but also benefits the Stomach/Spleen and protects against excessive cooling or purgation by these ingredients.

Dang Gui (Radix Angelicae Sinensis) is a Blood tonic ingredient which also moistens the Intestines and promotes bowel movements. Because Intestinal Fluids and Blood are all part of the Yin, tonifying the Blood can have a beneficial effect on Intestinal function. In addition, tonifying the Blood helps to harmonize the Liver. *He Gan* means to nourish and dredge the Liver simultaneously. By nourishing Liver Blood, the Liver is induced to relax, smooth, or soften itself, thus achieving free flow of Qi through moistening. Dang Gui also activates the Blood and transforms Stagnation. Since some element of Blood Stagnation often complicates chronic Qi Congestion, this too is beneficial in this formula. Dang Gui is Sweet, Acrid, Bitter, and Warm and enters the Heart, Liver, and Spleen. It treats menstrual complaints in general, whether due to Blood Deficiency or Stagnation, and is sometimes referred to (erroneously but tellingly) as woman's Ginseng.

Persica (Semen Pruni Persicae) is Bitter, Sweet, and Neutral. It enters the Heart, Liver, and Large Intestine. It is classified as a Blood-invigorating medicinal in Chinese medicine. It breaks up Congealed Blood and also lubricates Dryness and promotes bowel movements. Breaking Stagnation (*Po Yu*) is more forceful than activating the Blood and transforming Stagnation. In this formula, Persica assists Dang Gui and Milk Thistle in both moistening the Intestines and treating Blood Stagnation, while it also assists Cascara Sagrada and Barberry in their laxative function.

Atractylodes (Rhizoma Atractylodis Macrocephalae) is Bitter, Sweet, and Warm and enters the Stomach and Spleen Channels. It is a *Bu Qi* or Qi-tonifying medicinal which specifically tonifies the Spleen, benefits the Qi, and dries Dampness. Symptomatically, Atractylodes is used to treat fatigue, anorexia, abdominal distention, vomiting, and diarrhea. It also treats constipation due to prolapse of Central Qi. Because it consolidates the Surface to stop Deficiency sweating, it also has an effect both on the Lungs which rule the *Wei Qi* and the Heart which governs the sweat. Extending this logic, it is possible to also suggest salutary effects of the Large and Small Intestines as well.

Trichosanthes (Fructus Trichosanthis Kirlowii) is one of the grace notes of this formula. It is categorized as a Hot, Phlegm-transforming ingredient in contemporary TCM texts, but this categorization does not do this ingredient justice. Trichosanthes is Sweet, Bitter, and Cold. It enters the Lungs, Stomach, and Large Intestine. It clears Heat and generates Fluids at the same time as it transforms Dry, Hot Phlegm. It also helps to activate the Qi and broaden the Chest. Therefore, emotionally, it can help to relieve depression and pent-up emotions. Symptomatically, it relieves thirst and is used for Hot, Dry, purulent upper respiratory problems.

Because Trichosanthes both clears Heat from the Lungs and moistens the Stomach, it benefits the Large Intestine to no little degree. By clearing the Lungs of Evil Heat, the Lung Qi is rectified and can disperse and descend. This enables healthy Large Intestine function. Trichosanthes and Aurantium Immaturus are combined in TCM for exactly this reason, to promote bowel movements. Also, by harmonizing the Lungs and Stomach, the Kidneys, the ruler of the Intestines and the Prenatal Root, are also benefitted thus benefitting the Root of life.

Aurantium Immaturus (Fructus Immaturus Citri Seu Ponciri) is Bitter and slightly Cold. It enters the Spleen and Stomach Channels and is categorized as a *Li Qi* or Qi-regulating medicinal. It breaks up Stagnant Qi and reduces Accumulations. It also directs the Qi downwards and moves the stool. Therefore, it is used to treat epigastric and abdominal pain, distention and gas, and constipation due to Stagnant Qi. When combined with Atractylodes, it aids Atractylodes in treating Stomach/Spleen Deficiency and Stagnant Food which can also complicate and aggravate Stagnant Qi.

Cinnamon Twigs (Ramulus Cinnamomi Cassiae) are categorized as a Warm Acrid Surface-relieving medicinal. However, this categorization also does not adequately explain this medicinal's wide range of actions. Cinnamon Twigs are Acrid, Sweet, and Warm and enter the Lungs and Bladder. They harmonize the *Ying* and *Wei*, warm the Channels, disperse Cold, move the Yang and transform Qi, and strengthen Heart Yang according to contemporary TCM texts. As mentioned above, in chronic cases of Liver Qi Congestion, Yang Qi tends to transform into Heat and float upward. This leaves the Lower Burner with a tendency to be Cold. Cinnamon Twigs both release this Heat from the Surface and also redirect it back down to its Source, transforming it from a pathological accumulation (*Xie Re*) to the Fire of Life (*Zhen Yang*). Cinnamon Twigs activate the Qi and Blood with the *Jing* and *Luo* and therefore assist both Persica and Dang Gui in ridding Stagnant Blood from the Intestinal *Luo*.

Saussurea (Radix Saussureae Seu Vladimiriae) is a Qi-regulating medicinal which is Acrid, slightly Bitter, Sweet, and slightly Warm. It enters the Spleen, Stomach, Gall Bladder, and Large Intestine Channels. Saussurea activates the Qi and stops pain, adjusts and regulates Stagnant Qi in the Intestines, and strengthens the Spleen and prevents Stagnation. In this formula, Saussurea helps Aurantium, Cascara Sagrada, and Barberry disperse Liver Qi Congestion and therefore promote bowel movements. On the other hand, it also prevents these purgatives from causing tenesmus or griping of the colon. Coupled with Atractylodes, Saussurea assists in treating loss of appetite and epigastric and abdominal pain and distention. By strengthening the Spleen, it prevents Liver Wood from invading Earth and thus checks the Liver according to Five Phase theory.

Amomum (Fructus Seu Semen Amomi) is an aromatic herb which transforms Dampness. It is often combined with Saussurea above. It is Acrid, Warm, and Aromatic and enters the Stomach/Spleen. Amomum activates the Qi, strengthens the Stomach, and transforms Dampness. It is used to treat lack of appetite and epigastric or abdominal pain and distention. Combined with Saussurea, it assists in preventing griping or colic of the colon from purgatives. Combined with Atractylodes, it aids in transforming Dampness obstructing the Spleen. Amomum is especially useful in allaying flatulence and intestinal gas.

Licorice (Radix Glycyrrhizae Uralensis) is a *Bu Qi* herb. It is Sweet and Neutral and enters all Twelve Regular Channels (*Shi Er Zheng Jing*). It tonifies the Spleen, benefits the Qi, moistens the Lungs, clears Heat, soothes spasms, and moderates and harmonizes all the other herbs in this formula. Because it is Sweet, it promotes the Stomach from undue purging by Bitter, Cold ingredients. Dr. Sung Baek, a Korean doctor, says that Licorice helps restore Hot and Cold energies to their proper place in the body. Because Licorice helps to relieve spasm, it aids all the other Qi-regulating ingredients in this formula while also benefitting the Lungs, thus enabling Metal to control Wood.

Aloe (Herba Aloes) is both a Western and Chinese purgative. In Chinese medicine, Aloe is believed to be both safe and effective for the treatment of chronic constipation and it lends itself for administration in tableted form since so little is required for therapeutic effect. Aloe is Bitter and Cold and enter the Liver, Heart, and Spleen. It purges Fire and moves the stool and clears Heat and cools the Liver. It is used to treat epigastric pain, dizziness, headache, tinnitus, irritability, and constipation all due to Excess Heat in the *Jue Yin*.

Because of the Qi and Blood activating effects of this formula and its purgative function, it should not be taken during pregnancy. Likewise, because some of the active ingredients in these herbs are present in mother's milk, it should not be used by nursing mothers, otherwise it may cause infantile diarrhea. This formula is designed to be taken over a prolonged period of time during which time it is meant to have a systemic healing effect on the Liver, the root cause of this kind of constipation. Rather than being just a colonic irritant like some other herbal laxatives, this formula is meant to address the underlying cause of this complaint. Therefore, its continued use will not create dependency. For best results, it should be used in combination with regular exercise, stress reduction, a low oil and fats, high fiber diet, and regular abdominal massage.

ESSENCE CHAMBER TABLETS

FOR THE TREATMENT OF PROSTATIC HYPERTROPHY

Prostate problems are something most men don't like to talk about. However, both benign prostatic hypertrophy and prostate cancer are common amongst older middle-aged and elderly men. The prostate as such is not an Organ or Bowel of traditional Chinese medicine and therefore prostate diseases per se are Western, not Chinese medical categories of disease. However, the most common symptoms of prostate disease, difficult urination and distention and fullness of the lower hypogastrium, are categorized as *Long Bi* in Chinese medicine. *Long Bi* means both retention and difficulty of urination in Chinese. Also, many of the signs and symptoms of prostate disease can be categorized as species of *Lin Zheng* in TCM or Urinary Disturbance. *Lin Zheng* is classically subdivided into the *Wu Lin* or Five *Lin*: *Shi Lin*, Stone *Lin*, urinary disturbance associated with stones or gravel; *Qi Lin*, urinary disturbance due to Liver Qi; *Lao Lin*, Fatigue *Lin*, urinary disturbance due to exhaustion with Qi and Yin Deficiency below and flushing-up of Yang above; *Re Lin*, Heat *Lin*, urinary disturbance due to accumulation of Damp Heat in the Lower Burner; and *Xue Lin*, Blood *Lin*, urinary disturbance accompanied by hematuria. In addition, there is also the category *Zhuo Lin* or Turbid *Lin* which describes turbid or cloudy urination and penile discharge.

In my experience, prostate problems are usually due to long-term tendency for Damp Heat to accumulate in the Lower

Burner. This is typically complicated by Liver Qi and/or Heat and Stagnant Blood. As the Kidney Qi declines due to age, frequent urination due to Damp Heat causes the Kidneys to loose their astringency on the one hand, causing terminal dribbling, and to lose their motivating power on the other, causing a weak stream. Since the circulation of the Lower Burner as a whole is mutually interdependent with the individual Organs and Bowels which constitute it, Stagnant Liver Qi and Stagnant Heat and Dampness often also tend to give rise to Stagnant Large Intestine Qi and constipation. This constipation or sluggishness of the bowels aggravates Bladder Stagnancy and promotion of bowel movements helps unblock the urination.

Essence Chamber Tablets have been formulated to address the issues described above frequently found in older middle-aged and elderly men causing prostate enlargement and urinary dysfunction. The ingredients in these tablets 1) rid Damp Heat from the Lower Burner; 2) seep Dampness and promote urination; 3) promote the separation of Pure and Turbid in the Lower Burner; 4) activate and course the *Jue Yin* in the Lower Burner; 5) activate and destagnate the Blood; and 6) tonify the Kidneys and activate the Yang. The ingredients selected for this formula are a combination of traditional Chinese and traditional Western herbal medicinals. They have been selected based on both the discrimination of Chinese Patterns of Disharmony (*Bian Zheng*) and on their specific empirical and symptomatic effect on the prostate (*Bian Bing*, the discrimination of named disease categories). Using this combined methodology of *Bian Zheng* and *Bian Bing*, we can combine the best of both traditional Chinese and modern Western medicines in an attempt to create a global New Medicine (*Xin Yi*) for the 21st century. The ingredients in Essence Chamber Tablets (*Jing She Pian*) are:

Chaparral	9 parts
Hydrangea	9 "

Saw Palmetto Berries	9 "
Damiana	9 "
False Unicorn	9 "
Stone Root	9 "
Poria	9 "
Tokoro	6 "
Abutilon	6 "

Chaparral (Caulis Et Folium Larreae Divaricatae) is a famous Southwestern Amerindian medicinal. It is Bitter, slightly Acrid, Salty, and Cool. It enters the Liver and Bladder Channels. It should be classified in TCM as a Heat-clearing, Toxin-dissolving ingredient. Its functions are that is clears Heat (*Qing Re*), dissolves Toxins (*Jie Du*), and combats cancer (*Kang Ai*). Chaparral also reduces swelling, eliminates Dampness, and benefits urination. It is indicated in the treatment of Damp Heat Entanglement and Toxins causing skin infections and inflammations, dysmenorrhea, Damp Heat *Bi*, Liver/Gallbladder Damp Heat Jaundice, vomiting, and flank pain. Hot *Lin* and Stone *Lin* urinary dysfunction, and uterine prolapse due to Damp Heat. In addition, Chaparral is useful in treating various swellings and masses associated with Damp Heat, whether benign or malignant.

Chaparral is effective in the treatment of herpes and warts, both of which are viral infections. Therefore, Chaparral may prove beneficial in the treatment of human papilloma virus (HPV) as well. Being a Hidden Evil (*Fu Xie*), Damp Heat Toxin of the *Wen Bing* category, HPV causes cervical dysplasia in women. In men, it most often goes undetected due to lack of a male analogue to the Pap smear. However, it is my opinion that HPV is smoldering unknown in a large segment of the present middle-aged male population, and further, that this Hidden Evil will result in a dramatic increase in prostate problems as these men reach their late forties and fifties.

Chaparral and Damiana have proven an effective empirical combination for the treatment of prostate problems. Therefore, they have been combined in this formula. Other possible therapeutic combinations of Chaparral with Chinese anti-cancer medicinals include Herba Verbena Officinalis, Radix Polygonati Cuspidati, and Herba Desmodii Styracifolii, to name but three. Topical preparations including Chaparral may also prove effective in treating cervical dysplasia. Chaparral in many ways in similar in function to Herba Patriniae Heterophyllae and Frustus Bruceae Javanicae, the latter of which has also demonstrated anti-viral effect against HPV.

Hydrangea (Radix Hydrangeae Arborscentis) is also a Damp-draining medicinal specific to the treatment of either an inflamed or an enlarged prostate. It is Acrid and Cool and enters the Kidney, Bladder, and Large Intestine. It seeps Dampness and promotes urination. It clears and eliminates Damp Heat from the Lower Burner and benefits the separation of Pure from Turbid below. Therefore, Hydrangea treats nonspecific urethritis in men and mucosal irritation of the urethra in the elderly. In addition, Hydrangea expels Stones, whether Kidney or Gall Bladder. In this formula, Hydrangea assists Chaparral in promoting and smoothing urination.

Saw Palmetto Berries (Fructus Serenoae Serrulatae) are a *Bu Yang* or Yang tonic ingredient. They are Acrid, Sweet, and Warm and enter the Kidneys, Spleen, and Lungs. Saw Palmetto Berries tonify Yang and therefore are used in the treatment of impotence and infertility. They also benefit the Kidneys and tonify the Lungs, thus ensuring the Kidneys' grasping the Qi sent down by the Lungs. Because of this, Saw Palmetto Berries treat asthma and chronic bronchitis. They tonify the *Wei Qi* and therefore treat recurrent Cold invasions due to Deficiency of Defensive Qi accompanied by spontaneous sweating, fear of chill, and shortness of breath. And they also transform Phlegm due to Kidney Yang Deficiency. In addition, they are also useful in treating Lower Thirsting & Wasting Disease. Like Chaparral and Hydrangea above, Saw Palmetto Berries are a specific empirical treatment for enlarged prostate. Since Water is transported and transformed by the Lungs, Spleen, and Kidneys; since in the Lower Burner, Kidney Qi is primarily responsible for motivating urination; and since the Kidney Qi begins to decline around the age of forty, Saw Palmetto Berries ensure the coordinated descension and transformation of Water and adequate Kidney Qi to expel it.

Damiana (Folium Turnerae Aphrodisiaciae) is another *Bu Yang* herb. It is Acrid and Warm and enters the Liver and Kidneys. It tonifies Yang, activates Yang, and relieves depression. It also moistens the Intestines and moves the stools. Because Damiana promotes the circulation of Qi and Yang in the Lower Burner, both in the *Jue Yin* and the Intestines, it not only strengthens Kidney Qi but disperses Congestion. It is used to treat impotence and frigidity but also chronic urinary tract disorders. When Damiana is combined with Saw Palmetto Berries, this combination is specific for prostate disease.

False Unicorn (Radix Helionadis Dioicae) should be categorized as a Blood-activating medicinal. It is Bitter and Warm and enters the Heart, Spleen, and Liver. It activates the Blood and transforms Stagnation, primarily in the Lower Burner. It is used mostly in gynecology but is equally useful in men for Lower Burner Stagnant Blood disorders. In addition, it clears and eliminates Damp Heat in the Lower Burner manifesting as leukorrhea in women and nocturnal emissions in men. Since long-term accumulation of Damp Heat below eventually causes Blood Stagnation, dispersing Stagnation is usually necessary in treating prostate problems. This is based on the close mutual relationship between all Six Stagnations.

Stone Root (Radix Collinsoniae Canadensis) is a Heat-clearing medicinal in some ways similar to Moutan. It is Acrid, Sour, and Cool and enters the Liver, Pericardium, and Large Intestine. It clears ascending Liver Fire manifesting as tracheitis, asthma, and laryngitis. It clears and eliminates Damp Heat manifesting as gastritis, diarrhea, dysentery, and colitis. Stone Root also strongly seeps Dampness and expels Stones. In addition, it activates the Blood and disperses Stagnation. Therefore, it is used for dysmenorrhea, scanty or delayed menstruation, and functional uterine bleeding complicated by Stagnant Blood. For the same reason, it is also used to treat Stagnant Blood due to traumatic injury. Stone Root is a specific for the Lower Burner and especially the anal and perineal areas. It treats hemorrhoids due to Congestion and any sensation of pressure or lump in that region. Stone Root assists False Unicorn in dispersing Stagnant Blood and also aids Chaparral and Hydrangea seep Dampness and eliminate Damp Heat.

Poria (Sclerotium Poriae Cocoris) is another Damp-draining herb. It is Sweet, Bland, and Neutral and enters the Heart, Spleen, and Lungs. Poria promotes urination and leeches out Dampness; it strengthens the Spleen and harmonizes the Middle; it tonifies the Spleen and transforms Phlegm; and it quiets the Heart and calms the Spirit. This ingredient primarily assists the Spleen in transporting and transforming Liquids in the Middle Burner. It aids in sending the Pure part of the Liquids up to collect in the Heart to be transformed into Blood, while at the same time sending the Turbid part down to be excreted as urine. This is how it both nourishes and calms the Heart at the same time as it promotes urination. Since Dampness percolating down from the Middle Burner tends to become Damp Heat when it becomes associated with Liver Heat, Poria in this formula addresses the Middle Burner as the source of Dampness. Thus this ingredient helps ensure that this formula addresses and regulates each of the Three Burners in their role in transporting and transforming Liquids. Poria is also believed in China to have anti-tumor and anti-cancer properties as well.

Tokoro (Rhizoma Dioscoreae Bi Xie Seu Hypoglaucae) is a species of wild yam. It is a Damp-draining medicinal which is Bitter and Neutral. Tokoro, the Japanese name for this medicinal, enters the Liver, Stomach, and Bladder. It separates the Pure from the Turbid and resolves Turbid Dampness in the lower Burner. It can be used for either Deficiency or Damp Heat below. It expels Wind Dampness or Damp Heat *Bi* or Obstruction manifesting as low back pain and pain or numbness of the lower extremities. It also clears Damp Heat from the skin in cases of Damp eczema and pustular sores. In this formula, Tokoro assists Chaparral, Hydrangea, and Poria in draining Dampness and promoting urination. This ingredient is found in Chinese empirical prescriptions for prostatic hypertrophy.

Abutilon (Semen Abutilonis Seu Malvae) is again a Damp-draining medicinal. Malva is a species of Ground Mallow. In Chinese medicine, Abutilon or Malva seeds are used to drain Dampness and promote urination. They are used for *Re Lin, Xue Lin,* and *Shi Lin* as well as for edema. They also moisten the Intestines and move the stool. In addition, they benefit the breasts, which means they activate the circulation through the breasts. Therefore, they are used for insufficient lactation, painful, swollen breasts, or early stage breast abscess. In Western herbalism, Marshmallow and Ground Mallow are used as demulcents to soothe irritated mucous membranes, including the urethra. In this formula, Abutilon or Malva is used to assist the other Damp-draining herbs but also to assist Damiana in promoting bowel movements and thus decongesting the Lower Burner as a whole. Abutilon is Sweet and Cold and enters the Three Bowels of the Lower Burner and the Liver.

Prostate problems in men are the equivalent to uterine disorders in peri- and postmenopausal women. In both men and women in their fifties and sixties, there is the tendency for Dampness, Heat, and Stagnation to accumulate below, especially if there is a fatty, oily, Damp diet, stress, and insufficient exercise. As all Three Burners begin to decline with age, their harmonious function become inefficient. Righteous Qi is no longer produced in abundance and the *Yuan Qi*, the prime motivating force in the Lower Burner, declines. On the other hand, pathologic substances (*Yin Xie*) are not dispersed and discharged efficiently and so accumulate. In addressing this complicated but common scenario, Essence Chamber Tablets have been formulated to facilitate the transportation and transformation of Water by the Lungs, Spleen, and Kidneys and to disperse Evil Heat, Dampness, Phlegm, and Stagnant Blood.

Essence Chamber Tablets are available from Health Concerns, 2236 Mariner Square, Suite #103, Alameda, CA 94501; 1-800-233-9355.

Coenzyme Q$_{10}$

Its TCM Functions & Indications

Traditional Chinese Medicine (TCM) as a style of Chinese medicine is an orthodox system. That means that it is a coherent, rational system with a definite methodology and a professionally agreed upon terminology. At this point in time, TCM is, I believe, the dominant professional style of Chinese medicine in the United States. For instance, it is diagnosis and treatment based on the methodology of this system which make up the largest portion of the NCCA national board exams in acupuncture. Based on such an orthodox approach, there are stringent and time-tested guidelines and parameters to prescribing Chinese medicinal foods and substances.

America today is a culturally heterodox society, and American practitioners of TCM find ourselves in a unique historical position. On the one hand, we practice a very comprehensive system of medicine with a very precise and logical, conceptual methodology. On the other hand, we and our patients are constantly coming in contact with medicinals of proven empirical efficacy but which have yet to be described according to the rubric of TCM. Some American practitioners of TCM use only medicinals originating from China. They hew to a Chinese orthodoxy which is understandable in China but which is somewhat more difficult to justify in our American milieu. Others are more eclectic and use many non-Chinese medicinals as part of their practice. These practitioners run the risk of practicing purely empirical, shot-gun therapy.

Happily, between these two extremes, Chinese exclusivity and
eclectic empiricism, there is a third option. The cornerstone of
TCM as a system of medicine is its rational methodology. This
rational methodology is so universally valid that it can be
applied to describe any medicinal substance whether that
medicinal originated from China or from any other culture or
region of the earth. In previous essays I have attempted to
describe both Western herbal medicinals[1] and modern Western
synthetic pharmaceuticals[2] according to the methodology and
terminology of TCM so that these medicinals might be
integrated into a new, even more comprehensive healing
system. Although that system may find its theoretical roots
primarily in Chinese medicine, its treatment modes and
medicinals will come from any and every corner of the earth.

Western herbs and pharmaceuticals are only two of the
potential sources for new medicinals which might be added to
the TCM pharmacopeia. There are also a number of relatively
new nutritional supplements, such as selenium, germanium,
chromium, and B_{15}, which are currently available in the health
care marketplace and which seem to be both safe and
empirically effective. One example of such a popular new
nutritional supplement is Coenzyme Q_{10} or CoQ as it is known
to its aficiandos. This nutrient has been proven in clinical trials
to be an extremely effective medicinal treating or aiding in the
treatment of a wide range of commonly encountered disorders.
All that stands in the way of CoQ's being used in rational
clinical practice by TCM practitioners is its lack of a TCM
description. However, with a little thought and research, that
description can be generated the same way that our lineal
forebears in Chinese medicine generated rational TCM
descriptions of Ginseng and Dang Gui.

CoQ$_{10}$

CoQ's full scientific moniker is succinate dehydrogenaseco Q$_{10}$ reductase. It is also called ubiquinone because it is found in every tissue of the body. CoQ is an enzyme which allows the mitochondria to manufacture ATP in the Krebs cycle. CoQ$_{10}$ was first isolated and named by an American scientist, F. L. Crane, in 1957. Dr. Karl Folkers at the University of Texas in Austin was the first researcher to identify CoQ$_{10}$'s crucial importance in cell respiration and energy production. Dr. Folkers and his associates are responsible for a great deal of the research and literature on CoQ. But it has been Japanese clinicians and researchers who have generated the most interest and experience in using CoQ medicinally. In Japan, there are 252 commercial preparations of CoQ supplied by over 80 pharmaceutical companies to over 10 million Japanese patients who take CoQ$_{10}$ on a daily basis.[3] Of these 10 million, 6 million are estimated to use CoQ for cardiac conditions.[4]

A survey of the published literature on CoQ reveals that it is useful in the treatment of numerous diseases: angina pectoris, congestive heart disease, hyperthyroid heart failure, hypertension, CVA (both acute & sequelae), periodontal disease, ulcers, diabetes, obesity, allergies, asthma, HIV, neoplasms, and malaria. In addition, researchers suggest CoQ may help in retarding aging and in combatting the side-effects of chemotherapy. Because of its beneficial effects on the immune system and on aging, and based on its role in the creation of energy according to Western biology, it is tempting to think of CoQ as a tonic medicinal. However, although it might be considered such from a Western point of view, CoQ is not a tonic from the TCM perspective.

In TCM, tonic medicinals are divided into four categories: those which make more Qi, those which make more Blood, those which make more Yang, and those which make more Yin. In looking for the common disease mechanism in the diseases CoQ_{10} treats from the professional TCM standpoint, Deficiency is not it. The TCM disease mechanisms common to species of all the above-mentioned Western disease categories are Stagnant Qi, Hot Phlegm, and Excesses of the Liver and Stomach complicated by possible Stomach Yin Deficiency and Hot Toxins. Although this is a somewhat complicated scenario, it is not an uncommon one by middle age. And, although there are a number of different TCM disease mechanisms accounting for other species of ulcers, hypertension, allergies, and asthma, Stagnant Qi, Hot Phlegm, and Liver/Stomach Excess are the only mechanisms or patterns common to all these Western diseases.

As described in some detail elsewhere[5], when the Stomach gets Excess, and therefore Hot, so typically does the Liver, and vice versa.   Liver Excesses almost always begin as or include Stagnant Qi. Because of the relationship between Qi and Food & Liquid metabolism, when Qi gets stuck and the Stomach is Hot, Clear and Turbid are not separated properly and Phlegm is produced. Although this Phlegm is generated in the Middle, because of Heat's tendency to rise and because of Stagnant Qi's tendency to rebel upward, Phlegm is commonly drafted upward to lodge in the chest where it may be experienced as Chest *Bi* (chest pain and constriction, including angina) and *Chuan* (dyspnea, wheezing, asthma). Or it may be drafted up even further to lodge in the cervical and axillary nodes causing lymphadenopathy. If it drafts upwards further still, it may be experienced as nasal allergies. And, if it vents upwards suddenly as *Zhong Feng* or Penetrating Wind, it may cause a CVA or stroke.

In my experience, the majority of middle-aged male hypertensives suffer from Liver/Stomach Excess often complicated by Phlegm. This is evidenced by their tendency to redder than normal tongues coated with a yellow, greasy fur and a slippery, wiry pulse. This is a very different disease mechanism than most middle-aged female hypertension which is related to Stagnant Blood and the *Chong Mai*. These same men often also have a tendency towards heartburn, ulcers, and bleeding gums. They generally over-eat, are somewhat aggressive, and irritable.

Periodontal disease accompanied by bleeding, inflamed, and swollen gums is most often due to a combination of Stomach and Liver Heat. The stoma or mouth is the orifice of the Stomach. In addition, the Liver Channel runs internally through the gums. Likewise, in clinical practice, stomach ulcers are very commonly due to Liver and Stomach Heat. Over time, this Heat wastes or burns out the Stomach Yin, thus complicating this scenario. Diabetes is also very commonly due to this same scenario. When the Liver gets stuck and the Stomach Hot and Yin Deficient, the Spleen is often also Qi Deficient and Damp. Heat drafts up causing Heat and Phlegm to accumulate in the Lungs. Over time the Lung Yin is wasted and the Lung Qi impaired. While below, because the over-heated Stomach "side-tracks" too much Liquids to the Kidneys and because of the loss of harmony between above and below and pre and post natal, the Kidneys also become Deficient as well. However, although the Upper and Lower Burners may also be wasted, this process most often begins in the Middle with the Stomach/Liver becoming Excess and the Spleen becoming Damp and Deficient.

There are several ways a person can become obese according to TCM, but the above-described scenario is a commonly encountered one in clinical practice. Essentially, adipose tissue in TCM is Dampness and Phlegm. Although some obese persons may be Spleen Qi Kidney Yang Deficient, thus leading to Dampness and Cold Phlegm Accumulation, many obese persons are Damp and Phlegmatic on the Exterior and Hot, Stagnant, and even Dry on the Interior. It is exactly because

"One pattern may account for several diseases and one disease may be due to several different patterns" that CoQ is only effective for a percentage of cases in which it is used by Western clinicians and researchers. It is my opinion that CoQ may help reduce weight in persons with Hot Phlegm, Stomach Heat (possibly complicated by Yin Deficiency), and Stagnant Qi, but that it is not effective for reducing weight in persons simply Cold, Damp, and Deficient.

Similarly, many malignant neoplasms are a combination of Hot Phlegm and Stagnant Qi mixed with or due to Accumulation of Hot Toxins. They may also be, in part, Stagnant Blood due to the relationship of the Qi to the Blood and Blood flow to the presence of Phlegm. Malaria in TCM also shares a somewhat similar disease mechanism. Malaria is divided into two broad types: Excess and Deficiency. The common signs and symptoms of the Excess type are alternating fever and chills, chest discomfort, parched mouth, retching or vomiting, spitting up mucous, eventual hypochondriac distention, and perspiration.[6] The tongue typically has a thin, yellow coating and the pulse is wiry, often slippery, and rapid. TCM practitioners should be able to recognize once again elements of Heat, Phlegm, Stomach Disharmony, Injury of Stomach Yin, and Liver Qi.

CoQ10's TCM Description

Based on this common disease mechanism of Heat, Phlegm, Liver/Stomach Excess, Stomach Yin Deficiency, and possible Hot Toxins being the only real common denominator for all the diseases treated successfully as recorded in the current CoQ literature, I think we can make the following TCM description of the therapeutic functions of ubiquinone. CoQ_{10} clears Heat and transforms Phlegm. It regulates the Qi and expands the chest. It unbinds the Qi and dissipates nodules. It also generates Fluids and allays thirst and irritability due to injury by Heat. And it dissolves Toxins. As for meridian routes, I believe it enters the Liver, Stomach, and possibly the Lung Channels. Its taste is Sweet and Bland and its temperature is Cool.

Therefore, CoQ's TCM indications should include Chest *Bi* due to Stagnant Qi and Phlegm; *Chuan* due to Hot Phlegm, especially complicated by a Hot Stomach and Liver Qi; *Wei Tong* (epigastric pain) due to Stomach/Liver Heat and Stagnation complicated by Stomach Yin Deficiency; Middle Thirsting & Wasting due to a Hot, Yin Deficient Stomach and Damp, Qi Deficient Spleen; scrofula or lymphadenopathy due to Stagnation of Hot Phlegm in turn due to Upwardly Perverse Liver Qi; bleeding gums due to Liver/Stomach Heat or Fire; *Zhong Feng* due to Liver/Stomach Heat and Phlegm; hypertension due to Liver/Stomach Excess and Phlegm; and *Shao Yang Fen* malaria.

The fact that CoQ$_{10}$ can allay the often disastrous effects of chemotherapy is due to the fact that most chemotherapeutic agents are species of Hot Toxins. In general, the side-effects of chemotherapy are inflammation due to Invasion of Hot Toxins, thirst and dryness due to Injury of Yin, digestive impairment due to Disharmony of Stomach/Spleen with Upward Perversion of Stomach Qi, and eventual injury of the Qi and Blood and Deficiency of the Liver and Kidneys.[7] Based on the above description of CoQ as clearing Heat, dissolving Toxins, regulating the Qi (and therefore harmonizing the Stomach), and generating Fluids (and therefore benefitting Yin), it should be apparent why CoQ is so effective in both mitigating the side-effects of chemotherapeutic agents and in aiding in the treatment of malignancy.

Likewise, it should also now be clear why CoQ has proven itself as a promising medicinal in the treatment of HIV infection. HIV is a species of *Wen Bing*. It invades the Blood Phase where it can remain a *Fu Xie* or Hidden Evil. When it becomes active, it works its way from *Xue Fen* to *Wei Fen* and from Lower to Upper Burners. Because it is a Warm Toxic Evil, it creates Heat in the Liver, Stomach, and Lungs, eventually exhausting the Yin, but also giving rise to Hot Phlegm and Toxic Swellings. Dr. Karl Folkers and associates have published an account of their administration of CoQ_{10} to a group of American AIDS patients. In all six of the patients described in some detail, CoQ_{10} administration was coincident with relief of cough and fever, oral ulceration, and lymphadenopathy, especially of the cervical and axillary nodes.[8]

Furthermore, the above description of the TCM therapeutic functions of CoQ_{10} should also clarify why this medicinal seems to be effective in retarding aging[9]. Although most people think of the aging process solely in terms of Deficiency, the signs and symptoms of aging are not just due to Deficiency but are also due to long-term accumulation of pathogenic substances, such as Qi, Blood, Heat, and Phlegm. The withering and cachexia characteristic of aging are benefitted by CoQ's generation of Fluids. But liver spots, lumps and bumps, rashes and ulcers all attendant to aging are due to Stagnant Blood in the *Luo*, Stagnant Phlegm in the *Jing*, and festering of Stagnant Heat. Because CoQ_{10} regulates the Qi, transforms Phlegm, and generates Fluids, it most definitely should have a salutary effect on aging.

When attempting to describe a new medicinal according to the rubric and methodology of TCM, I also find it useful to compare such a new medicinal to descriptions of medicinals already described in the Chinese materia medica. It is my opinion that due to the patterns inherent in phenomenal existence, only certain characteristics tend to occur or group together. Although there is great individual diversity, yet still there are broad, discernible categories and groupings. When a newly described medicinal has a somewhat similar constellation of characteristics and functions to an already described TCM medicinal, this reinforces the phenomenal possibility of such a constellation. Whereas, if no other medicinal previously described in the 2000 year plus written history of Chinese medicine has ever been described in a similar way, I hesitate to suggest such a possibility. In the phenomenal world, certain things go together and others do not. TCM practitioners should already have noted the similarity in function between CoQ$_{10}$ and Trichosanthes Kirilowius[10]. Both are used in the treatment of a very similar group of diseases: asthma, chest pain, ulcers, diabetes, lymphadenopathy, and malaria. Also interestingly, Compound Q, the anti-AIDS medicine which has stirred up such controversy this past year, is derived from Radix Trichosanthis.

However, if CoQ$_{10}$ is so similar in TCM functions and indications to Radix Trichosanthis, why should the TCM practitioner use it instead? First of all, ease of administration and patient compliance are big reasons why American TCM practitioners should consider the incorporation of CoQ in our pharmacopeia. Because it comes encapsulated, CoQ is easy to take and patient compliance is high. Many American practitioners have some difficulty getting their American patients to take time-consuming to prepare, awful tasting, decocted herbs. Chinese formulas as desiccated extracts and rabbit-turd-like, Chinese patent pills are only slightly better accepted. Whereas, CoQ capsules do not require any paradigm shift for our patients to accept.

Secondly, it is my experience in American clinical practice that often Chinese herbal polypharmacy formulas are too difficult and time-consuming to tailor to my patients' personal needs so as to achieve therapeutic results without side-effects. For instance, in the treatment of periodontal disease with bleeding gums, *Long Dan Xie Gan Tang* is often too dispersing and Cool for long-term administration; but *Zhi Bai Di Huang Wan* does not effectively clear Heat from the Liver and Stomach nor regulate the Qi. Likewise the Gypsum in both *Yu Nu Jian* and *Bai Hu Tang* may not be well tolerated in long-term use. My patients are not just interested in treating acute exacerbations of pyorrhea. They want me to help them avoid repeated, painful cleanings and periodontal surgery over a period of many years. A safe, single medicinal such as CoQ_{10} fits such patients' needs better than complex, polypharmacy Chinese formulas which require constant adjustment.

And third, Chinese doctors in China themselves will admit that the therapeutic effectiveness of TCM is not one hundred percent. Just because a formula exists in a Chinese book for the treatment of a specific condition does not mean that treatment is effective or completely satisfactory. As any TCM practitioner with clinical experience I think has to admit, our medicine as we know it now can still use help in treating many diseases. New medicinals, such as CoQ_{10}, can help increase the efficacy of our treatments when added to our traditional repertoire. This is similar to adding other Western medicines along with TCM treatments for difficult, recalcitrant diseases, such as cancer and AIDS as described, for instance, in *The Treatment of Cancer By Integrated Chinese-Western Medicine*.[11] Often the depth and complexity of much modern disease seem to require more than just traditional Chinese herbs. On the other hand, many Western pharmaceuticals are too strong and too narrow in their application and thus cause too many side-effects. However, modern nutritional supplements, such as CoQ, appear to be both safe and effective and, when prescribed according to the discrimination of patterns (*Bian Zheng*) of TCM, in no way do violence to our rational methodology.

Case Histories

The following three cases histories are examples of how I use CoQ in my TCM practice. The first is of a 43 year old, Caucasian male. This patient complained of heartburn of more than four years' duration. Three years previously he had taken some Chinese herbal medicine in decoction for this problem which sometimes worked but sometimes didn't and sometimes caused intestinal cramping. He discontinued the Chinese herbal medicine because it was time-consuming and inconvenient. This patient also reported frequent bleeding gums, especially after eating spicy or greasy food or drinking alcohol. Stress made the heartburn and bleeding gums worse and also caused occasional transient episodes of chest pain. The patient's tongue was fluted, fat, and somewhat red with a thin, yellow, slightly greasy coating. His pulse was slippery and wiry.

My TCM diagnosis of this patient was chronic Liver Qi and Heat with a Hot Stomach and some tendency to Damp and Phlegm production. Besides counselling this patient on diet, exercise, and stress reduction, I prescribed CoQ$_{10}$ at 60 mg per day taken with a meal. After eight weeks, the patient reported complete cessation of the heartburn which had previously been constant. In addition, he also reported a cessation of bleeding gums when brushing except when he indulged in spicy food and alcohol. The patient was quite pleased with this therapeutic result and, because of the ease of administration, relatively low cost, and anti-aging benefits of CoQ, decided to continue taking it indefinitely.

The second case is of a 35 year old, Caucasian male. Recently his dentist suggested periodontal surgery with scraping of the bone. He was diagnosed as suffering from bone retreat due to infected gums. He did not have bleeding gums and the bone retreat had been diagnosed by x-ray. Based on his dentist's recommendation, he had had his teeth cleaned four times per year for the past four years with apparently insufficient therapeutic effect. The patient could not afford the periodontal surgery and so came to me looking for an alternative.

The patient was slimly built with a darkish complexion. He looked frail and haggard. He reported his sleep was light and disturbed by matitudinal insomnia. His low back was weak and knees were stiff. He had a big appetite but could never gain weight. He experienced nocturia 4 nights out of 7. This patient was fatigued a lot and also experienced some problems with premature ejaculation. His tongue had a dull, pale reddish tip. It was swollen but only faintly fluted. The coating to the rear was whitish yellow and a little greasy. His pulse was a little fast, a little fine, and wiry.

My TCM diagnosis was Kidney Yin Deficiency with some Stomach Heat and Liver Qi. Therefore, I prescribed *Zhi Bai Di Huang Wan* in its form as Temper Fire (K'an Herb Co.), 2 tablets, 3 times per day, plus 60 mg of CoQ once per day with a meal. After one month, the patient reported better energy and sleep. After three months, the patient reported less nocturia and less low back and knee problems. After five months, the patient's mouth was re-x-rayed and the periodontal surgery and bone-scraping were postponed indefinitely. The patient continues to take both Temper Fire and CoQ in order to maintain this therapeutic result.

In this case, Temper Fire alone would not have specifically addressed the patient's elements of Stomach Heat and Liver Qi. In addition, the CoQ added a specificity in treating the patient's gums which Temper Fire alone does not have. The treatment was, compared to periodontal surgery, easy, inexpensive, and painless. And, based on the above description of CoQ_{10}, it was completely logical according to the methodology of TCM. It was not just shot-gun, empirical therapy but was that combination of empiricism and rationality which is the goal of TCM.

The third case is of a 50 year old, Caucasian male who was HIV positive. This man knew he had been HIV positive for a couple of years but was almost symptom free. He had been off and on AZT twice in the year previous during which time he had received weekly acupuncture treatments as part of our clinic's nine step HIV positive program.[12] His only HIV related symptom was enlarged lymph nodes, especially of the neck and armpits. This patient's TCM diagnosis besides being infected by a latent *Wen Bing* was Liver Qi, Stomach Heat and Yin Deficiency, and Phlegm Nodulation. This was based on his thick, yellow but dry tongue fur, fine, wiry pulse, and palpable lymph node enlargement. I suggested that this patient try CoQ$_{10}$ based on the HIV study by Dr. Folkers cited above and on the patient's TCM diagnosis.

Six weeks after beginning CoQ at 60 mg per day, the patient reported complete elimination of all lymph node enlargement. Because he felt so good, he had himself reduced his AZT intake to two capsules per day. Although his tongue and pulse remained for the most part unchanged, his pulse did become very evenly balanced over all the positions in the *Cun, Guan,* and *Chi*. This patient continues to take CoQ daily as part of his AIDS prevention regime. Because the patient had already read about CoQ$_{10}$ as a possible treatment for HIV, he was well disposed to taking this supplement. And because its TCM functions and indications fit his pattern of disharmony, I felt confident of its ameliorating effect on his condition.

Conclusion

Hopefully more American practitioners of TCM will begin to

describe non-Chinese medicinals from every source according to the terminology of TCM. This process will enrich TCM and will enable us to give better, more effective, and more comprehensive care to our American patients. Vitamins, minerals, amino acids, and enzymes are, I believe, especially appropriate for incorporation into TCM since these substances in their naturally occurring forms have always been a part of Chinese medicine. In addition, their safety plus their efficacy recommend their usage.

Describing CoQ_{10} as a "Chinese" medicinal should also benefit practitioners of Western medicine as well. As alluded to above, in the scientific literature on CoQ, clinical trials based on administering ubiquinone for Western disease categories always leaves a percentage of patients unbenefitted. For instance, in studies on CoQ and angina, 47% failed to respond; in congestive heart disease, 47% again were unresponsive; and in hypertension, 46% did not improve.[13] The probable reason why these patients did not improve is that their disease mechanisms did not match the TCM indications for CoQ's TCM functions. Western disease categories are, by Chinese standards, not individualized enough for truly differential diagnosis. When Chinese diagnosis by *Bian Zheng* is added to diagnosis by disease category (*Bian Bing*), the amelioration rates for CoQ should go up markedly. Using CoQ_{10} based on TCM *Bian Zheng*, its administration can be honed to exactly those who will benefit by it. Such specificity through accurate differential diagnosis is not only the goal of TCM but should be the goal of any professional medicine.

CoQ_{10} is available over the counter at most health food stores. A high quality, clinical grade of CoQ can be ordered from **Bioenergy Nutrients**, 6395 Gunpark Dr. Suite A, Boulder, CO 80301; 1-800-553-0227. This company furnishes professional practitioners a certificate of analysis establishing product purity upon request.

ENDNOTES

1   Flaws, Bob, "A Perennial Spring, A Discussion of the TCM Properties of St. John's Wort in the Possible Treatment of AIDS and the Universal Applicability of Chinese Medicine", *Journal of Chinese Medicine*, UK, #31, September, 1989, p. 8-12

2   Flaws, Bob, "Valium: Its TCM Functions, Indications, & Contraindications", *Journal of the American College of Traditional Chinese Medicine*, San Francisco, Vol. 7, #3, 1989, p. 27- 30

3   Bliznakov, Emile G., M.D. and Hunt, Gerald L., *The Miracle Nutrient Coenzyme Q$_{10}$*, Bantam Books, NYC, 1987, p.2

4   Birkland, Gene, "CoQ$_{10}$, The Miracle Enzyme", *The American Chiropractor*, August, 1986, p. 43

5   Flaws, Bob, "Yin Yang and the Mechanisms of Internal Disease", *Blue Poppy Essays 1988*, Blue Poppy Press, Boulder, CO, 1988, p.251-256

6   Human Revolutionary Health Committee, *The Barefoot Doctor's Manual*, trans. by Titus Yu, Lam Wah Bong, and Kwok Chin, Cloudburst Press of America, Seattle, 1977, p. 110

7   Zhang Dai-zhao, *The Treatment of Cancer by Integrated Chinese-Western Medicine*, trans. by Zhang Ting-liang and Bob Flaws, Blue Poppy Press, Boulder, CO, 1989, p. 93

8   Folkers, Karl, et al., "Biochemical Deficiencies of Coenzyme Q$_{10}$ in HIV Infection and Exploratory Treatment", *Biochemical and Biophysical Research Communications*, Academic Press, Vol. 153, 1988, p. 888-896

9   Bliznakov & Hunt, op.cit., p. 184-202

10   I give the botanical name here instead of the pharmacological
        nomenclature because, in early Chinese *Ben Cao*, little dis-
        tinction was made therapeutically between the root, seed, and
        pericarpium. A much fuller understanding of Trichsanthes'
        medicinal functions is gathered when one looks at all three
        of these together. The modern TCM description of each do
        add some specificity in the use of each but by separating
        them, such TCM descriptions also reduce the fuller under-
        standing of Trichosanthes of the classic *Ben Cao*. Personally,
        I think Trichosanthes is a very important medicinal.

11   Zhang, op.cit.

12   Flaws, Bob, *Nine Ounces, A Nine Part Program for the
        Prevention of AIDS in HIV Positive Persons,* Blue Poppy Press,
        Boulder, CO, 1989

13   Lee, William H., R.Ph., Ph.D., "Coenzyme Q_{10}, Is It Our New
        Fountain of Youth?", *A Good Health Guide,* Keats Publish-
        ing, New Canaan, CT., 1987, p. 7, 8, 12

GE-132
ORGANIC GERMANIUM

ITS TCM FUNCTIONS & INDICATIONS

Among the six medicines authorized for clinical trials on aids patients at the International AIDS Treatment Conference held in Tokyo in 1987, two are derived from well-known Chinese herbs.[1] Lentinan is derived from the Shiitake mushroom and Glycyrrhizin is derived from Licorice root. A third, Organic Germanium, is found in relatively high concentrations in a number of famous Chinese herbs, including Ginseng, Garlic, Codonopsis, Lycium berries, and Galla Wisteriae Floribundae[2] Organic Germanium is sold in Japan in drugstores and traditional Chinese apothecaries and has become a household word there in the last 20 years.[3] Organic Germanium is one of the new nutritional supplements which might beneficially be added to the materia medica of Western practitioners of Traditional Chinese Medicine (TCM). The only impediment to such incorporation into our pharmacopeia is its lack of TCM description. However, that description can be generated based on two decades of Japanese clinical experience using Organic Germanium.

Organic Germanium, bis-beta-carboxyethyl germanium sesquioxide or Ge-132 for short, has been popularized in Japan through the works of the late Dr. Kazuhiko Asai and his collaborators. Although Dr. Asai had a great respect for and knowledge of Traditional Chinese Medicine, as a biochemist, he himself was content to describe the medicinal effects of Ge-132 in Western biomedical terms. But, by reviewing the case

histories of Japanese patients most remarkably responding to
Ge-132 therapy recorded by Dr. Asai and his associates, a clear
TCM pattern emerges. As I have written elsewhere, the basic
modus operandi for establishing any non-TCM medicinal's TCM
functions and indications is to find the TCM disease mechanisms
(*Bing Ji*) common to species of all the Western diseases
responding to that medicinal.[4] Although Morton Walker,
D.P.M., writing in the *Townsend Letter for Doctors*, has decried
Dr. Asai's book, *Miracle Cure: Organic Germanium*, due to its
anecdotal nature, it is precisely such case history reports which
contain the signs and symptoms that can be processed by the
TCM logic of the Four Diagnoses.[5]

Japanese case histories

The following case histories, taken from Dr. Asai's book, all
give clear clues to Ge-132's TCM functions and indications.
Some of the patients were treated by Dr. Asai himself and
others by Drs. Meiko Okazawa and Takahiro Tanaka.

A 50 year old woman with a confirmed diagnosis of subacute
myelo-optico-neuropathy or SMON, what here in the U.S. would
more likely be called MS, came to Dr. Asai's clinic complaining
of difficulty walking and muscular atrophy of her leg. In
addition, she was virtually blind. She was given Organic
Germanium at a dose of 40 mg per kg of body weight per day.
After 3 months, this woman could walk with the aid of a cane.[6]

A 25 year old man with cerebellar degeneration also had
difficulty walking and talking. He had nystagmus, tinnitus, and
trembling limbs. Dr. Asai gave him 40 mg Ge-132 per kg
weight divided into two doses per day. After 5 months,
everything but his walking had improved. After 10 months, this
patient could rise and walk short distances and his tinnitus and

trembling had disappeared.[7]

A 49 year old man with Bechet's disease had failing eyesight and difficulty walking. Dr. Asai gave him 1.5 g of Ge-132 per day and advised him on a low acid diet and developing a good mental attitude. After only 10 days, this patient's eyesight began to improve.[8]

A 75 year old man was cured of an enlarged prostate causing urinary difficulty. This man had been advised to have surgery but declined turning instead to Dr. Asai. Dr. Asai effected this cure by administering 800 mg of Ge-132 per day.[9]

Dr. Takahiro Tanaka, a 60 year old male, himself suffered from fatigue, enervation, a heavy head, and pain in his prostate. After taking Ge-132, Dr. Tanaka experienced re-establishment of erection upon awaking. His fatigue, languor, and prostate pain all disappeared by taking 80 mg of Ge-132 per day divided into two doses. His bowel movements improved; he lost weight; he slept more soundly; and his cold extremities also improved.[10]

Dr. Okazawa cured a 78 year old woman with cerebral thrombosis causing persistent headache and shoulder/neck tension within 1 month by administering Ge-132.[11]

Likewise, Dr. Okazawa cured the hardness of hearing of both a 70 year old and 80 year old woman by daily Ge-132 supplementation.[12]

Another case of Dr. Okazawa's was a 35 year old woman with autonomic ataxia. This patient complained of apprehension, cold extremities, loss of balance when standing, a heavy feeling in the head, insomnia, palpitations, and depression of unknown cause. This woman was also cured by taking Ge-132 as a daily supplement.[13]

A final case history, also Dr. Okazawa's, should suffice in elucidating a general TCM trend. The patient was a 41 year old woman. Dr. Okazawa describes her as constitutionally weak. She complained of asthma, hypertension, headaches, constipation, pains from abdominal adhesions, hypersensitivity to pharmaceuticals, generalized pruritus, and liver and kidney disorders. This patient had taken Chinese herbs for 2 years with little improvement. However, after 40 mg of Ge-132 per day for 6 months, all her complaints were eliminated.14

The common TCM denominator

The professional TCM practitioner should have no difficulty in recognizing the common thread in the TCM diagnosis of all these cases. Each of the above patients displayed signs and symptoms of Liver Kidney Deficiency. This is further borne out by Dr. Asai's statements that daily supplementation with Ge-132 is excellent for treating apoplexy in the elderly[15], is very effective for treating eye diseases in general but cataracts and glaucoma in particular[16], treats both hyper and hypotension[17], relieves pain and anxieties in climacteric women between the ages of 50 and 60[18], and also treats uterine, breast, and bladder cancers[19], all of which can be due to variations of Liver and Kidney Deficiencies. Dr. Tanaka also found that Ge-132 treats arteriosclerosis, cerebral apoplexy, the sequelae of CVA, heart problems (including angina pectoris), epilepsy, senile mental diseases, chronic rheumatisms, and Raynaud's disease.[20] In particular, Dr. Tanaka found that sclerotic heart disease characterized by pain in the chest, bradycardia, and a slow pulse responds well to Ge-132.[21] Dr. Okazawa additionally found that Ge-132 is beneficial in the treatment of articular rheumatism, especially of the hips and knees and especially in post middle-aged women[22], asthma with dropsical swelling[23], and

Guillain-Barre Syndrome[24] and can inhibit the progress of muscular atrophy and Down's Syndrome.[25]

Although there may be other TCM disease mechanisms accounting for varieties of each of the above named Western disease categories, the common TCM disease mechanisms of all of these are Liver Kidney Deficiency. By this is meant Liver Blood Deficiency/Kidney Yin Deficiency and/or Kidney Yang Deficiency. Though Liver Kidney Dual Deficiency (*Gan Shen Liang Xu*) most often means Liver Blood/Kidney Yin Deficiency, the Kidney Deficiency part of this pattern can be either Yin or Yang or both. This is based on the fact that, "The Kidneys and Liver share a common source" and that, "The Blood and *Jing* share a common source." Both these traditional Chinese statements describe the close reciprocal relationship between the Liver and Kidneys and the Blood and Kidney *Jing*, with the Kidney *Jing* being the "source" in both statements. *Jing* itself can be either Yin or Yang depending upon the context in which this term is used. Although compared to Qi, Jing is Yin, compared to Yin, *Jing* is often thought of as Yang.

Many patients successfully treated with Organic Germanium suffer from what in Chinese medicine are called *Wei Zheng* or Flaccidity Syndrome. *Wei Zheng* as a disease category covers a range of autoimmune diseases characterized by muscular atrophy, paralysis, and neurological impairment. These disease include multiple sclerosis (MS), lupus (SLE), rheumatoid arthritis (RA), scleroderma, Guillain-Barre Syndrome, and Bechet's disease. Although there are a number of TCM *Zheng* or patterns covering these various Western diseases, by far the most commonly encountered pattern is Liver Kidney Dual Deficiency. In such cases, insufficiency of Liver Blood fails to nourish and maintain the *Jin* Sinews which then dry out and become stiff and atrophic. Insufficiency of Kidney *Jing* with predominance of either Kidney Yin Deficiency in the young and middle-aged or Kidney Yang Deficiency in the elderly causes degeneration in any and all tissues nourished and activated by the Kidneys. These include the Brain, the Marrow (meaning in TCM the nerves as well as bone marrow), the *Gu* Bones, and the *Wai Shen*, the Outer Kidneys, i.e. the reproductive organs.

Liver Kidney Dual Deficiency with both Yin and Yang Deficiency also explains the majority of menopausal complaints. The *Tian Kui* (Heavenly Water or menstruation) ceases due to insufficiency of Liver Blood in turn due to decline of Kidney *Jing*, its source, due to aging. As the *Nei Jing* states, women cease menstruating at 7x7 years due to decline of Kidney *Jing*. Hot flashes are due to upward perversion of Yang energy from the Kidneys and Liver below due to its losing its root in the *Qi Hai/Tan Tian*. In such cases, there is flushing up of Liver Yang or Deficiency Fire in the Heart above, and Liver Blood and Kidney Yin and Yang Deficiency below. It is this same basic scenario which accounts for hip, sciatic, and knee pain in middle-aged and peri-menopausal women -- once again the Liver Blood failing to nourish the *Jin* Sinews and Kidney Yin and Yang failing to nourish and energize the *Gu* Bones. It should be remembered that the loins in Chinese medicine not only include the lumbosacral area but also the hips as well.

In looking at the overwhelming majority of case histories presented by Dr. Asai, it becomes clear that his most obvious and remarkable cures with Ge-132 were with elderly patients exhibiting symptoms of Kidney Deficiency due to aging and children and young adults suffering from Congenital Insufficiency. Congenital Insufficiency means Kidney Deficiency. This is why Dr. Okazawa found that Ge-132 has an inhibitory effect on the progression of Down's Syndrome.

Likewise, the asthma cases presented by Drs. Asai and Okazawa which were benefitted by Ge-132 are all clearly Kidney Qi Deficiency cases involving the elderly or the constitutionally weak with prominent Kidney Deficiency associated signs and symptoms, such as dropsy, loss of hearing, and cataracts. In addition, those cases involving constipation which improved after Ge-132 supplementation also involved the elderly. In the aged, constipation is most often due to Fluid Insufficiency of the Intestines. The Blood and Fluids share a common source, and, with the decline of systemic Yin attendant to aging, the Fluids of the Intestines become exhausted. In TCM, this aspect of constipation is typically remedied by Liver Blood tonics, such as Dang Gui. However, constipation in the aged is also concomitantly due to decline of Kidney Yang, remembering that, "The Kidneys rule the Intestines" and that Kidney Qi/Yang supplies the motivating force for transportation and transformation in the Lower Burner.

The TCM functions of Ge-132

Based on the above Japanese case histories of patients responding favorably to Ge-132, I believe Organic Germanium should be categorized as a Yang tonic. In Chinese medicine, there are a number of medicinals which are categorized as Yang tonics but whose functions include tonification of the Kidneys, nourishing of the Blood, strengthening of the *Jin* Sinews and *Gu* Bones, moistening of the Intestines, and benefitting of the *Jing* Essence. These include Herba Epimedii, Herba Cynomorii, Herba Cistanchis, Radix Morindae, Cortex Eucommiae, Radix Cibotti, and Radix Dipsaci. It is my opinion that Organic Germanium also has these same functions. Typically, because Yang Qi is both Warm and moving, these Chinese medicinals also activate the Blood and expel Wind and Dampness, thus also stopping pain. In addition, Herba Epimedii also harnesses Ascendant Liver Yang and prevents up-flushing above.

Because such a constellation of TCM functions is consistent with other traditionally described TCM medicinals and because of Organic Germanium's demonstrated clinical efficacy, as evidenced by the above case histories, I believe Ge-132's TCM functions should be listed as:

-Tonifies the Kidneys and fortifies the Yang

-Nourishes the Blood and benefits the *Jing* Essence

-Nourishes the *Jin* Sinews and strengthens the *Gu* Bones

-Moistens the Intestines and promotes bowel movements

-Promotes the flow of Qi and activates the Blood

-Dispels Dampness and Wind and stops pain

-Tonifies Yin and Yang and harnesses Ascendant Liver Yang

-Benefits Water and promotes urination

-Benefits hearing and brightens the eyes

-Strengthens the loins and knees

-Warms and consolidates Lung Qi and enables the Kidneys to grasp the Qi

To some TCM practitioners, this may seem like an improbably long list of functions since modern *Ben Cao*, such as Bensky & Gamble's *Chinese Medicine: Materia Medica*[26], typically only list three or four functions per medicinal. However, such modern *Ben Cao* tend to highlight the most obvious uses of medicinals so neophytes can discriminate their predominant usage. Older, classical *Ben Cao* tend to give much fuller descriptions of the benefits of Chinese medicinals and list more functions as I have above for Ge-132. The professional practitioner should be able to understand the theoretical ramifications which make these functions reasonably hang together.

The TCM indications for Ge-132

The TCM indications for Organic Germanium include most, if not all, Kidney Yang Deficiency conditions and most, if not all, Liver Kidney Dual Deficiencies where Kidney Yang Deficiency also plays a part. The potential list of such diseases and conditions is long, including musculoskeletal problems, mental problems, circulatory disorders, hearing and vision disorders, and even some urogenital, sexual, and endocrine disorders. Ge-132 may be indicated or should be considered in any disease condition for which a TCM practitioner might prescribe Ramulus or Cortex Cinnamomi, Radix Rubra Panacis Ginseng Koreani, or any of the Yang tonics, such as Herba Epimedii and Cortex Eucommiae.

The Western medical indications for Ge-132

According to the authors of the *American Institute for Biological Research Scientific Reviews,* an abstract publishing resource for Western clinicians, animal and human clinical trials suggest organic germanium to be of therapeutic value for the following conditions or diseases:[27]

        Cancer
        Chronic Viral Infections
        Heart Disease

Although I would not like to see Organic Germanium overlooked in the treatment of autoimmune diseases, such as MS, SLE, RA, etc. for which it seems extremely appropriate, TCM theory can help explain why and help refine exactly which species of the above three listed diseases Ge-132 is likely to benefit.

Cancer

Zhang Dai-zhao, in *The Treatment of Cancer by Integrated Chinese-Western Medicine*, lists four broad TCM categories of pathogenesis for cancer.[28] The fourth of these is Deficiency Injury of the *Zang Fu (Xu Shang Zang Fu)*. This Deficiency Injury is then subdivided into Internal and External *Bing Yin* or disease factors. Of the Internal factors, three of the four factors discussed (Internal Injury by the Seven Emotions, Dietary Imbalance, Exhaustion, and Deficiency Injury due to Advanced Age & Senility) may directly cause Liver Kidney Dual Deficiency.

It is said in Chinese medicine that, "The Seven Passions all transform into Fire." Fire, a Yang Evil, injures and exhausts True Yin. This includes Liver Blood and Kidney Yin. Since Yin is the foundation of True Yang, Yin Deficiency eventually may result in both Yin and Yang Deficiency, in which case tonification of Yang is necessary to catalyze transformation of Yin. Exhaustion due to overwork, prolonged fatigue, or excess sex directly consumes Qi and Blood and eventually injures the Liver and Kidneys, the Blood and the *Jing*. Whereas, the aging process is the consumption and attendant exhaustion of Yin by the act of living (Yang). Life is the consumption of Yin substance as the fuel for Yang activity and consciousness (*Shen Ming*).

The fourth *Bing Yin*, dietary irregularity or imbalance, may also indirectly cause Liver Kidney Dual Deficiency. Any foods which cause or aggravate Heat in the Stomach and/or Liver, such as alcohol, fatty, greasy, fried foods, and spicy, acrid foods, may eventually lead to Deficiency Injury of the Blood and Yin. Whereas, coffee can waste the Blood and Fluids and directly exhausts the Kidney *Jing*.

As for External Evils, based on Liu Wan-su's Principle of Similar Transformation, any of the Six *Yin* may transform into Evil Heat. When either Excess Heat flourishes or Deficiency Heat lingers, Yin Fluids are consumed. In particular, Deficiency Heat often leads to and complicates Liver Kidney Dual Deficiency. The Heat injures the Blood and Yin, but it also injures the Qi as well. Qi Deficiency eventually leads to Kidney Deficiency, including Yang Deficiency below. This scenario describes the long-term effects and sequelae of polio, mononucleosis, brucellosis, and even CEBVS. Such exogenous febrile diseases may, according to Chinese medical theory, create an internal environment which eventually evolves into cancer.

Zhang Dai-zhao lists nourishing the Liver and tonifying the Kidneys among the eight TCM therapeutic principles for treating cancer.[29] He also lists Liver Kidney Dual Deficiency as one TCM pattern describing varieties of colon cancer[30], liver cancer[31], and uterine/cervical cancer.[32] Zhang lists Lung Kidney Dual Deficiency as one TCM pattern covering lung cancer[33], and we have already discussed the Kidney Qi's role in grasping the Qi sent down by the Lungs. Hong-yen Hsu, in *Treating Cancer With Chinese Herbs*, lists Yin and Yang Deficiency with Floating Yang as a possible TCM pattern describing some types of brain cancer.[34] Likewise, Hsu gives Liver Blood/Kidney *Jing* Deficiency with Depressed Qi, Internal Heat, and Downward Percolation of Damp Heat as a TCM pattern covering penile cancer.[35] In addition, Hsu describes two Chinese herbal prescriptions for the treatment of giant cell osteosarcoma which are obviously designed to correct Liver Blood/Kidney Yin Deficiency with Ascension of Yang due to Loss of Root in the Lower Burner.[36]

Based on my above description of the TCM functions of Ge-132, it makes sense that this medicinal would treat malignancies when their TCM diagnosis fits this Liver Kidney Dual Deficiency pattern. Because Kidney Yang is the Root of all Yang in the body, it is also possible that Organic Germanium would have an ameliorating effect on any Qi Deficiency/Yang Deficiency/Deficiency Cold condition as well.

Zhang Dai-zhao states that radiation and chemotherapy often cause Deficiency Injury of the Liver and Kidneys due to Hot Toxins.[37] In such Deficiency Damage cases, Organic Germanium might be reasonably be expected to help redress the side effects of these Western allopathic therapies. Using such a description of the TCM functions and indications of Ge-132, practitioners should be able to better differentiate when to use Organic Germanium in treating cancer and the side effects of modern cancer therapies.

Chronic viral infections

Viral infections are the bane of modern Western medicine which offers relatively little effective treatment for them. In particular, EBV (Epstein-Barr virus), HIV (human immune-deficiency virus), HPV (human papilloma virus), and herpes are all implicated in widely disseminated, debilitating, persistent, and even life-threatening diseases. These viral infections have come to dominate the health concerns of large segments of the American population which has been offered little in the way of assurance of cure.

In Traditional Chinese Medicine, all these viral conditions are species of Hidden Evils (*Fu Xie*) of the *Wen Bing* category. After entering the body, they typically cause an initial inflammatory reaction. Then they go into a latency or hidden stage where they can remain relatively dormant for months, years, and even decades. Chinese medicine's first recorded reference to such Hidden Evils is in the *Nei Jing*, the premier classic of Chinese medicine dating from the 2nd century B.C. In the *Nei Jing*, it is said that such Hidden Evils may remain latent as long as the Kidney *Jing* is in sufficient supply. If, through diet, exhaustion, stress, or excessive sex, the *Jing* Essence is consumed to the point of insufficiency, it may allow such Hidden Evils to go from latent to active within the body.

Therefore, maintaining the *Jing* in good supply through proper diet, exercise, rest and relaxation, and regulation of one's sex life is the most important part of keeping such Hidden Evils latent. More detailed instructions on how this can be done are given in my *Nine Ounces, A Nine Part Program for the Prevention of AIDS in HIV Positive Persons.*[39] However, Liver Blood and Kidney *Jing* tonic medicines, such as Seven Forest's Restorative Tablets and Health Concern's Astra Isatis, have proven preliminarily effective in keeping such viruses latent in the case of hiv and herpes respectively. For the same reason, Ge-132 or Organic Germanium likewise appears to be relatively effective in controlling EBV, HIV, and herpes. This, to me, seems logical given its TCM functions. It especially seems logical to me that Ge-132 would be most effective in treating hiv, when the patient has yet to develop full-blown AIDS, i.e. when the Evil Qi is still more or less latent. In my clinical experience, the most common pulse abnormality in HIV infected persons is a deep right *Chi* Foot pulse accompanied by a prominent right *Guan* Gate pulse.

Heart disease

Heart disease is a very large and diverse category of diseases. Given my TCM description of Ge-132, however, and based on one of Dr. Takahiro Tanaka's case histories, I think it is possible to suggest which specific heart patients should benefit most from treatment with Organic Germanium. The case involved a 66 year old man with sclerotic heart disease. His signs and symptoms included pain in the chest, bradycardia, and a slow pulse. He was also very fatigued and short of breath. Upon taking Ge-132, he quickly experienced relief of chest pain and eventually he could walk uphill without frequent rests.[39]

This type of case history is much more enlightening to a TCM practitioner than scores of controlled studies analyzing the tissues of dissected rats since it includes signs and symptoms we can read according to the Four Diagnoses. Based on the patient's age and signs and symptoms and especially his pulse, it seems clear he suffered from what we would diagnose as Chest *Bi* due to Yang Deficiency and Blockage of the Heart Channel. Dr. Henry Lu, translating an unspecified Chinese text, gives the signs and symptoms of this *Zheng* or pattern as: congested chest, feeling suffocated, periodic heart pain, palpitations, shortness of breath, a pale complexion, fatigue and weakness, fear of cold and cold limbs, occasional excessive perspiration, inability to sleep well, poor appetite, discharge of copious, clear urine, and thin stools. The tongue is pale, fat, and tender with a white, possibly greasy coating. The pulse is deep and relaxed or slow and clotted.[40]

From the above signs and symptoms, we can infer that Yang Deficiency of the Heart is due ultimately to Yang Deficiency of the Kidneys. This is why there is copious, clear urine and the thin, loose stools. Dr. Liu Yan-chi, in *The Essential Book of Traditional Chinese Medicine*, lists "weakened function of the

kidney in the elderly and feeble" as the first cause of Blockage
of the Heart Channel causing coronary atherosclerotic disease.[41]
Since Ge-132 is a Yang tonic by TCM definition, patients
suffering from specifically this type of heart disease should
benefit from Organic Germanium.   Likewise, Raynaud's
Syndrome is most often a Yang Deficiency disease and this is
why Raynaud's sufferers often feel warmth tingling in their
extremities only minutes after ingesting Ge-132[42]. In addition,
hypotension and hypertension can both be due to Kidney Yang
Deficiency in TCM and Ge-132 should be considered especially
in such cases.

Other diseases responding to Ge-132

Betty Kamen, Ph.D., in *Germanium, A New Approach to
Immunity*, mentions reports by physicians prescribing Ge-132
curing a diverse group of symptoms. These include warts and
corns, backaches, headaches, eczema, and frequent urination[43].
Warts and corns are an accumulation of Yin substance.
Acupuncture and moxibustion treatments of these conditions
essentially supply more Yang Qi to the local area, thus
transforming and transporting these local Yin Accumulations.

Backaches are a common Kidney Deficiency symptom and it is
not surprising some peoples', and especially the elderly's
backaches are treated by Ge-132. Just as Radix Dipsaci and
Cortex Eucommiae can be prescribed in combination with other
medicinals for the treatment of low back pain even due to
other mechanisms than Kidney Deficiency due to their special
tropism for this area of the body, likewise we might posit this
same kind of special tropism and action for Ge-132 on the low
back and loins.

In TCM there are species of chronic, recalcitrant headaches due to non-arisal of Clear Yang to the head and failure of Kidney *Jing* to fill the Sea of Marrow. Such headaches are encountered in constitutionally weak patients, the chronically debilitated, and the aged. Since Ge-132 is a Yang tonic which also benefits the *Jing* Essence, it is logical that it would benefit these specific types of headache. In addition, since Ge-132 has a nourishing effect on Liver Blood, it might also be effective for treating post partum, post menopausal, and post menstrual headaches in women.

Chronic eczema is usually due to Insufficient Blood nourishing the skin. This same mechanism also leads to formication and senile pruritus. These conditions tend to get worse at night and in the winter which confirms their Kidney Deficiency origin. The TCM treatment of these conditions is based on tonifying the Liver and Kidneys.[44]

Frequent urination may be due to several different mechanisms. In the young and early middle-aged, it is rarely due to Kidney Deficiency and is routinely misdiagnosed and mistreated by neophyte American practitioners. In younger patients, side-tracking of Fluids by a Hot Stomach mutually inflamed by a Hot Liver is much more commonly encountered. There are also Spleen Damp, Heart Fire, and Lung Deficiency mechanisms which often cause polyuria in the young. However, by the time a person approaches 60, most polyuria does include some Kidney Qi Deficiency in which case the Kidney Qi is insufficient to transform and transport Fluids back upwards as is their job. This dysfunction also, in part, accounts for the gravelly voice, dry skin, and hair loss in the aged. It is for just this type of polyuria that Ge-132 should be effective.

Ge-132 & aging

Many Western writers, such as Betty Kamen, suggest that Ge-132 may be a longevity medicinal. Since it appears to be a Yang tonic, this also seems likely from a Chinese medical perspective as well. In the late Ming dynasty (circa 1570), Zhang Jie-bin, aka Zhang Jing-yue, stated that since life is Yang, a person cannot have too much True Yang since it is impossible to say a person has too much life. This is in contradiction to Zhu Dan-xi of the Yuan who felt most chronic disease is due to Yin Deficiency in turn due to an Excess of Yang. Although Zhu was not wrong (since he was talking about pathologic Yang, i.e. Heat), still Zhang Jie-bin, speaking as he was about Kidney Yang, had a point.

Zhang and his associates later came to be known as the School of Prenatal Tonification. This means tonification of the Prenatal Root of Life -- the Kidneys. Further, this school was also called the School of Warm Tonification since their emphasis was on strengthening and banking the Fire of Life, the *Ming Men Zhi Huo*, Kidney Yang. Zhang and his associates liked to use Liver Blood/Kidney *Jing* tonics like Radix Rehmanniae (Zhang was often called Dr. Rehmanniae) in combination with Warm, Yang tonics such as Cortex Cinnamomi. Cortex Cinnamomi reroutes Yang back to the *Qi Hai/Tan Tian*, its source or root. There it catalyzes Yang transformation of Yin Essence, initiating the creation of both Qi and Blood. *Jing* transformed into Qi becomes the *Yuan Qi* which catalyzes the creation of Source Qi in the Lungs; and *Jing* sent up to the Heart becomes the material substrate for that Organ's creation of the Blood.

This is essentially what Ge-132 seems to do well according to the logic of TCM. Since aging is identical to the decline and exhaustion of Kidney Yin and Yang, it is only reasonable that

Ge-132 should have a retarding effect on the aging process. The ears, the eyes, urination, sex, and the bones are all tissues and functions particularly nourished and energized by the Kidneys. Therefore, it is not surprising that it is these tissues and functions which seem to respond so markedly to Ge-132. In particular, osteoporosis, according to Dr. Parris Kidd, one of the foremost authorities on and proponents of the medical use of Ge-132, is prevented by regular supplementation of Organic Germanium: "Ge-132 protected against bone mass decrease in osteoporosis, normalizing calcium metabolism possibly via an effect on parahormone production."[45] The TCM practitioner would say rather, or in addition, via tonification of Kidney *Jing*.

Dosages of Ge-132

The effective dosage levels of Ge-132 spans a wide range depending upon the severity of the condition under treatment, whether it is being taken preventively or remedially, and whether it is being taken synergistically with other supplements or medicinals. Preventively, 25-30 mg per day is usually recommended. For minor problems, this dosage may be increased to 50-100 mg per day. Dr. Kendall reports good therapeutic and remedial results with doses ranging from 100-400 mg per day.[46] And for serious, life-threatening and malignant diseases, 1-2 g per day can be taken.

Dr. Kidd reports complete cessation of pain in terminally ill cancer patients within 20 minutes of taking 3-4 grams of Ge-132.[47] Dr. Asai never used more than 2.5 g per day even in cases of cancer and reported numerous cures at 500 mg per day.[48] Dr. Serafina Corsello, M.D., of the Stress Center of Huntington, N.Y., administers Ge-132 for 5 days in a row and then rests the patient for 2 days before beginning Ge-132 again. She describes this 2 day rest between courses as a "cooling off" period, an interesting choice of words given Ge-132's TCM description.[49]

Most authorities agree that Ge-132 is best administered in several equal doses over a 24 hour period rather than taking the full dose one time per day. It is also felt by many that taking Ge-132 sublingually rather than swallowing it results in greatest utilizable absorption and, therefore, efficacy.

Side effects & contraindications of Ge-132

Although Organic Germanium has, as Dr. Kidd puts it, a "uniquely low toxicity", it is not completely free of side effects. The reported side-effects of Ge-132 include softening of the stool, diuresis, and an occasional rash about the neck and shoulders. Some persons also have reported insomnia and dizziness, especially if they began right away taking high doses of Organic Germanium.[50] These side-effects are all consistent according to TCM logic with Ge-132's being a Yang tonic.

Tonification of Yang means adding warmth or Heat to the body. If this Heat is not adequately circulated, it can flush upwards and outward causing rash, tingling, headache, dizziness, and insomnia. That all these side-effects seem to be transient confirms my opinion that, like Herba Epimedii and Cortex Cinnamomi, Ge-132 promotes its own circulation and also harnesses and returns Ascendant Yang. I myself experienced transient dizziness five days after beginning taking Ge-132 at 100 mg per day divided in two equal doses. This dizziness lasted only one day. I tend to have a Hot Liver and Stomach with occasional episodes of Arrogant Liver Yang. Loose stools and polyuria may be explained as over-transportation of the digestate and Liquids in a system that has been sluggish. I also experienced such polyuria for two or three days after the disappearance of the slight dizziness.

Dr. Kamen tends to think that these side-effects are signs that toxicity is being discharged from the body. However, describing every crisis and side-effect as a healing discharge is too easy an answer all too often given by practitioners and proponents of alternative healing. If something is powerfully good, it also has the potential for being powerfully bad in the wrong situation. Therefore, like Herba Epimedii, Cortex Cinnamomi, and other Liver Kidney Yang tonics of their class, I suggest Ge-132, especially in large doses, be carefully considered in Yin Deficiency patients with Flaring of Deficiency Heat. Although Warm tonification may prove effective in some cases of this *Zheng*, it may also aggravate others.

Also, Yang tonification is generally more appropriate in the aged as opposed to the young. Some young people in our culture think that if a little is good, more must be better and therefore take any and sometimes all OTC medicinals touted as retarding aging. With Ge-132, this could cause problems. Younger and middle-aged persons wishing to use Ge-132 preventively should only take small doses of this medicinal. This caveat does not extend to Ge-132's remedial use as long as it is indicated according to TCM diagnosis by *Bian Zheng*.

Toxicity

Dr. Kidd, based on toxicity and safety tests conducted in Japan, states:

> In acute, subacute and chronic toxicity studies it (Ge-132) has been tested orally, intravenously, subcutaneously, and intraperitoneally on mice, rats, rabbits, beagle dogs, and human volunteers. Heart and brain function, behavioral parameters, and reproductive effects also were evaluated. Ge-132 was confirmed to be a highly safe compound, up to

the equivalent in humans of tens of grams per day.[51]

However, there are several different types of germanium offered in the marketplace. Only one is Ge-132 and only Ge-132 has been proven non-toxic as described above. Ge-132 or Organic Germanium, developed by Dr. Asai and his associates, has a low toxicity and a high therapeutic index or favorable benefit/risk ratio.

Germanium citrate-lactate may have beneficial effects on immunity and cardiovascular function. It may also have anti-cancer effects as well. However, tests on its toxicity and safety have yet to be concluded in Europe. Spirogermanium, investigated by the National Cancer Institute as a potential chemotherapy agent has proven itself unsafe for human consumption. Its benefit/risk ration is unacceptable due to its toxicity. Germanium dioxide, investigated as a treatment for anemia in the 1920s, has proven both ineffective for that purpose and toxic to the human system when taken long-term. Recent clinical reports from Japan have documented several cases of kidney failure due to long-term ingestion of germanium dioxide.[52]

Therefore, it is important that practitioners prescribing germanium and patients taking germanium be sure that the germanium they use is Organic Germanium or Ge-132. This is the form of germanium which has the best benefit/risk ration and the form of germanium that has been proven to be safe and non-toxic. Practitioners can purchase Ge-132 from Bioenergy Nutrients Inc. 6395 Gunpark Dr., Boulder, CO 80301, (800) 553-0227. This firm is happy to furnish certificates of analysis testifying to their Ge-132's purity. Further, Bioenergy Nutrients also furnishes copious literature and reprints on Ge-132 to professional practitioners enabling them to more knowledgeably prescribe this substance and also various brochures and pamphlets for patients and laypersons.

Ge-132 in combination with other therapies

Professional Chinese medicine is based on the writing of polypharmacy or multi-ingredient formulas. Although describing a single medicinal's TCM functions and properties is the beginning of its journey towards incorporation into our materia medica, it is also important for TCM practitioners to also work out the common, effective combinations of a new ingredient. This is based on TCM's holistic vision of restoring balance to the entire organism. Most chronic conditions are multifaceted. Since every part and function in the human organism is interrelated, chronic problems almost always involve more than one Humour, more than one Phase, and more than one Organ. It is this emphasis on internally balanced prescription writing that has enabled Chinese medicine to develop a therapeutics almost entirely devoid of side-effects. Because of this, the professional TCM practitioner will want to know or consider how Ge-132 can be combined within a holistic and comprehensive treatment plan.

Ge-132 & Chinese Herbs

First, Ge-132 can be effectively combined with traditional Chinese formulas in order to make them more effective. On the one hand, Ge-132 can be combined with such Yang tonics as *Jin Gui Shen Qi Wan* (aka *Ba Wei Di Huang Wan*). It can also be combined with formulas which warm the Interior and dispel Cold, such as *Fu Zi Li Zhong Wan* and *Chen Wu Tang*. It can also be used with Liver Kidney tonic formulas, such as *Er Xian Tang* which nourishes Liver Blood, tonifies Kidney Yin and Yang, and harnesses Ascendant Yang. Likewise, Ge-132 can be combined with Lung Kidney tonic formulas for asthma, such as *Shen Jie San,* and Heart Kidney tonic formulas for heart disease, such as *Shen Fu Tang* and *Si Ni Tang.*

In particular, I have routinely begun administering Ge-132 to my female menopausal patients who are concurrently taking my version of *Er Xian Tang* called Two Immortals manufactured and distributed by Health Concerns of Alameda, CA. Since this formula itself is designed to address all the issues and functions which Ge-132 addresses, this addition to this formula I believe potentizes it and makes it all the more effective. I have been very successful using this protocol in eliminating hot flashes, night sweats, depression, insomnia, constipation, and low back and sciatic pain attendant to the climacteric.

Ge-132 & Acupuncture

Some acupuncturists may have not yet mastered Chinese herbal medicine, since these two therapies, although conceptually related, are not always taught as a unit. The TCM style of acupuncture as developed in the Peoples' Republic of China, is based on multiple, closely spaced, repetitive treatments. Because of the differences in the American health care delivery system and financial and time constraints, most American patients cannot afford such intensive acupuncture treatment. In such cases, less frequent acupuncture treatments can be supplemented by nutritional supplements like Ge-132 in order to make up for the therapeutic short-fall. Often, such an approach is better accepted and more cost and time effective for American patients. In such cases, Ge-132 is of benefit in supplementing the acupuncture/moxibustion treatment of Kidney Yang Deficiency low back and knee pain, polyuria, nocturia, spermatorrhea, impotence, cold extremities, and Heart Kidney Yang Deficiency and Lung Kidney Qi Deficiency patterns. Internal administration of Ge-132 might also prove a useful substitute for moxa which is often prohibited or frowned upon in American office complexes.

Ge-132 & other nutritional supplements

Personally, I have found that in many complex, intractable
conditions, Chinese herbs and acupuncture just are not enough.
As mentioned elsewhere, even Chinese doctors in China will
admit this. TCM as developed in China is not a totally effective
system of medicine even though it is a superior one. For such
complex, intractable conditions which are so often encountered
in American clinical practice, I find that vitamin and mineral
supplementation often adds to the effectiveness of Chinese
herbs and acupuncture. For instance, again in the treatment of
menopausal complaints due to Liver Kidney Dual Deficiency
complicated as it so often is by Yang Deficiency below,
combining Ge-132 with Two Immortals and Metagenics' Fem
Estro tablets achieves much quicker, long-lasting, and better
effect than administering any one of these alone. Fem Estro
tablets contain Korean (Red) Ginseng which itself tonifies
Kidney Yang and raw adrenal concentrate which tonifies Liver
Blood and Kidney *Jing*. In addition, it contains Vitamin C to
clear Heat and Bioflavonoids to clear Heat and stop bleeding,
Para-aminobenzoic Acid (PABA) to nourish the Blood and Body
Fluids and to irrigate the skin, and Vitamin B_5 which dredges
the Liver and harmonizes Wood and Earth. Therefore, based
on TCM functions, all three of these medicinals--Ge-132, Two
Immortals, and Fem Estro tablets--share a common TCM
approach, and their combined use gives a more potent yet
rounded and balanced effect than using any one of these alone.

In the future, I look forward to the creation of a New Medicine
for the 21st century which will be a combination of TCM theory
and medicinals from any and all sources. In that medicine,
practitioners will craft their prescriptions combining herbs from
around the world, nutritional supplements such as Ge-132, and
even Western pharmaceuticals, yet all based on the logic and
methodology of Chinese medicine as the dominant surviving,

professionally practiced, rational, holistic medicine in the world today. As a move in this direction, I recommend Ge -132 or Organic Germanium to my fellow American practitioners for incorporation into our pharmacopeia.

ENDNOTES

1   Kidd, Parris, Ph.D., "AIDS NEWS", *GINA Speaks*, Vol. 1,
     #1-3, 1988, Germanium Institute of North America, p.4

2   Kidd, Parris, Ph.D., "Ge-132: Research Breakthrough from
     the Orient", *Science Studies Ge-132-01* (1-89), p.1

3   Kamen, Betty, Ph.D., *Germanium, A New Approach to
     Immunity*, Nutrition Encounter, Inc., Larkspur, CA, 1987, p.3

4   Flaws, Bob, "The Pill and Stagnant Blood, The Side-Effects
     of Oral Contraception According to Traditional Chinese
     Medicine", *The Journal of Chinese Medicine*, #32, Jan. 1990,
     UK, p. 19-21
     Flaws, Bob, "Valium: Its TCM Functions, Indications and
     Contraindications", *Journal of the Am. Coll. of TCM*, Vol. 7,
     #3, S.F., 1989 p. 30
     Flaws, Bob, "Bactrim/Septra: TCM Properties, Functions,
     Indications and Contraindications", *Journal of the Am. Coll.
     of TCM*, Vol. 7, #4, S.F., 1989 p. 29-30
     Flaws, Bob, "A Perennial Spring: A Discussion of the TCM
     Properties and Uses of St. Johnswort in the Possible
     Treatment of AIDS and the Universal Applicability of
     Chinese Medicine", *The Journal of Chinese Medicine*, #31,
     Sept. 1989, UK, p. 8-12

5   Walker, Morton, D.P.M., "Germanium Oxygenation/Immune
     Enhancing Effects Sparks Excitement", *Townsend Letter for
     Doctors*, #52, 8711

6   Asai, Kazuhiko, Ph.D., *Miracle Cure, Organic Germanium*,
     Japan Publications, Inc., Tokyo and N.Y., 1980 p.58

7   Ibid., p.59

8   Ibid., p.61

9   Ibid., p.68

10   Ibid., p.69

11   Ibid., p.75-76

12   Ibid., p.76

13   Ibid., p.77

14   Ibid., p.79

15   Ibid., p.62

16   Ibid., p.65

17   Ibid., p.67

18   Ibid., p.67

19   Ibid., p.70

20   Ibid., p.71

21   Ibid., p.77

22   Ibid., p.77

23   Ibid., p.78

24   Ibid., p.86

25   Ibid., p.85

26   Bensky, Dan and Gamble, Andrew, *Chinese Herbal Medicine: Materia Medica*, Eastland Press, Seattle, 1986

27   *AIBR Scientific Reviews, Botanical Medical Series*, #7, 1987. American Institute of Biological Research, Tacoma, WA

28   Zhang Dai-zhao, *The Treatment of Cancer by Integrated*

Chinese-Western Medicine, trans. by Zhang Ting-Liang and Bob Flaws, Blue Poppy Press, Boulder, CO 1989, p. 17-19

29   Ibid., p.22

30   Ibid., p.66

31   Ibid., p.69

32   Ibid., p.83

33   Ibid., p.76

34   Hsu, Hong-yen, *Treating Cancer with Chinese Herbs*, Oriental Healing Arts Institute, LA, 1982, p.143

35   Ibid., p.170

36   Ibid., p.154-156

37   Zhang, op.cit., p.93

38   Flaws, Bob, *Nine Ounces, A Nine Part Program For the Prevention of AIDS in HIV Positive Persons*, Blue Poppy Press, Boulder, CO, 1989

39   Asai, op.cit., p.70-71

40   Lu, Henry, *Doctor's Manual of Chinese Medical Diet*, Vol.2, Chinese Foundations of Natural Health, Vancouver, B.C., 1981, p.11

41   Liu Yan-chi, *The Essential Book of Traditional Chinese Medicine*, Vol.2: Clinical Practice, trans. by Fang Jing-yu and Chen Lai-di, Columbia University Press, N.Y., 1988, p.287

42   Asai, op.cit., p.64

43   Kamen, op.cit., p.17

44   Liang Jian-Lui, *A Handbook of Traditional Chinese Dermatology*, trans. by Zhang Ting-Liang and Bob Flaws, Blue Poppy Press, Boulder, CO, 1988, p.23

45   Walker, op.cit., quoting Dr. Parris Kidd

46   Ibid.

47   Ibid.

48   Kamen, op.cit., p.34

49   Ibid., p. 34
50   Kidd, Parris, Ph.D., "Your Questions Answered", *GINA Speaks*, op.cit., p.6

51   Kidd, "Ge-132: Research Breakthrough from the Orient", op.cit., p.5

52   Summerfield, Frank W. and Kidd, Parris, Ph.D., "Germanium Dioxide: A Risk Not Worth Taking", *GINA Speaks*, op.cit., p.8

FEM ESTRO®

A WESTERN NUTRITIONAL FORMULA AND ITS TCM RATIONALIZATION

Traditional Chinese Medicine (TCM) is a rational medicine. Professional practitioners of TCM are used to reading rationalizations of both acupuncture and herbal formulas. However, up until now, these rationalizations have always described the functions and indications of medicinal substances and therapies originating in China. In the last year, I have written a number of essays and articles describing Western herbs and Western pharmaceuticals, including nutritional supplements, as if they were TCM medicinals.[1] This I have done as a preliminary step in laying the groundwork for a truly universal New Medicine for the 21st century. This New Medicine I envision bases its theory and rationale on TCM. TCM is the dominant, professionally practiced, literate, time-tested holistic medicine in the world today. Its theory is both broad enough to be universally applicable and wise enough to be the foundation of the humane, preventive, and whole-person, wellness-oriented medicine modern patients are looking for. Any therapy or medicinal substance from any source can be incorporated in a rational manner into this New Medicine once its properties, functions, indications, and contraindications are described according to TCM.

However, as mentioned above, describing individual medicinals according to TCM is only the first step. The next step is formulating comprehensive treatment plans incorporating these new medicinals. This encompasses the writing of prescriptions combining Chinese and non-Chinese medicinal "herbs" and synthetic pharmaceuticals in a single formula. It also includes rationalizing non-Chinese, non-"herbal" formulas and treatments as if they were TCM formulas and treatments. One such non-Chinese formula is Fem Estro tablets distributed by Metagenics International. The ingredients of this formula are:

Vitamin E (d-alpha tocopheryl succinate)	500 IU
Radix Rubra Panacis Ginseng Koreani	1000 mg
Bioflavonoids	500 mg
Vitamin B_5 (calcium d-pantothenate)	300 mg
paba (para-aminobenzoic acid)	300 mg
Vitamin C	250 mg
Raw Adrenal Concentrate	125 mg

The above amounts of each ingredient are achieved by a three tablet dose. The recommended daily dosage for this formula is one tablet four times per day.

This nutritional formula is an effective treatment for menopausal complaints, including hot flashes, breakthrough bleeding, low back, hip, and knee pain, and anxiety and palpitations. However, with the exception of Korean Ginseng, none of the ingredients in this formula are listed in standard TCM *Ben Cao*. Therefore, many TCM practitioners may feel incapable of or uncomfortable including these supplements in their treatment plan. The fact that these medicinals do not come from China is completely irrelevant. If this formula can be described according to the rationale of TCM, it can then be rationally prescribed by TCM practitioners.

Vitamin E (d-alpha tocopheryl succinate) is a Yang tonic which both nourishes Liver Blood and fortifies Kidney Yang. Therefore, Vitamin E benefits the *Jing* Essence and strengthens the *Jin* Sinews. This TCM description of Vitamin E is based on its clinically proven benefits as recorded in the Western biomedical literature. Therapeutic use of Vitamin E reduces nocturnal leg cramps, exercise cramps, and restless leg syndrome.[2] In TCM, these conditions are usually due to Insufficiency of Liver Blood nourishing the *Jin* Sinews resulting in their contraction. Sterility was one of the first conditions noted in Vitamin E deficiency.[3] This can cause irreversible testicular atrophy in males and reduced spermatogenesis. In TCM, this is due to Deficiency of Kidney *Jing*. Vitamin E therapy has proven successful in treating osteoarthritis and polymyositis, especially in the aged.[4] This is because, in TCM terms, most musculoskeletal complaints in the aged are due to Liver Kidney Dual Deficiency patterns. Likewise, in older patients, Vitamin E has proven effective in treating neurological and visual deficits.[5] These are also due to Liver Kidney Deficiency which is the dominant mechanism of aging. This is why many people consider Vitamin E a longevity supplement and age retardant. Even the fact that Vitamin E has been proven to benefit chronic cystic mastitis confirms this TCM description.[6] Chronic fibrocystic disease often involves Liver Blood/ *Chong Mai* Deficiency with up-flushing of Liver Stomach Yang and/or Deficiency Fire.

Although Radix Alba Panacis Ginseng is a Qi tonic primarily entering the Spleen and Lungs which also generates Fluids, Radix Rubra Panacis Ginseng Koreani tonifies the Qi and fortifies the Yang. It goes to the Kidneys as well as the Stomach/Spleen. It enters or travels to the *Qi Hai/Tan Tian* first and then spreads its influence from there. Its temperature is Warmer that White Ginseng and it is used in TCM only in cases where there is decline or collapse of Yang. In China, therefore, it is primarily thought of as an older person's tonic and is most often taken in the winter.

Bioflavonoids are produced in photosynthesizing cells. They are responsible for the majority of the yellow, red, and blue pigmentation of plants. Because therapeutically Bioflavonoids are used primarily to prevent bleeding and to combat viral infections, they should be classified as a Blood-regulating (*Li Xue*) medicinal which clears Heat and stops bleeding. Because they treat both periodontal disease[7] and herpes[8], both of which are manifestations of Heat in the Liver Channel, I beleive we can say that Bioflavonoids enter the Liver and Gall Bladder Channels. Heat arising from the Liver/Stomach is also responsible, in part, for diabetic cataracts, another condition Bioflavonoids are used to treat.[9] Liver and Stomach Heat mutually aggravate each other, and both the Liver and Stomach Channels arise to the eyes either externally or internally.

Vitamin B_5 is also known as Pantothenic Acid. Deficiency in humans has been shown to cause low blood pressure, dizziness, fatigue, infections, weakness, stomach distress, and constipation.[10] Therapeutically, Pantothenic Acid has been found effective for reducing fatiguability and nervousness and for improving gastric secretions.[11] In addition, it seems to promote endurance, speed wound healing, and help in the treatment of ulcerative colitis.[12] One last fact which helps to clarify Vitamin B $_5$'s TCM functions is that its deficiency is also implicated in herpes zoster.[13]

Pantothenic Acid seems to treat a very similar constellation of signs and symptoms as Radix Bupleuri Flacati and, therefore, I would describe its functions as relaxing constrained Liver Qi, raising the Clear Yang, harmonizing Wood and Earth, and clearing and eliminating Damp Heat. This includes Liver Heat, Gall Bladder Damp Heat, and also Damp Heat in the Intestines. Pantothenic Acid seems to enter the Liver and Gall Bladder with special tropism for the Middle Burner. In terms of classifying this ingredient in the TCM pharmacopeia, it might be placed with Bupleurum and Rhizoma Cimicifugae, Radix Peurariae, and Herba Menthae among the Cool, Acrid medicinals which relieve the Surface.

PABA or Para-aminobenzoic Acid's TCM functions seem to be similar to Radix Polygoni Multiflori. It tonifies Liver and Kidneys, nourishes the Blood, and benefits the *Jing* Essence. This explains why it helps treat premature greying of the hair, fatigue, headaches, and irritablity. paba also moistens the Intestines and, therefore, benefits constipation and promotes bowel movements. In addition, PABA expels Wind from the skin by nourishing the Blood. This explains why PABA is so often used topically for skin problems which, by the time they manifest as diseases Chinese medicine recognizes, are mostly Blood Deficiency problems with Stagnant Blood in the *Luo Mai*. These include wrinkles, dry skin, and dark spots.[14] When there is vitiligo, which PABA has also been used to treat, the TCM diagnosis is Wind and Dampness invading and lingering in the skin which then impede the Blood's nourishing of the skin in the affected areas.[15] This lack of Blood locally and the presence of Dampness then causes the white dyschromia.

Vitamin C is a Heat-clearing medicinal according to the logic of Chinese medicine. It is for this reason that Vitamin C or Ascorbic Acid is effective in the treatment of colds, flus, and various infections, the vaste majority of which tend to be Hot or Warm diseases. Vitamin C seems to be beneficial for clearing both Excess and Deficiency Heat similar to Rhizoma Picrorrhizae. For this reason, it has also proven useful in the treatment of *Wei Zheng*, such as MS, which usually have a Deficiency Fire component. Vitamin C also has the function of stopping bleeding when that bleeding is due to Heat entering the *Xue Fen* causing the Blood to run recklessly outside its pathways. Since Heat is the most common *Bing Ji* or disease mechanism causing bleeding in TCM, this underscores Vitamin C's wide-ranging utility as a styptic.

The fact that megadoses of Vitamin C tend to cause diarrhea is due to Vitamin C's Cool or Cold temperature energetically. Too much Vitamin C depresses the Righteous Warmth of the

Middle Burner leading to the Stomach/Spleen's inability to *Hua* or transform foods and liquids. The fact that Vitamin C is often deficient in patients with neurosis, hypochondria, hysteria, schizophrenia, and other affective disorders further corroborates its Heat-clearing function, since most mental disorders likewise are due to the presence of Evil Heat disturbing the *Shen*. The process of life is the consumption of Yin by Yang and, therefore, most pathogenesis is due to Evil Heat. That is why Vitamin C is such a widely applicable medicinal. Its use therapeutically can be seen as an example of Liu Wan-su's emphasis on Cool and Cold (*Liang Han*) medicines.

The use of animal glands and tissues in Chinese medicine has a long history. In the Tang dynasty, Sun Si-miao prescribed liver for the treatment of eye diseases, and Chinese dietary therapy is replete with animal organ recipes for the treatment of various Deficiencies.[16] In general, organs are tonifying medicinals. Animal medicinals are considered more "compassionate" than their vegetable counterparts, although their donors might balk at the use of this word. What this means is that their effect is more immediate and stronger due to their greater similarity to the Organ or tissue to be tonified.

Raw Adrenal Concentrate is a Yin tonic medicinal. Although some may be tempted to make a simplistic analogy of the kidneys to Yin and the adrenals to Yang, it must be remembered that the Chinese *Shen* Kidneys are not identical to the Western biomedical kidneys. And, if we look at the conditions that are benefitted by adrenal glandular supplementation, their common TCM disease mechanism is Yin Deficiency/Deficiency Fire: allergies, autoimmune diseases (*Wei Zheng*), asthma, sinusitis, bronchitis, and immune deficiency, burnout, and stress/exhaustion reactions.

Looking at the above described ingredients as a formula, it is striking that the rationale, in TCM terms, for its composition is almost identical to the famous Chinese menopausal formula *Er Xian Tang* (Two Immortals Decoction). The ingredients of this formula developed at the Shu Guang Hospital in Shanghai are:

Rhizoma Curculiginis	6-15 g
Herba Epimedii	9-15 g
Radix Morindae	6-9 g
Radix Angelicae Sinensis	6-9 g
Cortex Phellodendri	4-9 g
Radix Anemarrhenae	6-9 g

The first three ingredients in this formula are all Yang tonics. Curculigo tonifies the Kidneys and fortifies the Yang. Epimedium does the same, but it also tonifies both Yin and Yang and harnesses Ascendant Liver Yang due to Liver Kidney Deficiency. Morinda tonifies the Kidneys and fortifies the Yang as well. However, because it strengthens the *Jin* Sinews as well as the *Gu* Bones, I think Morinda must also have some Liver Blood nourishing properties as well. *Dang Gui* tonifies the Blood and inparticular Liver Blood. It also invigorates and harmonizes the Blood and mositens the Intestines. Invigoration of the Blood means that *Dang Gui* promotes Blood circulation. Harmonization of the Blood means harmonization of the Blood with the Qi. This, in turn, has to do with harmonization of the *Chong* and *Ren* and regulation of the menses. Phellodendron drains Damp Heat. It also quells Kidney Fire and, therefore, in this formula checks any tendency of flaring or congestion due to over-tonification of Yang by the first three ingredients. Anemarrhena likewise clears Heat and quells Fire. However, it nourishes Yin as well and generates Fluids. Anemarrhena and Phellodendron are commonly matched for clearing Flaring of Deficiency Heat due to Yin Deficiency.

The functions of this formula as a whole are to replenish both Yin and Yang, to clear Heat, and to regulate the *Chong* and

Ren.[17] The Yin which is nourished encompasses both Liver Blood and Kidney Yin. The Heat this formula clears is Deficiency Heat/Liver Heat flaring upwards. Although various TCM texts list the disease mechanisms of menopausal complaints as Liver Kidney Yin Deficiency, Ascendancy of Liver Yang, Kidney Yang Deficiency, and Heart Blod/Spleen Qi Deficiency as if menopausal women are either one *Zheng* of the other[18], in clinical practice, the most common presenting condition is a combination of Liver Blood/Kidney Yin Deficiency, Kidney Yang Deficiency, Arrogant Ascension of Liver Yang and/or Flaring of Deficiency Fire, Liver Qi Stagnation, and a disturbed *Shen* due to both lack of nourishment and the presence of pathologic Heat. Since this is exactly the composite disease mechanism *Er Xian Tang* is designed to treat, it is little wonder it is so effective and widely employed by TCM practitioners in China.

However, based on this same composite disease mechanism, it is also no wonder that Metagenics' Fem Estro tablets are also so effective. Vitamin E tonifies both Kidney Yinand Yang as well as nourishes Liver Blood. Red Korean Ginseng tonifies Kidney Yang. Raw Adrenal Concentrate tonifies Kidney Yin and clears or harnesses Deficiency Heat. PABA nourishes Liver Blood and Kidney Yin and benefits the *Jing* Essence which itself can be transformed into Yin or Yang. Vitamin C and Bioflavonoids clear Heat, stop bleeding, and calm the *Shen*. And Vitamin B_5 or Pantothenic Acid regulates the Liver Qi, relieves constraint, harmonizes the Liver/Spleen, and clears Heat. Especially if one keeps in mind that most often in clinical practice at least one of *Er Xian Tang*'s Yang tonics is deleted and replaced by more Yin tonics, such as Fructus Zizyphi Spinosae, and that also often Q-regulators, such as Cortex Albizziae Julibrissinis or Fructus Akebiae, are added to dedge the Liver Qi that is alsmost always a component of this scenario, then the similarity in rationale and composition between *Er Xian Tang* and Fem Estro tablets is all the more apparent.

Because current menopausal-aged women tend to be of a slightly older generation than most current American practitioners of TCM, they often have more trouble making the paradigm shift to Chinese medicine in general and to bitter, Chinese herbal "teas" in particular. Therefore, Fem Estro tablets are a very useful way of treating our American menopausal patients via a medicine they can relate to well. First of all, they are a tablet and do not require any preparation. Secondly, they can be swallowed without bitter taste. Third, since they typically work a little slower than a 150 gram plus, standard dose, TCM decoction (30-45 days versus 7-14 days for the eradication of hot flashes), they also tend to produce less side effects and, therefore, require less adjustment and represcription. Fourth, they look like medicine and come packaged similar to American expectations about medicine. And fifth, they can be understood by this generation of American patients either according to the theory of TCM or Western biomedicine, whichever they prefer and relate to best. And yet, based on the TCM description suggested above, a TCM practitioner can prescribe these tablets strictly according to the rubric and rationale of our ancient discipline.

I myself have begun prescribing Fem Estro tablets in tandem with the tableted version of Two Immortals I developed for Health Concerns of Alameda, CA. My preliminary impression is that this combination is both well accepted by my patients with high compliance and works extremely well. One complaint often voiced by American TCM practitioners is that tableted medicines are too low potency. By combining Fem Estro tablets with Two Immortal tablets, I beleive the vitamins potentize the herbal medicinals; while the herbs help to round out and soften the effects of the vitamins on the patient's system. This combination is cost-effective and time-efficient, and I think it merits serious consideration by American TCM practitioners.

Such combination prescribing of herbal medicinals with vitamins and other nutritional supplements and even with low doses of Western pharamceuticals opens exciting vistas for polypharmacy in the future. Already, Metagenics International markets, mostly to Chiropractors, MDs, and Naturopaths, a number of Chinese herbal/Western vitamin and mineral composite formulas. And in China, patent medicines are currently being manufactured combining Western pharmaceuticals and Chinese herbs. I beleive it is very important for American practitioners to recognize, accept, and advance our unique position in the shaping of this New Medicine.

Western medicine focuses on extremely small details, and yet its diagnostic categories are amorphous and abstract, based as they are on inferences about chemicals rather than on real life, symptom/sign situations. Chinese medicine, on the other hand, tends to see things from a larger, more general perspective. Yet in its diagnosis and therapeutics, TCM is far more precise, based as it is on individualized signs and symptoms. Although Western biomedical bits of information are useful and informative, I beleive it is the broad and wise theory and methodology of Chinese medicine which should provide the rational foundation of the New Medicine I envision.

As demonstrated above, we TCM practitioners can describe by our methodology any and every potential medicinal whether that be a simple or a compound formula. And, based on our diagnosis according to *Bian Zheng* or the discrimination of Patterns (of Disharmony). I think we TCM practitioners can actually prescribe Western nutritional formulas, such as Fem Estro tablets, with more accuracy than Western biomedical practitioners. Because not evey woman's climacteric exhibits the same imbalances and mechanisms, no single formula, be it

Western or Eastern, will comprehensively address every woman's menopause. It is Chinese medical theory which allows for more individualized and, therefore, precise prescription. Based on the above TCM description of Fem Estro tablets, I feel I have a very exact picture of just which menopausal patients will benefit most by its use.

Fem Estro can be purchased from **Metagenics International,** 971 Calle Negocia, San Clemente, CA, 92629, 1-800-692-9400.

ENDNOTES

1   Flaws, Bob, "A Perennial Spring, A Discussion of the TCM
         Properties of St. Johnswort in the Possible Treatment of
         AIDS and the Universal Applicability of Chinese Medicine,"
         Journal of Chinese Medicine, UK, #31, Sept., 1989, p. 8-12

         Flaws, Bob, "Valium: Its TCM Functions, Indications, and
         Contraindications," *Journal of the American College of
         Traditional Chinese Medicine*, San Francisco, Vol 7, #7, 1989,
         p. 27- 30

         Flaws, Bob, "Bactrim/Septra: TCM Properties, Functions,
         Indications, and Contraindications," *Journal of the American
         College of Traditional Chinese Medicine*, San Francisco, Vol.
         7, #4, 1989, p. 29-30

         Flaws, Bob, "Co-enzyme Q10: Its TCM Functions and
         Indications", *Science Studies*, Bioenergy Nutrients, Boulder,
         CO, Feb. 1990

2   Ayres, S. Jr. & Mihan, R., "The Restless Legs Syndrome:
         Response to Vitamin E," *Journal of Applied Nutrition*, #25,
         1973, p. 8-15

         Ayres, S. Jr. & Mihan, R., "Nocturnal Leg Cramps: A
         Progress Report on Response to Vitamin E," *Southern
         Medical Journal*, Vol. 67, 1974, p. 1308-1312

         Cathcart, R.F., "Leg Cramps and Vitamin E," *Journal of
         American Medical Association*, #219, 1972, p. 216

3   Jennings, I.W. *Vitamins in Endocrine Metabolism*, Charles C.
         Tomas Pub., 1970, p. 101

4   Killeen, et.al., "Polymyositis: Response to Vitamin E,"
         Southern Medical Journal, Vol 69, #10, October, 1976, p.
         1372

Machtey, I. & Ouaknine, L., "Tocopherol in Osteoarthritis: A Controlled Pilot Study," *Journal of American Geriatric Society,* Vol 26, #7, July, 1979, p. 328

5   Dunne, Levon J., *Nutrition Almanac,* 3rd Edition, McGraw-Hill Publishing, NY, 1990, p. 53

6   Abrams, A.A., "Use of Vitamin E in Chronic Cystic Mastitis," *New England Journal of Medicine,* #272, 1965, p. 1080

7   Dunne, op.cit., p. 62

8   Hausteen, B., "Flavonoids, A Class of Natural Products of High Pharmaceutical Potency," *Biochemical Pharmacology,* Vol. 32, #7, 1983, p. 1141-1148

9   Varma, S.D., Mizuno, A., Kinoshita, J.H., "Diabetic Cataracts and Flavonoids," *Science,* #195, 1977, p. 205

10   Dunne, op.cit., p. 27-28

11   Ibid., p. 28

12   Williams, F.J., *Nutrition Against Disease,* Pitman Publishing Corp., NY, 1971

13   Hodges, R.E., Bean, W.B., Ohlson, M.A., & Bleiler, R.E., "Factors Affecting Human Anti-body Response," *American Journal of Clinical Nutrition,* Vol 11, #2, 1962, p. 85-93

14   Pfeiffer, Carl, as cited by Dunne, op.cit., p. 43

15   Liang Jian-hui, *A Handbook of Traditional Chinese Dermatology,* translated by Zhang Ting-liang & Bob Flaws, Blue Poppy Press, Boulder, CO, 1988

16   Flaws, Bob & Wolfe, Honora Lee, *Prince Wen Hui's Cook, Chinese Dietary Therapy,* Paradigm Publications, Brookline, MA, 1983

17   Yeung Him-che, OMD, PhD., *Handbook of Chinese Herbs and Formulas*, Vol. II, self-published, 1983, p. 91

18   Song Guang-ji & Yu Xiao-zhen, *A Handbook of Traditional Chinese Gynecology*, translated by Zhang Ting-liang, Blue Poppy Press, Boulder, CO, 1987, p. 47-48

AN ORTHOMOLECULAR BEN CAO

Orthomolecular medicinals include vitamins, minerals, essential fatty acids, enzymes, coenzymes, cofactors, and amino acids. These are the building blocks of the human organism. They are called orthomolecular because they are made up from the same molecules as the human body. Therefore, they are *ortho* or the same as our bodies' own constituents. This is opposed to zenomolecular and ultramolecular medicinals. Zenomolecular medicinals introduce into the body molecules which are different from those of which we are composed. Ultramolecular medicinals generally refer to homeopathics. Homeopathic preparations which are diluted beyond Avagadro's number do not contain a single molecule of the original mother tincture from which they are made. They are, therefore, *ultra* or beyond molecular.

Orthomolecular medicinals are both extremely effective and extremely safe. When orthomolecular medicinals are prescribed in the proper combinations and amounts, patients can expect to see a definite improvement in their signs and symptoms within 45 days. According to Donald Loomis, during the years 1983-1987, 1182 Americans died due to complications due to Western drug therapy. During that same time period, no Americans died due to complications associated with orthomolecular therapy.[1]

In addition, according to a United States Department of Agriculture 10 state nutrition study, a large percentage of the American population is not getting the RDA or recommended daily amounts of crucial micronutrients. According to this survey, 68% of the population is getting the RDS of Calcium, 57% less than the RDA of Iron, and 75% less tha the RDA of

Magnesium. 45% of the persons studied were getting less than the RDA of B_1; 34& had less than the RDA of B_2; 33% had less than the RDA of B_3; 80% had less than the RDA of B_6; 34% had less than the RDA of B_{12}; and 41% had less than the RDA of Vitamin C. When one considers that this government established RDA is only a minimum intake in order to prevent the signs and symptoms of vitamin deficiency disease and is not the optimum levels of these nutrients for insuring good health, the necessity for orthomolecular supplementation becomes all the more obvious.

Many patients ask why eating a healthy, well balanced diet is not enough in terms of getting the nutrients they need. The problem is that what passes for a healthy, balanced diet amongst many people here in America in fact is not. Overconsumption of simple sugars, simple carbohydrates, salt, fats, and proteins all cause imbalances in our metabolism of crucial micronutrients. Add to this increased demands for certain nutrients due to stress, environmental pollutants and toxins, and widespread persistent viral and yeast infections plus the depletion of our soil and, therefore, the decline in nutrition of our foods, and it becomes apparent why most of us can benefit from taking additional orthomolecular supplements.

Many TCM practitioners here in the United States consider vitamins and minerals outside their provenance. However, in China, vitamin supplements are a part of *Fu Zhong Xi Yi* or Integrated Chinese-Western Medicine. This is evidenced by the use of water soluble vitamins in *Shui Zhen* or Water Needle therapy in many Chinese acupuncture clinics. In addition, the back covers of *The Journal of Traditional Chinese Medicine* Vol. 10, Nos. 1 & 2 published in Beijing both contain full page advertisements for a product called Vitamin E Royal Jelly. The main components of this TCM medicinal are Vitamin E, Royal Jelly, and Vitamins B_1 and B_6. Nonetheless, American TCM practitioners may hesitate to prescribe orthomoleculars since their grasp of Western clinical nutrition may not be that good. However, if we TCM practitioners had TCM descriptions of orthomolecular medicinals, then we could prescribe these based both on the Western clinical nutrition literature and our own TCM diagnoses. In fact, that is exactly what I propose.

It is my experience that Western orthomolecular can be both understood and prescribed based on TCM theory. If one understands the TCM functions and descriptions of individual orthomolecular supplements, than one can analyze a Western orthomolecular formula just as if it were a TCM herbal formula. In many instances, such a TCM understanding actually adds clarity and depth of understanding to the Western use of these orthomolecular singles and formulas. Included in this compendium are essays devoted to TCM analyses of Western orthomolecular formulas. These formulas, once understood as any other TCM formula, can be prescribed either alone or in tandem with TCM herbal formulas. Based on such a combined approach, Metagenics, a leader in the manufacture and marketing of orthomolecular medicines, has designed a number of formulas which contain Chinese herbs and even classical TCM prescriptions as integral components of their formulas.[2]

However, before we can talk of formulas, we must first have a vocabulary of individual orthomolecular singles in the same way that before we can study Chinese herbal prescriptions we must first have a sound knowledge of the TCM *Ben Cao*. Therefore, the following is a brief *Ben Cao* of the main vitamins, minerals, and amino acids used in Western orthomolecular formulas. I have worked out these descriptions based on extensive literary research read from the perspective of TCM and my clinical experience utilizing orthomolecular supplements.

In my experience using Metagenics' formulas, if their use is based on correct *Bian Zheng* diagnosis, successful amelioration can be expected in 45 days from the commencement of therapy.

In addition, our American patients are, for the most part, well conditioned to taking vitamin and mineral supplements. Their shape, size, and color are all expected and present no paradigm shifts for most people. This means that their method of administration itself helps catalyze the placebo effect which is so important in healing. When Chinese herbal ingredients or formulas are added to such formulas, this only adds the *cachet* of the East to an otherwise already accepted therapeutic modality. Patients think that they are getting the best of both East and West, which indeed they are. This only adds to their positive response. At the same time, it insinuates the use of Chinese herbs into the consciousness of more American patients. When and if these patients need to take Chinese herbs in decoction, they are already primed.

TCM Functions of Vitamins

Vitamin A: Tonifies the Blood, benefits the *Jing* Essence, brightens the eyes, nourishes the Skin, clears Heat from the Blood, treats Deficiency Fire Patterns

Vitamin B$_1$: Regulates the Qi, activates the Qi, strengthens the Spleen, dries Dampness, helps prevent Stagnation, expedites the free flow of Liver Qi, stops pain

Vitamin B$_2$: Tonifies the Blood, nourishes & tonifies Liver & Kidneys, treats Deficient Yin & Blood Patterns including *Lao Bing* and Wasting Disease, nourishes Stomach Yin, benefits the *Jing* Essence

Vitamin B$_3$: Relaxes constrained Liver Qi, harmonizes the Liver/Stomach, Liver/Spleen, clears Heat from the Stomach, raises Yang Qi

Vitamin B$_5$: Regulates the Qi, relieves Liver Qi Constraint, harmonizes the Liver/Spleen/Stomach, raises Clear Yang, clears & eliminates Damp Heat, clears Heat from the Liver

Vitamin B$_6$: Clears Heat from the Liver/Gallbladder, extinguishes Wind, harmonizes Wood & Earth, relieves depression, clears Heat from the Stomach and Damp Heat from the Gallbladder

Vitamin B$_{12}$: Tonifies the Qi, tonifies the Qi to transform the Blood, stops bleeding

Vitamin B$_{15}$: Regulates the Qi, activates the Blood, disperses Stagnation, benefits the Heart, and, therefore indirectly the Lungs

Biotin: Nourishes the Blood, relaxes the Liver, nourishes the Skin, tonifies the Heart Blood, clams the *Shen* Spirit

Choline: Nourishes the Blood, extinguishes Wind, nourishes the *Jin* Sinews, moistens the Intestines

Folic Acid: Nourishes the Blood, relaxes the Liver, calms the *Hun*, secures the Fetus

Inositol: Nourishes the Blood, moistens the Intestines, Nourishes the Skin, calms the *Hun*

PABA: Tonifies the Liver & Kidneys, tonifies the Blood, benefits the *Jing* Essence, moistens the Intestines, promotes bowel movements, expels Wind from the Skin, blackens the hair, and retards aging

Vitamin C: Clears Heat, stops bleeding, clears Heat & dissolves Toxins, clears Heat from the Heart and calms the *Shen*

Vitamin D: Tonifies the Kidneys, benefits the *Jing* Essence, mends the Sinews & Bones, brightens the eyes, calms the Fetus

Vitamin E: Tonifies the Yang, nourishes Liver Blood, tonifies Kidney Yang, benefits the *Jing* Essence, nourishes the *Jin* Sinews

Vitamin K: Stops bleeding, astringes the Intestines, contains leakage of Lung Qi, restains leakage of Blood

Bioflavonoids: Regulate the Blood, clear Heat, stop bleeding, clear Heat from the Liver

Beta-carotene: Activates the Qi and dredges the Liver, clears Heat and dissolves Toxins, disperses Stagnations & Accumulations, combats cancer

TCM Functions of Minerals

Calcium: Settles and calms the *Shen*, benefits the Yin and restrains Floating Yang, absorbs acid and stops pain, descends Yang and extinguishes Wind, clears the Liver and brightens the eyes, strengthens the Bones and promotes the generation of new tissue

Chromium: Tonifies the Qi, tonifies the Spleen and benefits the Qi, tonifies the Qi & Blood

Cobalt: Tonifies the Qi, tonifies the Qi to transform Blood

Copper: Drains Dampness, promotes urination and leeches out Dampness, strengthens the Spleen, clears & eliminates Damp Heat

Flourine: Tonifies the Kidneys and nourishes Yin, strengthens the Bones and teeth

Iodine: Clears Heat, clears the Liver, disspiates Nodulations

Iron: Clears Heat and cools the Blood, nourishes the Yin & Blood, invigorates & dispels Congealed Blood, clears Deficiency Fire & Ascendant Fire

Magnesium: Settles & calms the *Shen*, benefits the Yin and restrains Floating Yang, prevents leakage of Fluids, absorbs acidity and stops pain

Manganese: Nourishes the Yin and benefits the *Jing* Essence, nourishes the *Jin* Sinews and strengthens the Bones, benefits the hearing

Molybdenum: Tonifies the Blood and nourishes Yin, cools the Blood and clears Heat, clears Heat and generates Fluids

Phosphorus: Tonifies the Kidneys, nourishes the Yin, benefits the *Jing* Essence, nourishes the *Jin* Sinews, strengthens the Bones, promtes the healing of the *Jin* & Bones

Potassium: Drains Dampness, promotes urination, strengthens the Spleen, stops diarrhea, clears Heat and expels pus, expels Wind Dampness, clears & eliminates Damp Heat including Damp Heat in the Liver/ Gallbladder

Selenium: Benefits the Yin, restrains Floating Yang, settles & calms the *Shen* Spirit, astringes the *Jing* Essence, brightens the eyes and relieves superficial visual obstruction

Silica: Tonifies the Kidneys and strenghtens the Bones

Silicon: Tonifies the Kidneys and strenghtens the Bones, nourishes the *Jin* Sinews

Sodium: Consolidates the Kidneys and astringes the *Jing*

Essence, stops excessive loss of Fluids, tonifies the Liver & Kidneys, stops sweating and, therefore, can adversely inhibit the Lungs' descension & dispersion, softens the Hard and disperses Nodulations

Sulfur: Nourishes the Blood and the Liver, nourishes the Skin, blackens the hair, cools the Blood, and benefits the Skin

Zinc: Benefits the *Jing* Essence, nourishes the Blood, strengthens the Bones, brightens the eyes, tonifies the *Jing* Essence to check Evil Qi

TCM Functions of Amino Acids

Alanine: Tonifies the Qi, benefits the Spleen, nourshes the Blood, calms the Heart Spirit

Arginine: Tonifies the Kidneys, strenghtens the Yang, moistens the Intestines, promotes bowel movements; contraindicated in Yin Deficiency & Depressive Fire conditions; strenghtens the *Jin* Sinews & Bones, expels Wind Cold Dampness

BCAA (Leucine, Isoleucine, & Valine): Nourish Yin and benefit the *Jing* Essence

Carnitine: Tonifies the Blood & Yin, benefits the *Jing* Essence

Cysteine: Nourishes the Blood and tonifies Yin, benefits the Skin and promotes the generation of new tissue, blackens the hair, cools the Blood and clears Heat, dissolves Toxins, treats Thirsting & Wasting Disease

Glutamic Acid: Tonifies Yin, benefits the *Jing* Essence

Glutathione: Clears Heat, dissolves Toxins, nourishes & cools the Blood, benefits lactation

Glycine: Nourishes the Blood, promotes the growth of new tissue, may benefit the *Jing* Essence

Histidine: Tonifies the Blood & Yin, benefits the *Jing* Essence, may cool the Blood

Lysine: Tonifies Yin, benefits *Jing* Essence, may clear Heat as well and dissolve Toxins

Methionine: Nourishes the Blood, benefits the *Jing* Essence, cools the Blood, relaxes the Liver, calms the *Hun*

Ornithine: Tonifies Yang

Phenylalinine: Relieves the Surface, clears Heat, dissolves Toxins, raises Clear Yang, activates the Qi, stops pain; contraindicated in *Yin Xu*, Deficiency Fire Patterns

Taurine: Clears Heat, dissolves Fire Toxins, clears the Liver, clears & eliminates Damp Heat from the Liver/Gallbladder, promotes lactation

Threonine: Nourishes the Blood, nourishes the *Jin* Sinews, relieves spasticity, relaxes the Liver, relieves constraint

Tryptophan: Calms the Spirit, improves sleep, relieves irritability and constraint, improves the appetite, invigorates the Blood, stops pain

Tyrosine: Regulates the Qi, dredges the Liver, relieves constraint, reverses Counterflow chilling of the extremities, harmonizes Wood & Earth; contraindicated in *Yin Xu* Parched Viscera mania

ENDNOTES

1   Loomis, Donald, "Fatalities Resulting from Poisoning by Vitamin Supplements in the United States," *Townsend Letter for Doctors*, January, 1990, p.41

2   Metagenics International, 971 Calle Negocia, San Clemente, CA, 92629; 1-800-692-9400

TCM Orthomolecular Therapy For PMS

Over the years numerous women have come to me for the treatment of PMS with Chinese medicine. Many of these women ask me about vitamin/mineral supplements. Some have been concurrently under the care of clinical nutritionists. Others have simply read about various orthomolecular supplements in the popular press. And others have had such supplements for the treatment of PMS suggested to them by friends or health food store clerks. For a long time, I simply said that I am a professional practitioner of Traditional Chinese Medicine or TCM, that orthomolecular supplements are not a part of TCM, and, therefore, there was little I could say about such medicinals. At the same time, however, women frequently told me that taking this supplement or that on top of the Chinese herbs I prescribed had significantly improved their PMS over and above what my Chinese herbs had done for them. In addition, I also came across women who had treated themselves for PMS entirely with orthomolecular medicinals and had achieved just as good results as I aim for with TCM.

Approximately two years ago I received in the mail a bunch of coupons with which one could send away for further information regarding a number of alternative health care products. These included one for a vitamin/mineral treatment for PMS. Being a TCM gynecologist and having written the first English language discussions of PMS in the TCM literature, my curiosity was immediately piqued and I sent the card out requesting further information. I received back a flier about an orthomolecular supplement which suggested that it could substantially eliminate PMS in 45 days. Because I normally allow 3 months for the TCM treatment of PMS, I sent away for even more information and eventually the company's entire professional catalogue. What I received at first irritated me. It was a catalogue full of orthomolecular formulas combined with Chinese herbal singles and classical formulas. I felt like I as a professional practitioner of TCM was being ripped off. I have to admit, my first reaction was proprietary. How dare these capitalists play on the mystique of the East and co-opt "my" medicine.

Then I began thinking about the formulas in this company's catalogue. As a student at the Boulder School of Massage Therapy, back when that school's curriculum embraced the entire range of alternative healing arts, I had taken a course in clinical nutrition which was essentially a study of orthomolecular therapy. I dug out my textbook from that course and started analyzing the formulas in this catalogue in terms of the appropriateness of linking specific Chinese herbs and formulas with specific vitamins and minerals. However, I quickly realized that in order to really judge the logic of these formulas I needed to work out a TCM description for these orthomoleculars. Therefore, I called this company's regional sales representatives and asked for the research literature upon which their formulations were based.

The company was Metagenics International and they were more than happy to supply me with literature and research materials. They answered my questions over the phone and even visited my office on a number of occasions in order to supply me with the information for which I was looking. Eventually I did work out a basic, although still tentative TCM description of the most common vitamins, minerals, and amino acids. Based on these descriptions I then analyzed the Metagenics' gynecological formulas and found them to be quite well crafted even from a TCM point of view. Therefore, I began prescribing these to my patients either alone or in conjunction with other TCM medicinals.

Immediately it was apparent that my patients liked these Metagenics products. They could immediately relate to them in a positive way. They are packaged according to American standards and expectations. They look like medicine to a Westerner. And, better yet, they combine the best of Western clinical nutrition with the mystique and *cachet* of herbs from the East. They are easy to take, can be explained from both Western and Eastern points of view, and are cost effective. Besides, they work.

At the time I came across these combined orthomolecular *cum* Chinese herbal formulas, I was already primed to consider a broader approach to TCM. I was already delving into Western herbs and combining these with Chinese herbs in my practice. Likewise, I had already begun looking at Western pharmaceuticals as TCM medicinals. Therefore, looking at Western vitamins and minerals seemed a natural progression in this opening up of my professional horizons. As mentioned above, my first reaction was negative, possessive, and paranoid. I felt my professional identity and, therefore, my livelihood threatened by what I considered interlopers. I mention this to be truthful but also because I think many of my coprofessionals may also initially experience the same feelings and reaction. However, having put aside those initial, ego-centric feelings I now have access to a far larger repertoire of healing modalities without in any way abandoning my TCM methodology or logic.

In particular, I have found Metagenics' orthomolecular supplements to be so beneficial in the treatment of PMS that I would like to share with my fellow TCM practitioners these protocols and formulas. They can be used either in tandem with other TCM formulas or in their stead. They can be "mixed and matched" any way the TCM practitioner wants as long as they are prescribed based on a TCM *Bian Zheng* diagnosis and a TCM understanding of *Bing Ji* or disease mechanism.

Western clinical nutrition identifies 4 subcategories of PMS. These are labelled PMS-A, PMS-D, PMS-C, and PMS-H. PMS-A stands for PMS primarily characterized by anxiety, irritability, mood swings, and nervous tension. PMS-D is characterized by depression, crying, forgetfulness, confusion, and insomnia. PMS-C is characterized by cravings, increased appetite, headache, fatigue, dizziness, fainting, and palpitations. And PMS-H is characterized by hyperhydration, fluid retention, weight gain in excess of 3 lbs., swollen extremities, breast tenderness, and abdominal bloating. Although women can have a combination of all of these various signs and symptoms of PMS, typically one or another of these groups of symptoms will predominate.

TCM practitioners should be able to understand the disease mechanisms responsible for each of these PMS symptoms and, therefore, assess the TCM logic of formulas suggested for their treatment. That is what I have done below. TCM practitioners are cautioned, however, that making a Western differential diagnosis of PMS-A or PMS-D in no way relieves us of the professional responsibility of doing an individualized TCM *Bian Zheng* diagnosis. The above Western diagnostic categories can be added to our own differential diagnosis but should not be allowed to replace it since ours is ultimately the wiser system.

PMS-A: Anxiety, irritability, mood swings, & nervous tension

TCM *Bing Ji*: Primarily Stagnation and Upward Perversion of Liver Qi

Metagenics' Protocol: Fem-PMS, Mag Citrate, Cortico B_5B_6, Inflavonoid, Lipogen, and/or Ultradophilus

Fem-PMS®

This is a woman's multivitamin/multimineral formula. Although it is called Fem-PMS, it can be used as a daily background supplement by many American women regardless of whether they have PMS or not. TCM practitioners will immediately recognize that included in this formula are the Chinese herbal ingredients of *Xiao Yao San*. I have written at length about this formula *vis a vis* PMS elsewhere.[1]   Basically, this formula dredges and regulates Liver Qi, relaxes the Liver, nourishes the Blood, tonifies the Spleen, and transports and transforms accumulated Dampness. Since PMS almost always is due to a combination of Liver Qi Congestion, Blood Deficiency, Spleen Deficiency and Dampness, the inclusion of the formula's ingredients in Metagenics' Fem-PMS is a wise choice.

The orthomolecular ingredients in Fem-PMS are: Vitamin A, Beta-carotene, B_1, B_2, B_3, B_5, B_6, B_{12}, Folic Acid, Choline, Bioflavonoids, Vitamin D, Vitamin E, l-Tyrosine, Calcium, Magnesium, Potassium, Manganese, Zinc, Iron, Copper, Chromium, Iodine, and Selenium.   What makes this a specifically woman's multivitamin/multimineral tablet is that the proportions of these nutrients are designed to correct the excessive estrogen which Western medical theory posits as one of the causes of so many women's complaints, including PMS, menorrhagia, metrorrhagia, endometriosis, and dysmenorrhea. Estrogen and its relatives, estrone, estradiol, and 17-methoxy-estradiol are not simply secreted by the ovaries. They are made by fat cells and by lecithin-negative clostridia bacteria in the large intestine. Therefore, diets high in protein and fat such as the typical American diet, obesity, and dysbiosis of the colon can all play a part in excessive levels of estrogen. In addition, Western medicine says that it is the liver which deconjugates or breaks down estrogen and is relatives, and therefore, anything which adversely effects the functioning of the liver can also have an adverse effect on estrogen metabolism.

The Western medical signs and symptoms of an estrogen imbalance are:

1) Cyclic symptoms at ovulation and/or the premenstruum

2) Abnormally elevated of blood levels of estrogen

3) Abnormal estrogen to progestrone ration

4) Low serum levels of Vitamins A, E, and B_6

5) Excessive blood loss and/or dysmenorrhea

6) Midcycle spotting

Western clinical nutrition believes that increased amounts of B vitamins, Magnesium, EFAs (Essential Fatty Acids), Zinc, Vitamin C, Bioflavonoids, and Vitamins A & E can help to decrease estrogen in women with excess estrogen and its related compounds. In particular, abundant research supports the thesis that supplemental B_6, between 80-200 g p.d., can benefit between 70-80% of women with premenstrual lability, breast distention, and headache. Therefore, Fem-PMS contains proportionately more of the following nutrients than general, all-purpose multi's: B_6, B_3, Folic Acid, Bioflavonoids, Magnesium, Manganese, Chromium, Iodine, and Selenium. Whereas, Vitamin D is reduced proportionately in this formula. In addition, the amino acid, l-Tyrosine, is added to improve the mood and decrease cravings and Choline is added as a lipotropic or fat metabolizing ingredient. Likewise, Chromium reduces sugar cravings by regulating blood sugar levels and thus also evens out energy swings.

Because this formula contains so many ingredients and is meant not only for the remedial treatment of various estrogen excess conditions but also as a general female nutritional supplement, I am not going to describe each of its ingredients singly. Suffice it to say that the vitamins, minerals, and amino acids in Fem-PMS essentially mimic and complement the functions of the *Xiao Yao San* it contains.

Mag Citrate®

This formula is composed of two orthomolecular ingredients: Magnesium and Calcium Citrate. Magnesium settles and calms the Spirit, benefits Yin, and restrains Floating Yang. Calcium likewise settles and calms the Spirit, benefits the Yin and restrains Floating Yang, but also descends Yang and extinguishes Wind. One of the ways nervous tension manifests is as muscular tightness in the upper back, shoulders, and neck. This is due in PMS to the non-descension of Yang Qi down into the pelvis to mobilize the Blood in the *Xue Hai/Bao Gong*. This up-flushing of Yang Qi also collects in the Heart and Lungs causing instability of the *Shen* housed there. Prescribing Mag Citrate, therefore, is like prescribing Os Draconis and Concha Ostreae for heavily sedating upwardly perverting Yang Qi. In the case of PMS, this Yang Qi first collects in the Liver and Middle Burner until it, being Yang, naturally accumulates to the point it flushes or floats up disturbing the Heart/Lungs.

Cortico B₅B₆®

This formula is composed of Vitamin B_5, Vitamin B_6, Vitamin C, Bioflavonoids, and again Magnesium. Vitamin B_5 regulates the Qi, relieves Liver Qi Constraint, harmonizes the Liver with both the Spleen and Stomach, raises Clear Yang, and eliminates Damp Heat. As such, it is very similar energetically to Radix

Bupleuri.   Vitamin B_6 clears Heat, extinguishes Wind, harmonizes Wood and Earth, relieves Depression, and clears Heat from the Stomach and Damp Heat from the Gallbladder. Vitamin C in this formula clears Heat from the Liver, Stomach, Heart, and Large Intestine, although it can clear Heat from the entire Triple Heater. Bioflavonoids regulate the Blood, clear Heat from the *Xue Fen* or Blood phase, and clear Heat from the Liver. Their functions are somewhat similar to Cortex Radicis Moutan. And Magnesium, as we have seen above, calms the Spirit, descends Yang, and extinguishes Wind.

From a Western point of view, this formula is beneficial for inflammation due to hyperadrenal exhaustion. Stress causes the adrenals to produce cortisol and if stress continues unabated, as it so often does here in the West, eventually patients become hyperadrenal. This situation is essentially what TCM describes as Depressive Liver Heat causing mutual aggravation of all the Organs participating in the *Ming Men* leading to eventual accumulation of Heat above in the Heart and Lungs. Over time, this then leads to Kidney Yin Deficiency below.

Inflavonoid®

This formula is composed of Rhizoma Curcumae Longae, Bioflavonoids, Vitamin C, and Ginger Extract. Rhizoma Curcumae Longae is a TCM medicinal. Its TCM functions are to invigorate the Blood, break up Congealed Blood, circulate the Qi, relieve Liver Qi Constraint, clear Heat, cool the Blood, and facilitate or benefit the Gallbladder. Ginger (Rhizoma Zingiberis Officinalis) is also a standard TCM medicinal. Its functions are to benefit the Middle, eliminate Dampness, descend Turbidity, disperse Accumulations such as Food, Phlegm, and Dampness, ascend the Pure, and regulate Stomach Qi. Vitamin C and Bioflavonoids have been described above.

This formula is meant to treat muscular pain due to Upwardly Perverse Liver Qi and Depressive Liver Heat. That means it treats headache, stiff neck and shoulder pain, chest and flank pain. However, it also takes into account the TCM fact that long-term Stagnation of Qi tends to result in Stagnation of Blood, Dampness, and Phlegm as well.

Lipogen®

This is one of Metagenics' most important formulas. It contains Choline, Inositol, Taurine, Methionine, Vitamin C, Black Radish Powder, Beet Leaf Powder, Trimethylglycine HCL, Magnesium, Chionathus, Celandine, and Raw Liver Concentrate. Choline nourishes the Blood, extinguishes Wind, stops spasms, pacifies the Liver, nourishes the *Jin* Sinews, moistens the Intestines, and promotes bowel movements. Inositol nourishes the Blood, moistens the intestines, promotes bowel movements, nourishes the skin, and calms the *Hun*. Taurine clears Heat and dissolves Fire Toxins, clears the Liver, clears and eliminates Damp Heat from the Liver/Gallbladder, and promotes lactation. Vitamin C in this formula clears Heat from the Liver/Gallbladder.

Black Radish Powder is Cool, Acrid, and Sweet. It enters the Lung and Stomach Channels. It clears Heat and dissolves Toxins, disperses Food Accumulation downward, promotes digestion, and transforms Hot Phlegm. Trimethylglycine HCL tonifies the Spleen/Stomach. In particular it benefits Stomach Yang in relationship to the *Ming Men*. It tonifies the Qi to transform Blood and Yin substance. Magnesium has been discussed above. Chionathus is Fringetree Bark (Cortex Radicis Chionathi Virginici). It is Bitter and Cold and enters the Liver and Gallbladder Channels. It promotes urination, clears Heat and eliminates Dampness in Liver/Gallbladder Damp Heat conditions, and clears Heat and relieves the Surface *Shao Yang Fen* afflictions. Celandine, also called Greater Celandine in the Western herbal literature is Radix Chelidonii Maji. It is Bitter, a bit Acrid, and Cool. It likewise enters the Liver and Gallbladder Channels. It clears Heat and dissolves Fire Toxins, reduces abscesses and dissipates Nodulations, clears Heat and promotes urination, and clears Heat and relieves the Surface. Celandine also combats cancer. Raw Liver Concentrate tonifies the Kidneys and strengthens the Yang, nourishes the Blood, benefits the *Jing* Essence, tonifies the Liver and Kidneys, brightens the eyes, and nourishes the *Jin* Sinews.

This formula is for the treatment of Damp Heat in the Liver/Gallbladder. Damp Heat in the Liver/Gallbladder usually starts as Dampness accumulating in the Spleen which then becomes mutually entangled with Depressive Liver Heat transformed out of Food Stagnation, Stomach Heat, and Liver Qi. Although I do not find Damp Heat of the Liver/Gallbladder that often in my PMS patient population, when such Damp Heat is part of a patient's PMS, this is a very effective formula.

Ultradophilus®

Metagenics' Ultradophilus is made from a patented strain of live Lactobacillus Acidophilus bacteria guaranteed to survive the hydrochloric acid in the stomach and bile in the small intestine so as to implant in the colon. Acidophilus' TCM description is that it regulates the Middle, ascends the Pure, descends the Turbid, regulates the Qi of the Large Intestine, tonifies the Spleen, benefits the Stomach, and kills yeast or *Sha Jun*. Because of the close inter-relationship between the Liver and Large Intestine and the Large Intestine and the Spleen/Stomach, regulation of the Large Intestine is one of the most important ways of regulating the Qi of the entire Triple Heater. I have written about this at length in *Scatology & The Gate of Life: The Role of the Large Intestine in Immunity, An Integrated Chinese-Western Approach*.[2] Although treatment of the Liver/Stomach/Spleen by way of the Large Intestine is a much overlooked strategy in TCM, it can produce dramatic results. It is especially indicated if the patient has alternating constipation/diarrhea and a tendency towards flatulence.

PMS-D: Depression, crying, forgetfulness, confusion, & insomnia

PMS *Bing Ji*: Depression is mostly due to Liver Qi Constraint. Crying is up-flushing Liver/Uterine Qi to the Lungs. Confusion and insomnia can be due premenstrually to either Blood and/or Yin Deficiency, Heat, or Hyperactivity of Liver Yang. Typically in PMS patients, emotional lability is due to some combination of Heart Blood Deficiency, Spleen Qi Deficiency, and some degree of Heat up-flushing to the Heart and Lungs.

Metagenics' Protocol: Fem-PMS, Mag Citrate, and/or Tyrosine

Tyrosine

We have already discussed above both Fem-PMS and Mag Citrate. Tyrosine regulates the Qi, dredges the Liver, relieves constraint, reverses Counterflow chilling of the extremities, harmonizes Wood and Earth, and extinguishes Wind. *Si Ni* or Counterflow chilling of the extremities is a very important symptom in TCM. It indicates that Heat has imploded within due to Liver Qi Stagnation aggravated by Spleen Qi Deficiency and, therefore, Blood Deficiency. This is a common complicating symptom amongst many PMS patients. When it is encountered, one way of treating it is with Tyrosine.

PMS-C: Cravings, increased appetite, headache, fatigue, dizziness, fainting, palpitations

TCM *Bing Ji:* Mostly Spleen Deficiency causing Heart Blood Deficiency. If there is increased appetite, this suggests concomitant Stomach Heat and Large Intestine Deficiency and Stagnation.

Metagenics' Protocol: Fem-PMS and/or Meta-EPO

Meta-EPO®

The ingredients in this Metagenics' formula are Evening Primrose Oil, Cis-linoleic Acid, Gamma-linoleic Acid, and Vitamin E. Evening Primrose or Herba Oenotherae Biennis has a long Western history as a treatment of PMS. Modern research has centered on its fatty acids as its main active ingredients. My TCM description of Evening Primrose is that it regulates the Qi, dredges the Liver, relaxes Constraint, harmonizes the Liver and Spleen, clears Heat from the Stomach and Lungs, descends Rebellion, stops coughing, activates the Qi, and stops pain. Cis-linoleic and Gamma-linoleic Acids are constituents of Evening Primrose Oil which have been added to increase its potency. Vitamin E is a Yang tonic which nourishes Liver Blood and tonifies Kidney Yang, benefits the *Jing* Essence, and nourishes the *Jin* Sinews.

Looking at Evening Primrose Oil's TCM functions, it is no wonder it has proven itself such a boon in the Western treatment of PMS. Adding Vitamin E to Evening Primrose is similar in terms of TCM methodology to adding *Dang Gui* and Peony to *Xiao Yao San*. The EFAs of Evening Primrose, Cis-linoleic, and Gamma-linoleic Acid all help to regulate prostaglandin metabolism which is the other main Western factor in the causation of PMS.

GLA Forte®

GLA Forte is another Metagenics' formula which can be used instead of Meta-EPO. From the Western point of view, its therapeutic use is also based on the relationship between EFAs, prostaglandin production, and PMS. It is composed of Borage Oil (Oleum Boraginis Officinalis) Gamma-linoleic Acid, and Vitamin E.

Borage Oil is a Cool, Acrid, Surface-reliever which enters the Lungs and Liver. It expels Wind and clears Heat from the Lungs and is also used for Lung Dryness and Lung Heat Patterns. It clears the Liver, releases the Surface, and pushes out rashes, stops coughing, benefits the throat, relieves Constraint and Depression, and dissolves Fire Toxins especially of the mouth and throat.

Although it is seen by many Western clinical nutritionists as simply a cheaper, more cost-effective source of EFAs than Evening Primrose, I believe that Borage Oil's overall medicinal functions are slightly different from Evening Primrose's and that practitioners should take into account these differences when prescribing one or the other. I believe that Borage clears Heat more than Evening Primrose and that Evening Primrose harmonizes the Liver and Spleen better. When a patient presents with more pronounced breast distention and pain along with premenstrual acne, I prescribe GLA Forte. But when a patient presents with more hypoglycemic symptoms and energy fluctuations affecting their mood, I prescribe Meta-EPO.

PMS-H: Hyperhydration, fluid retention, weight gain in excess of 3 lbs., swollen extremities, breast tenderness, and abdominal bloating

TCM *Bing Ji:* Breast tenderness and abdominal bloating are mostly due to Qi Congestion. Swollen extremities are categorized under *Shui Zhong* or Water Swelling in TCM. This may be due to faulty transportation and transformation of Body Fluids by either the Lungs, Spleen, or the Kidneys. In PMS, such edema of the extremities is typically due to a combination of faulty Lung and Spleen metabolism. Qi Congestion and Water Swelling, although related, are different *Zheng* in TCM.

Metagenics' Protocol: Fem-PMS, Cortico B_5B_6, E-400 Selenium, Meta-EPO

E-400 Selenium®

We have already discussed the other three Metagenics' protocols for PMS-H above. E-400 Selenium is composed of Vitamin E and Selenium. Vitamin E nourishes Liver Blood and Kidney *Jing*. Selenium benefits Yin and restrains Floating Yang at the same time that it settles and calms the Spirit. These two ingredients treat the root of PMS which is Yin *vis a vis* Yang. During the premenstruum, the Yang Qi should descend to mobilize the Blood for discharge. In women with PMS, this Yang Qi tends to float upwards and does not descend. This is due to accumulation of Qi due to Liver Constraint and also to a tendency to Blood Deficiency, since part of the mechanism of the Qi's descension into the pelvis is its magnetization by the Blood in the *Bao Gong/Xue Hai*. This formula seeks to nourish the Blood below at the same time as pushing the Yang down from above. It also underscores the fact that TCM often sees symptoms, such as swollen breasts, very differently from Western medicine. Western medicine sees such swollen breasts as a species of localized edema, but TCM sees these as a sign of localized Qi accumulation in the upper body.

There are three other Metagenics' orthomolecular formulas specifically for women which I would like to discuss in relation to PMS which are not included in Metagenics' suggested protocols for PMS-A, -D, -C, or -H. These are Fem-FBS, Fem-Relief, and Fem-UBF.

Fem-FBS®

Fem-FBS is for the treatment of premenstrual breast distention and tenderness. It is composed of Beta-carotene, Vitamin A, Vitamin E, Vitamin B_1, Bioflavonoids, Iodine, Selenium, Tyrosine, and Rhizoma Curcumae Longae.

Beta-carotene activates the Qi and dredges the Liver. It clears Heat and dissolves Toxins, disperses Stagnations and Accumulations, and combats cancer. Vitamin A tonifies the Blood, benefits the *Jing* Essence, brightens the eyes, nourishes the skin, and clears Deficiency Heat. Vitamin E nourishes Liver Blood and tonifies Kidney Yang, benefits the *Jing* Essence, and nourishes the *Jin* Sinews. Vitamin B_1 regulates the Qi, activates the Qi, strengthens the Spleen, dries Dampness, helps prevent Stagnation, expedites the free flow of Liver Qi, and moves the Qi and stops pain. Bioflavonoids regulate the Blood, clear Heat, stop bleeding, and clear Heat from the Liver. Iodine clears Heat from the Liver and dissipates Nodulations. Selenium benefits Yin, restrains Floating Yang, settles and calms the Spirit, astringes the Essence, and brightens the eyes. Tyrosine regulates the Qi, dredges the Liver, relieves Constraint, reverses Counterflow chilling of the extremities, harmonizes Wood and Earth, and extinguishes Wind. Rhizoma Curcumae Longae invigorates the Blood, breaks up Congealed Blood, circulates the Qi, relieves Liver Qi Constraint, clears Heat, cools the Blood, and facilitates the Gallbladder.

Premenstrual breast distention, tenderness, pain, and nodulation are primarily due to Liver Qi, Depressive Fire of the Liver giving rise to Stomach Heat which travels up the *Yang Ming* and accumulates in the breasts, and Phlegm drafted up with this perverse Qi and Heat. This formula taken as a whole activates the Qi and disperses Stagnation. It dredges the Liver and relieves Depression. It clears Heat and scatters Nodulation. In addition, it relaxes the Liver by nourishing the Blood, thus also magnetizing the Qi downwards as discussed above. I often prescribe Fem-FBS in tandem with Fem-PMS. Quite frankly, this regime typically gets just as good results in a similar amount of time as individually prescribed, bulk dispensed, and freshly decocted herbal formulas at a comparable cost with a great deal less trouble.

Fem-Relief®

This formula is for the treatment of body pain during the premenstruum, such as upper back and neck pain, headache, sciatic and sacroiliac pain, and flank pain. Its ingredients are: Vitamins B_3, B_5, B_1, B_6, Magnesium, Radix Polygoni Multiflori, Stigma Humuli Lupulae, Rhizoma Curcumae Longae, and Radix Valerianae Officinalis.

B_3 relaxes constrained Liver Qi, harmonizes the Liver and the Spleen/Stomach, raises Clear Yang, clears Heat from the Stomach, and clears Heat from the Liver by relieving the Surface and dispersing Heat outward. B_5 regulates the Qi and relieves Liver Qi Constraint. It also harmonizes Wood and Earth, raises the Clear Yang, clears and eliminates Damp Heat, and clears Heat from the Liver by relieving the Surface. B_1 regulates the Qi, strengthens the Spleen, dries Dampness, helps prevent Stagnation, expedites the free flow of Liver Qi, and moves the Qi and stops pain. B_6 clears Heat, extinguishes

Wind, harmonizes Wood and Earth, relieves Depression, clears Heat from the Stomach and Damp Heat from the Gallbladder. Magnesium settles and calms the Spirit, benefits Yin, restrains Floating Yang, prevents leakage of Fluids, absorbs acidity and stops pain.

Radix Polygoni Multiflori is, of course, a famous Chinese medicinal. It tonifies the Liver and Kidneys, nourishes the Blood, benefits the *Jing* Essence, moistens the Intestines, promotes bowel movements, expels Wind from the skin, and specifically treats low back and lower extremity pain due to Liver/Kidney Dual Deficiency. Likewise, Rhizoma Curcumae Longae is also a traditional Chinese medicinal. We have already discussed its TCM description above.

Hops or Stigma Humuli Lupulae clears Heat and purges Fire from all three Burners but particularly from the Stomach which may rise to the Heart via the *Xu Li,* thus disturbing the Heart Spirit or which may rise to the Lungs causing cough. Because it clears Heat from the Heart, it calms the *Shen* and thus allays anxiety. Because it clears Heat from the Liver, it calms the *Hun* and thus allays irritability. It also clears and eliminates Damp Heat from the Stomach/Intestines, the Lower Burner, and the skin. Because it clears Heat from the Liver/Stomach, it also benefits the digestion, stops *Wei Tong* and nausea due to *Gan Fan Wei,* and promotes bowel movements. Likewise, because Depressive Liver Heat is so often associated with scanty and painful periods, Hops are useful in treating Mutual Entanglement of Damp Heat in the Lower Burner *Tong Jing* or dysmenorrhea. And finally, because Hops clear Heat from all three Burners, it also reduces the *Ming Men Zhi Huo* when it is flaring in cases of priapism, satyriasis, and premature ejaculation. Like Taraxacum, Hops also has a special empirical effect on promoting lactation and a special tropism for the breast/chest.

Radix Valerianae Officinalis, more commonly known as Valerian, promotes the free flow of constrained Liver Qi. It invigorates the Blood, calms the Spirit, stops pain, promotes menstruation, and harnesses Ascendant Liver Yang.

Frequently, body pain in women which worsens with their premenstruum is due to a combination of Depressive Liver Heat and Blood Deficiency. If this Heat transformed from Stagnant Qi in the Middle vents upwards, it causes upper back, shoulder and neck pain, and headache. If it spreads laterally in the chest, it causes chest pain and oppression, heart and rib pain. If it becomes mutually entangled with Damp Heat and Stagnant Blood below, it can cause lower abdominal pain, sacroiliac pain, and sciatica. Metagenics' Fem-Relief formula treats pain in all these areas by activating the Qi and Blood, dispersing Stagnation, clearing Depressive Heat, eliminating Damp Heat, harnessing Ascendant Liver Yang, and nourishing the Blood.

Fem-UBF®

This formula is for the orthomolecular treatment of dysfunctional uterine bleeding. In the case of PMS, it can be used to treat breakthrough bleeding or periods ahead of schedule. Typically, if Depressive Heat becomes severe enough, it will cause early periods in which case other PMS signs and symptoms will be minimal or non-existent. This does not mean the PMS has been cured and is, in fact, a worsening of the patient's overall condition. Although it may be less uncomfortable, it will eventually lead to Yin Deficiency, Deficiency Heat, and exhaustion of Kidney *Jing*.

Fem-UBF is composed of Vitamins A, C, and E, Beta-carotene, Bioflavonoids, Iron, Tyrosine, Raw Liver, and *Xiao Yao Wan*.

In general, its functions are similar to *Dan Zhi Xiao Yao Wan* plus added styptic ingredients. It treats menorrhagia, metrorrhagia, breakthrough bleeding, and early periods due to Depressive Liver Heat causing the Blood to flow recklessly outside its *Dao* or Pathways.

Vitamin A tonifies the Blood and *Jing*, clears Heat, and cools the Blood. Beta-carotene activates the Qi and dredges the Liver, clears Heat, dissolves Toxins, disperses Stagnations and Accumulations, and combats cancer. Bioflavonoids regulate the Blood, clear Heat, stop bleeding, and clear Heat specifically from the Liver. Vitamin C clears Heat, stops bleeding, clears Heat from the Heart, and calms the *Shen*. Vitamin E nourishes Liver Blood, tonifies Kidney Yang, benefits the *Jing* Essence, and nourishes the *Jin* Sinews. Iron clears Heat, cools the Blood, nourishes the Yin and Blood, invigorates and dispels Congealed Blood, and clears Ascendant Fire. Tyrosine regulates the Qi, dredges the Liver, resolves constrained Qi and reverses Counterflow, regulates the menses, and harmonizes Wood and Earth. Raw Liver tonifies the Liver, especially Liver Blood and Kidney *Jing*, tonifies the Kidneys and promotes Yang, brightens the eyes, and nourishes the *Jin* Sinews.

Because this formula includes *Xiao Yao San*, TCM practitioners should take care not to prescribe it as an all-purpose *Beng Lou* or uterine bleeding panacea. The *Xiao Yao* formula may aggravate uterine bleeding due to Kidney Yin Deficiency, Deficiency Fire, and Loss of Astringency due to decline of Kidney Qi. Raw Liver and Vitamins A and E offset somewhat Bupleurum's tendency to plunder Yin, but still, I think, care should be taken. Fortunately, in my clinical experience, most early periods and menorrhagia are due to Depressive Heat.

Conclusion

Modern Western orthomolecular supplements can be a useful addition to the TCM repertoire in general but especially in terms of treating PMS. In the above essay I have focused on a series of formulas manufactured and marketed by Metagenics. I use this company's products in my practice because they themselves are interested in the combination of TCM medicinals and formulas with orthomolecular supplements. I also like this company because of its prompt service and excellent product information. However, Metagenics is only one orthomolecular distributor and other companies may market orthomolecular formulas equally as effective. While suggesting that American TCM practitioners add orthomolecular medicinals to our practice, I am also suggesting that that addition be made based on a TCM analysis of such medicinals and formulas. Whether a practitioner chooses to use Metagenics, Standard Process, or any other orthomolecular company's products, it is important that the practitioner understands the TCM mechanisms, functions, and *Bian Zheng* diagnosis for each and every formula. Unless such a TCM understanding exists, the practitioner is no longer practicing TCM.

I remember clearly the first time I prescribed only Western orthomoleculars to one of my patients and not Chinese herbs. It felt somewhat strange and I was internally reluctant to do it. I had developed a professional *persona* based on prescribing Chinese medicinals and the dispensing of Western orthomoleculars pushed the limits of my professional identity. Happily that first patient responded very well to my orthomolecular prescription. Now I have no qualms about prescribing non-Chinese medicinals from a number of different sources. But, and this is a very important but, I still consider myself a professional practitioner of TCM and every prescription

I write is based on a TCM *Bian Zheng* diagnosis and the understanding of the treatment as a TCM therapy.

ENDNOTES

1   Flaws, Bob, "Premenstrual Syndrome (PMS)", *Free and Easy: Traditional Chinese Gynecology for American Women*, Blue Poppy Press, Boulder, CO 1986

2   Flaws, Bob, *Scatology & The Gate of Life: The Role of the Large Intestine in Immunity, An Integrated Chinese-Western Approach*, Blue Poppy Press, Boulder, CO, 1990

Inhalant Therapy

Ding Chuan Xi Ru Fang
Relieve Asthma Inhalant Formula
& Lan Hua Zhi Ke Ding Chuan Gao
Blue Flower Stop Cough Relieve Asthma Paste

Before I ever studied Chinese medicine and Chinese herbs, I studied Western herbs and Western naturopathic medicine. At the time, Win Smith, who is now himself a practitioner of TCM in Taos, NM, taught a course in herbal medicine at the Boulder School of Massage Therapy. Our classes were essentially herb walks where we would go out into the fields and mountains. There Win would identify for us herbal medicinals and explain how they were used in the Western herbal tradition. At that time, I had more time than money. I would forage most of my greens and vegetables and spent a lot of my time making up salves, tinctures, lotions, poultices, and plasters either from books or Win's instructions. When it comes to herbal medicine, I have a long history as a tinkerer.

At the same time, being a Tibetan Buddhist, I was very interested in Tibetan herbal medicine. One day I came across a picture in the Ven. Rechung Rinpoche's *Tibetan Medicine*. It showed a number of Tibetan medical apparati including two inhalant machines. These were closed pots which had spigots which were inserted into the two nostrils on one and into the two nostrils and mouth on the other. At the bottom of each

pot, there was a squeeze bulb acting as a small bellows.
Medicinal herbs are put in these pots and lit. The patient then
puts these spigots up their nostrils and, in the one case, in their
mouth. They then breath in at the same time as they squeeze
the bulb at the bottom of the apparatus thus forcing medicated
smoke up their nose and into their mouth.

Some years later, after having become a professional
practitioner of Traditional Chinese Medicine, I ordered a
Chinese patent medicine for the treatment of asthma from one
of our supplier's catalogues. I had assumed that it was an
herbal medicine, but when it came, it turned out to be
theophyllin manufactured in Hong Kong. Because I am not a
Western MD, I threw the theophyllin away. However, in each
box was a stick of medicated incense made from Chinese herbs
specifically for the first aid relief of an acute asthmatic attack.
From time to time I used these incense sticks during acute
asthmatic episodes in my patients and was impressed by their
efficacy. However, eventually I could no longer justify the
expense and waste of buying this Chinese medicine just for the
medicated incense sticks inside. Remembering both Western
inhalant remedies for asthma and the pictures of Tibetan
inhalant therapy apparati, I created the following formula,
called *Ding Chuan Xi Ru Fang* or Relieve Asthma Inhalant
Formula, for the treatment of acute asthmatic episodes. It
consists of:

> Herba Verbasci Thaspi
> Herba Lobeliae Inflatae
> Folium Tussilagi Farfarae
> Herba Thymi Vulgaris
> Herba Nepetae Catariae
> Flos Lavendulae Officinalis

These are all Western herbal medicinals. However, they can all
be described according to the rubric of TCM, in which case

they can also be prescribed according to its *Bian Zheng* methodology.

Folium Verbasci Thaspi, aka Mullein, is Bitter and Cool. It enters the Lungs, Liver, Gallbladder, and Stomach. It clears Heat and moistens Dryness. It stops coughing due to Lung Heat.

Herba Lobeliae Inflatae, aka Lobelia, is Bitter and Cool and enters the Liver, Lungs, and Stomach Channels. It unbinds Chest Qi, stops coughing, and relieves *Chuan* or asthma/wheezing. It clears Heat, especially Wind Heat, and relieves spasms. It promotes urination by regulating the functions of the Lungs *vis a vis* their domination of the Water Passageways. In addition, Lobelia clears Heat and dissolves Toxins when applied locally to sores and felons.

Folium Tusslagi Farfarae, aka Coltsfoot, is a Chinese medicinal. However, in TCM it is the flower bud which is used and not the leaf. It is my feeling that the medicinal uses of the two are essentially the same. In this formula, the leaves are used since they burn better. Coltsfoot is Acrid and Warm and enters the Lungs. It redirects Lung Qi downward and stops coughing. It astringes the Lungs, clears Heat, and benefits the throat. Like Lobelia above, it also clears Heat and dissolves Toxins when applied topically in the treatment of sores.

Herba Thymi Vulgaris, Garden Thyme, is used medicinally in China. However, as Dr. Albert Leung says, because it has only been used there medicinally, its TCM properties and description has not yet been determined.[1] In China, Garden Thyme, as opposed to Wild Thyme which is also known and used in China, is called *She Xiang Cao* or Musk Herb. This name coupled with both this herb's traditional Western usage and its contemporary Chinese usage I think gives us the necessary clue to working out such a description since Musk is Chinese medicine's most famous Aromatic Orifice-opener.

Thyme is Acrid, Bitter, Aromatic, and Warm. It enters the Lungs, Spleen, Liver, and possibly the Large Intestine depending upon how one views that organ. I believe Thyme should be classified under the TCM category of Aromatic Orifice-openers. I believe it opens the Orifices and transforms Phlegm and harmonizes the Middle and transforms Turbid Dampness. By transforming and permeating Phlegm in the Lungs, it both stops coughing and benefits urination. By clearing Phlegm from the Orifices of the Heart and activating the Qi, Thyme benefits the Spirit and eliminates nightmares. Ultimately, Aromatic Orifice-openers are Qi herbs which disperse and transform. By transforming Turbid Dampness, the Middle Burner is benefitted and thus ascension and descension are also regulated. This results in Thyme's treatment of nausea, borborygmus, and flatulence. In the same way, these Qi-activating and dispersing properties also enable Thyme to treat menstrual problems such as dysmenorrhea due to Stagnation. And finally, Garden Thyme also expels worms.

Herba Nepetae Catariae, aka Catnip, is Acrid, Bitter, and Cool. It enters the Lungs and Liver. It is a Surface-reliever which disperses clears Wind Heat. In addition, Catnip clears the head and benefits the throat. It relaxes constrained Liver Qi, activates the Qi, and harmonizes the Middle. Although it is similar to Herba Menthae, Catnip's ability to relax the *Jin* Sinews and calm the mind is greater. For this reason, Catnip is especially good for treating hysteria in the truest sense of that word and mental/emotional distress.

Flos Lavendulae Officinalis, aka Lavender, is Acrid and Cool. It enters the Heart, Lungs, and Liver. It calms the Spirit and relieves Depression at the same time as it activates and releases constrained or pent-up Qi.

These herbs taken together as a formula clear Heat, redirect Lung Qi downward, relieve constraint and spasm, and stop cough. In particular, they clear Heat not only from the Lungs but also from the Liver and Stomach as well which are the source of chronic Evil Heat wafting up to disturb the Lungs. In addition, they also release the pent-up Liver Qi which is so often associated with chronic asthmatic attacks. Therefore, the TCM *Bian Zheng* diagnosis for which this formula is indicated is Lung Heat asthma and wheezing possibly complicated by Liver Qi and Stomach/Liver Heat. I think clinicians will recognize this as the most common disease mechanism for recurrent asthma attacks in both American children and young adults.

A handful of this mixture is placed in a ceramic or otherwise nonflammable bowl and lit. It is allowed to burn momentarily and then blown out. The patient is then instructed to breath in the smoke which results. This process can be facilitated in children if a sheet is draped like a tent over their heads and the herbs lit at the level of their chest. The smoke will accumulate under this tent bathing their entire head and making the inhalation of this medicated smoke unavoidable.

When prescribed based on a correct *Bian Zheng* diagnosis, the effects of this inhalant therapy can be remarkable. Acute asthmatic attacks are difficult to abort through acupuncture. Herbs in decoction also take too long to get into the system. Inhalant therapy gets the medicine to the bronchi immediately where it gets immediate results. Such inhalant therapy is almost universally a part of folk medicines around the world. American Indians used it. It was used in the European Wise Woman tradition, in Ayurvedic and Tibetan medicine, and in Chinese medicine. Unfortunately, in the last two hundred years, there has been a global tendency on the part of professional medicines to downplay or delete therapies other than internal medicines. Here in the United States, TCM largely confines itself to acupuncture and internal medicine. However,

the panoply of traditional Chinese therapies is much wider than
that. In my experience, often it is the addition of such other
therapies which spells the difference between success and
failure in the clinic.

After having created the above inhalant formula, I remembered
seeing various *Ding Chuan Gao* for sale in Chinese pharmacies
in Shanghai. *Gao* means a medicated paste. *Ding Chuan* means
to relieve asthma or wheezing. Likewise I also remembered the
Vick's Vaporub my mother used to use on my chest when I
suffered from bronchial asthma as a child. Therefore, I created
Lan Hua Zhi Ke Ding Chuan Gao or Blue Flower Stop Cough
Relieve Asthma Paste as a companion remedy to the above
inhalant formula. The ingredients in this medicated paste are
somewhat similar to *Ding Chuan Xi Ru Fang*.
They include:

> Herba Lobeliae Inflatae
> Flos Tussilagi Farfarae
> Folium Marrubii Vulgaris
> Radix Et Herba Verbasci Thaspi
> Oleum Lavendulae Officinalis
> Oleum Eucalypti Globuli
> Gummum Benzoin
> Beeswax
> Lard
> Oleum Semenis Sesami

We have discussed Lobelia, Coltsfoot, Mullein, and Lavender
above. In this case, I use Flos Tussilagi Farfarae instead of the
leaves since we cook the herb in sesame oil instead of burning
it. For the same reason I use Radix Et Herba Verbasci instead
of just its leaves and also simply add Lavender Oil instead of
using Flos Lavendulae.

Folium Marrubii Vulgaris, aka Horehound, is Bitter, Acrid, and Cool. It enters the Lungs, Liver, and Spleen. It unbinds Chest Qi and directs the Qi downward. It transforms Phlegm and stops coughing. It also benefits urination and the throat while at the same time relieving the Surface.

Oleum Eucalypti Globuli, aka Eucalyptus Oil, is Bitter, Acrid, Aromatic, and Cool. It enters the Lungs. It clears Heat and dissolves Toxins, transforms Phlegm and stops coughing. It also kills parasites or *Chong* in the broad sense of my usage of that term.

Gummum Benzoin is Sweet, Acrid, Aromatic, and Warm. It enters the Heart and Spleen. It opens the Orifices, deobstructs Stagnation, activates the Qi and Blood, and penetrates Turbidity.

Beeswax, Lard, and Sesame Oil are used as the medium for this *Gao*. The herbs are fried at a low heat in the sesame oil until they are dark brown but not burnt. The dregs are strained out and the Lavender and Eucalyptus Oils are added. Then the lard and beeswax are added until the right consistency is obtained. This *Gao* should not be too stiff. Rather it should go on easily.

This paste is spread directly on the chest, back and front, in the treatment of upper respiratory tract infections and asthma due to Lung Heat, Hot Phlegm, and Constrained Qi. It is a very useful adjunctive remedy when used in tandem with acupuncture, internal medications, and inhalant therapy. Such medicated herbal pastes for upper respiratory complaints are also universal in traditional medicines around the world. American TCM practitioners need not search their suppliers for Chinese versions. Our own naturopathic tradition includes the American Indian, European Scholastic or Galenical, Wise Woman, and Eclectic traditions within it and, as such, contains a rich storehouse of indigenous healing wisdom.

Mao Ze-dong resurrected TCM when he recognized the great storehouse of indigenous Chinese remedies while on his Long March. It is time we American practitioners of Chinese medicine recognize the treasure chest of remedies upon which we are sitting. All we have to do to make rational use of these or any remedies from around the world is to describe these according to the rubric of TCM. Then we can prescribe and apply these based on TCM *Bian Zheng* diagnosis. TCM *Bian Zheng* diagnosis is, perhaps, the best professional holistic system of diagnosis in the world today. It is certainly the most important gift TCM has to offer towards the creation of a universal or planetary New Medicine.

ENDNOTE

1   Leung, Albert, *Chinese Herbal Remedies*, Universe Books,
        New York, 1984, p. 160-162

AZT & Compound Q As TCM Surface-Relieving Medicinals

A Preliminary Discussion of Their Taxonomy & Treatment of Side Effects

AZT and Compound Q are two pharmaceuticals employed in the battle against AIDS. AZT (zidovudine) is a standard and accepted, albeit not entirely satisfactory treatment. According to Western medicine, it is a transcriptase inhibitor. Compound Q, also known as trichosanthin and simply Q to its aficionados, is a highly purified extract obtained from Radix Trichosanthis Kirlowii. According to Western medicine, it kills HIV infected macrophages leaving other, uninfected cells of the immune system intact. It is a more controversial treatment which has gained considerable exposure in the public media in the last 12-18 months. Since many HIV positives and PWAs seek treatment by Traditional Chinese Medicine (TCM), and since, in my experience, they often want to do TCM concomitantly with AZT and/or Compound Q, it is important for TCM practitioners to have a TCM description of these medicinals.

Without such a TCM description, TCM practitioners have no way of assessing the TCM impact of these medicinals on their patients. Without being able to distinguish between these drugs' intended TCM effects and their true unwanted side effects, TCM practitioners have no way of rationally deciding upon concurrent TCM therapy. As a rational *cum* empirical system of medicine, TCM treatment is based on *Bian Zheng* diagnosis which is, in turn, partially based on an understanding of the *Bing Ji* or disease mechanisms at work. These mechanisms must also include those induced by concurrent therapy. Although certain Western biomedical information can be used in order to establish a TCM description of a previously non-TCM medicinal, TCM treatment itself is predicated primarily on TCM therapeutic principles derived from the *Bian Zheng* diagnosis.

Elsewhere I have written that the human immunodeficiency virus (HIV) can be described in TCM terms as a *Fu Wen Xie* or Warm Hidden Evil which typically enters the Lower Burner and quickly or immediately penetrates to the *Xue Fen* or Blood phase where it can remain hidden or latent for an indefinite period of time.[1] This persistent, hidden Hot Evil wastes the Yin, Blood, and Body Humors and injures the Righteous or *Zheng Qi*. According to classical Chinese theory derived, in part, from the *Nei Jing*, such a Hidden Hot Evil may flourish proportionate to the Internal accumulation of Heat and the decline and exhaustion of *Jing* Essence.

When a Hidden Warm Evil flourishes and becomes more active, it travels from Lower to Upper Heaters and from *Xue Fen* to *Qi Fen* and eventually to *Wei Fen* causing a predictable sequence of signs and symptoms while at the same time wasting the Kidneys, Spleen, Lungs, and Heart. This progression from Inside to Outside and from Bottom to Top is retrograde compared to standard *Wen Bing* or Warm Disease theory. However, such retrograde progression is characteristic of other viral *Wen Bing*.

Rubella, rubeola, and varicella are also viral *Wen Bing* which tend to move in a somewhat similar retrograde fashion. These commonly pediatric diseases are due in TCM to a new Warm Evil invading the *Wei Fen* or Defensive layer or phase. This then provokes inherited or gestational *Tai Du* or Fetal Toxins through systemic aggravation of Internal Heat. Such Fetal Toxins also reside in the *Xue Fen* and are a species of *Fu Wen Xie* or Warm Hidden Evil. In Chinese medicine, when a new External Invasion causes activation of a Hidden Evil, this is called *Xing Gan Yin Dong Fu Xie*. In the case of rubella, rubeola, and varicella, externally invading Wind Heat is typically the catalyst for these Hidden Warm Evils' activation, in which case the appropriate TCM therapeutic principles for their treatment are to release or relieve the Surface, expel Wind, clear Heat, and promote the exteriorization of the Hidden Hot pathogen. This is called promoting the expression of rash or pox. It is also sometimes called ripening a rash or pox. Using Surface-relieving, dispersing medicinals, Warm Evils lurking in the Blood phase are brought to the Surface. There the *Zheng Qi* can do battle with the *Xie Qi* and neutralize it.

Warm Hidden Evils can also go from latent to active due to macrocosmic seasonal changes in microcosmic energetics. According to *Nei Jing Su Wen*, Chapter 4, a Cold Evil may penetrate the body in the winter and lie latent until spring. In the spring, Yang Qi moving up and outward as it does at that time also exteriorizes or stirs up the Hidden Hot Evil. However, anything which causes the upward and outward movement of Yang Qi in the body may also provoke the activation of a Warm Hidden Evil. It does not necessarily have to happen only in the spring. Such factors include the development of Internal Heat which tends to vent upwards and to the Surface and the exhaustion of Blood, Yin, and Body Humors which allows the Yang Qi to float up and away from its Root.

Therefore, Latent Heat, or *Fu Re* as it is called in Chinese, may express itself in two different ways according to the theory of TCM. First, it may manifest concurrently with a new External Wind Heat Invasion. The signs and symptoms of such a *Xin*

Gan Yin Dong Fu Xie or new disease stirring up a Hidden Evil
are chills, sore throat, fever, slight sweating, muscle aches,
possible swollen glands, runny nose, stuffy nose, or cough, thirst,
dark, scanty urine, a red tongue with thick, sticky coating, and
fine, rapid pulse which is also floating in the *Cun* position.
These signs and symptoms indicate both an External Wind Heat
Invasion and concurrent Internal Heat.

Secondly, Latent Heat may also become active due to Internal
changes without necessarily being provoked by a new External
disease. In this case, there will be signs and symptoms of
Internal Heat without chills, muscle aches, upper respiratory
disorders, etc. There will still be thirst and the urine will be
dark, but the tongue is red with a scantier than normal, dry
yellow or mirror-like coating. The pulse is fine and rapid but
is also floating or rootless in the left *Chi*. There may be
swollen glands and sore throat due to the upward perversion of
Liver Heat drafting with it Phlegm but this alone does not
constitute an Exterior Pattern.

As mentioned above, the appropriate TCM therapeutic
principles for treating a concurrent Wind Heat/Latent Internal
Heat disease are to relieve the Surface, expel the Wind, clear
the Heat, and to promote the expression of the rash. This rash
is the exteriorized expression of Heat in the *Xue Fen* or Blood
phase. In the case of active Hidden Heat without any Exterior
or Superficial signs and symptoms, the appropriate therapeutic
principles are to clear Internal Heat and to cool and nourish
the Blood.

It is my opinion that both AZT and Compound Q are both
Surface-relieving medicinals from the TCM point of view. This
opinion is based on these drugs' published side effects and on
my clinical experience with patients who have used them. I
believe that both drugs attempt to treat HIV infection by
exteriorizing the pathogen so that it is no longer hidden to the

Zheng Qi or the immune system. It seems to me that both AZT and Compound Q attempt to provoke the arisal and exteriorization of Hidden Heat by dispersing Yang Qi to the Surface and by raising the temperature of the body. Therefore, both medicines tend to provoke signs and symptoms of Heat congested in the Surface. AZT seems to do this at an often unacceptable cost; whereas, in many patients, Compound Q has a much better benefit/risk ratio.

According to James W. Long, MD in *The Essential Guide to Prescription Drugs 1990*, AZT's side effects include skin rashes, hives, and itching; headache, weakness, drowsiness, dizziness, nervousness, and insomnia; nausea, stomach pain, diarrhea, loss of appetite, vomiting, altered taste, lip sores, and swollen mouth and tongue; muscle aches, fever, sweating, confusion, loss of speech, twitching, tremors, and seizures; and bone marrow depression evidenced by fatigue, weakness, fever, sore throat, and abnormal bleeding and bruising.[2] Of these so-called side effects, I believe that the skin rashes, hives, itching, headache, lip sores, muscle aches, fever, and sweating are all signs of dispersal of Evil Qi to the Surface and are due to exteriorization. The fatigue, weakness, drowsiness, dizziness, nervousness, and insomnia are due to this Acrid, Dry, probably Warm Surface-reliever's wasting and exhausting Yin Humor and ultimately *Jing* Essence. The fact that AZT's side effects are made worse by acetominaphen, acyclovir, aspirin, cimetidine, indomethacin, and sulfonamides corroborates my hypothesis since these are also dispersing medicinals which activate the Qi and Blood from the point of view of TCM.

It should be remembered that there is a close relationship between *Li Qi* or Qi-regulating medicinals which activate and disperse the Qi and Surface-relievers. Many TCM medicinals in both categories have both functions. This is because relief of the Surface is accomplished by activation and dispersion of the Qi. Both categories of medicinals tend to be Dry, Light, and

Airy. They also tend to be more Aromatic than other medicinals and have more *Qi* than *Wei* or Flavor.[3] In general, the ingredients in both these categories of TCM medicinals are Yang as compared to Yin.

In my experience, Compound Q also causes skin rashes, muscle aches, fluey feelings, headache, fever, and chills followed by fatigued, drowsiness, and dizziness. Usually, however, these effects of Q are short-lived and relatively minor. In some cases, there may also be swollen glands. So far, Compound Q does not seem to wreck or injure the *Sui* Marrow the way AZT does in some patients. Many patients who take AZT experience depression of hemapoiesis which may be irreversible using Chinese Qi, Blood, and Marrow-nourishing medicinals.

If my hypothesis about the TCM description of AZT and Compound Q is correct, this suggests several amendments to their use. First of all, they should not be used to treat a patient who already has developed skin lesions. TCM theory says that once skin rashes have been expressed, Surface-relieving, rash-promoting medicinals should be suspended. Secondly, they should only be used in patients whose *Zheng Qi* and *Zhen Yin* are relatively robust. These medicinals scatter *Zheng Qi* and waste *Zhen Yin* as an inescapable part of their dispersion. Bringing a pathogen to the Surface is not particularly meaningful if there is not enough *Zheng Qi* to combat it.

In the treatment of measles, if a rash begins to express itself but then fades back into the body, this is considered due to a lack of the patient's *Zheng Qi*. Rather than giving further rash-promoting medicinals, tonics are prescribed to boost the *Zheng Qi* and to combat the *Xie Qi*. As a corollary of this, during or after using a Surface-relieving, rash-expressing medicinal, it is often necessary to support the Blood and Yin below. This becomes all the more important in AIDS since the *Fu Wen Xie* may already have exhausted many PWAS' *Yin Jing* in their Lower

Burner. In general, the TCM guidelines for using other Acrid,
Warm, Surface-relieving, rash-promoting medicinals, such as
Flos Schizonepetae and Rhizoma Cimicifugae should be
followed. These are typically contraindicated in Deficient
Blood, Deficient Yin, and Deficient Exterior conditions.

In addition, great care should be taken when treating either
with modern Western or traditional Chinese medicines the
seeming side effects of these two drugs. For instance, Benadryl
is often taken along with Compound Q in order to suppress
rash. Also, antipyretics and anti-inflammatories are often used
to relieve accompanying fever and muscle aches. However, as
I see it, these are not necessarily unwanted side effects but
rather are the intended effects of these medicines. Their arisal
is a sign of reverse or healing vicariation.[4] Suppression of such
signs and symptoms may be suppression of this reverse
vicariation and, therefore, negate the therapeutic benefits of
these drugs. TCM practitioners should treat such seemingly
negative side effects the same way they would in the case of
measles or chickenpox. This will not cause reverse vicariation
but will, in fact, facilitate the *Zheng Qi*'s neutralization of the
Evil Qi. On the other hand, drowsiness, nervousness, tremor,
seizures, and abnormal bruising and bleeding should all be
treated with Chinese medicine as unwanted iatrogenic
complications.

There are three formulas I would especially like to mention for
the treatment of the initial complications of taking Compound
Q. These are *Sheng Ma Ge Gen Tang* (Cimicifuga & Pueraria
Decoction), *Xuan Du Fa Biao Tang* (Dissipate Toxins/Release
the Exterior Decoction, aka Cimicifuga & Peucedanum
Combination), and *Ze Gen Mu Li Tang* (Lithopsermum &
Oyster Shell Decoction). The first two come from the *Dou Ji*
or Pox category of TCM formulas, while the third comes from
the *Yong Yang* or carbuncle category.

Sheng Ma Ge Gen Tang is one of the most famous TCM rash-promoting formulas. It is composed of:

> Radix Puerariae
> Rhizoma Cimicifugae
> Radix Paeoniae Albae
> Rhizoma Recens Zingiberis
> Radix Glycyrrhizae

This formula is meant to release the muscle layer and vent rashes. It is commonly employed in the treatment of rubella and rubeola. According Bensky & Barolet, if there is Exterior Heat, add Herba Menthae, Periostracum Cicadae, Fructus Arctii, and Flos Lonicerae. If there is a sore throat and swollen glands, add Radix Platycodi, Radix Scrophulariae, and Fructicatio Lasiospherae. If the rash is dark red suggesting more prominent Heat in the Blood, add Radix Lithospermi Seu Arnebiae. And for rashes due to viral origin, again add Lithospermum.[5] Of these additional ingredients, Arctium, Lithospermum, and Lonicera have all demonstrated anti-viral activity in general[6] and anti-HIV activity in particular.[7] In addition, Lithospermum clears Heat, cools the Blood, dissolves Fire Toxins, and promotes the complete expression of rashes.

Hsu and Hsu say that, "The Measles-ripening effect of (*Xuan Du Fa Biao Tang*) is superior to that of *Sheng-ma-ko-ken-tang*."[8] It is indicated for the treatment of fever, muscle aches, mild fear of chill, flu-like feelings, possible sore throat and swollen glands, no *pronounced* rash, and darkish urine.[9] Its ingredients include:

> Rhizoma Cimicifugae
> Radix Peucedani
> Flos Schizonepetae
> Radix Puerariae
> Semen Pruni Armeniacae

Radix Platycodi
Fructus Arctii
Fructus Forsythiae
Herba Lophatheri Gracilis
Radix Ledebouriellae
Caulis Akebiae Mutong
Fructus Citri Seu Ponciri
Herba Menthae
Radix Glycyrrhizae

Personally, I don't think this formula is better *per se* than *Sheng Ma Ge Gen Tang* since, in TCM clinical practice, that formula is seldom prescribed in its simple, unmodified form. A TCM analysis of the ingredients in this second formula suggest that it is more appropriate as a guiding formula if there is also cough and more obvious Phlegm.

Zi Gen Mu Li Tang is prescribed for lymphadenitis, swollen glands, breast lumps, and skin cancer. However, although it is not classified as a *Dou Ji* formula, based on a TCM analysis of its ingredients, it too can exteriorize Heat hidden in the *Xue Fen*. It is composed of:

Radix Lithospermi Seu Arnebiae
Concha Ostreae
Radix Angelicae Sinensis
Radix Astragali Seu Hedysari
Radix Paeoniae Albae
Radix Ligustici Chuanxiong
Rhizoma Cimicifugae
Rhizoma Rhei
Flos Lonicerae Japonicae
Radix Glycyrrhizae

Cimicifuga releases the Exterior and promotes the expression of rash. Lithospermum clears Heat from the *Xue Fen* and promotes the expression of rash. Dang Gui and Peony nourish the Blood and, therefore, assist Lithospermum's cooling the Blood. Oyster Shell in this case disperses Nodulation. Astragalus nourishes the *Zheng Qi*. Rhubarb clears Heat through purgation of the bowels. However, it can be omitted if there is no constipation. Lonicera clears Heat and dissolves Fire Toxins, expels Wind Heat, and is used in the treatment of dermal eruptions. Licorice clears Heat and dissolves Toxins. And Ligusticum, aka Cnidium, activates the Blood to assist in the dispersal of the Blood towards the Surface. I find this formula especially useful for treating fever and swollen glands after the administration of Compound Q.

Although the above three formulas may be modified in a myriad of ways depending upon the individual patient's presenting signs and symptoms, I routinely add Herba Ecliptae to such patient's post-Q formulas. Zhang & Hsu[10] and Tsung[11] identify Eclipta as Alternanthera Philoxeroides and both say that this medicinal has demonstrated anti-HIV activity. According to TCM, Eclipta nourishes Liver Blood and tonifies Kidney Yin, it cools the Blood, and stops bleeding. Additionally, however, Zhang & Hsu report that Eclipta has been used to good effect in China for the treatment of measles.[12] Since it is a known HIV-antagonist, since it cools the Blood and nourishes Yin, and since it is effective in the treatment of measles, a rash or pox disease, I believe its inclusion in the above formulas is a useful one when these formulas are administered to HIV positives post-Q.

It is currently believed that AZT should be started early before an HIV patient's condition deteriorates too far. If AZT is a Warm, Acrid, Surface-relieving, rash-expressor, this makes some sense. However, I believe that TCM diagnosis by *Bian Zheng* is the best methodology for assessing who should take AZT and when. TCM has diagnostic parameters for assessing the strength of a patient's *Zheng Qi* and the repletion of their Yin and *Jing*.

Western medicine, by and large lacks the theory or the diagnostic parameters to make such assessments.

Further, I question the necessity of continuing such drugs once signs of successful exteriorization cease to manifest. It is not uncommon for HIV positives taking Compound Q to develop rash and flu-like symptoms the first few times they take Q. Later on, no such symptoms may be provoked. In such cases, I assume that no further profitable exteriorization is taking place and, therefore, no further therapeutic benefit. At that point, I wonder whether a different therapeutic approach should not be taken.

One of my HIV positives experienced flu-like muscle aches, fever, and rash the first time he took Q. I treated him with acupuncture for Wind Heat. Several days after taking this first dose of Compound Q, his right *Chi* position pulse came up from being deepish. The second time he took Q, he experienced less muscle ache, less fever, and no rash. His pulse did not change further at this time. The third and fourth times he took Q, he experienced only fatigue and lethargy but no fever, muscle aches, or rash. After the fourth dose of Q, this patient's pulse went from being relatively full and a little slippery-wiry to fine and wiry overall with a floating right *Cun* and left *Chi*. Likewise, his tongue coating went from being slightly thicker than normal to being scanter than normal with the tongue itself looking tender. My assessment of this patient is that the first two doses of Q benefitted this patient but that the second two doses did no further benefit and seems to have harmed him instead.

It is a medical fact that life-threatening diseases must often be treated with such powerful therapies that side effects are inescapable. Sometimes such side effects are the signs of healing. Other times, they are truly unwanted and deleterious. In Chinese AIDS clinics, it is recognized that concomitant therapy is necessary to mitigate the negative effects of Compound Q therapy. According to oral sources, it seems that the Chinese are using similar protocols as those used for treating the side effects of chemotherapy in cancer patients. Therefore, I refer TCM practitioners to Zhang Dai-zhao's *The Treatment of Cancer by Integrated Chinese-Western Medicine.*[13] This book contains good discussions and instructions for the treatment of drug-induced side effects.

Other oral sources suggest that the medicinal Spica Prunellae Vulgaris in high doses is especially appropriate for combatting the side effects of Compound Q. This seems reasonable to me during the initial few days after administration of Q if there is sore throat, fever, *and* swollen glands or the basic TCM indications for this medicinal. However, for the patient described above, after his pulse became fine and floating, I prescribed a formula called Ecliptex. This is a formula manufactured and marketed by Health Concerns as a tablet specifically for the treatment of liver damage due to chemical toxins whether dietary, environmental, or iatrogenic. Its ingredients are:

> Herba Ecliptae
> Fructus Sylibi (Milk Thistle Seed)
> Tuber Curcumae
> Radix Salviae Miltorrhizae
> Fructus Lycii Chinensis
> Fructus Ligustri Lucidi
> Radix Bupleuri
> Fructus Schizandrae
> Radix Pseudoginseng
> Radix Angelica Sinensis
> Semen Plantaginis
> Radix Glycyrrhizae

In this patient's case, I began by grinding these bulk ingredients into a fine powder. The patient was then instructed to take 1 heaping tablespoon in hot water 3-4 times per day. I chose to use this formula in powder form instead of pill based on cost effectiveness and the patient's preference.

Unfortunately, although I have tried to build patients' Blood and Marrow which has been wrecked by AZT using Subhuti Dharmnanda's Seven Forest formulas, such as Antler 8, I have not been able to reverse such damage in patients whose T_4 cell count plummeted after taking AZT. Although I have been able to alleviate the pronounced signs and symptoms of Qi, Blood, and Yin Deficiency, these signs and symptoms have tended to recur. Nor have I been able to catalyze an elevation in Western blood values. This suggests to me that AZT is an especially dangerous drug which must be prescribed with the utmost discrimination and care. I believe that TCM diagnostic and therapeutic theory can provide the wisdom for that discrimination.

ENDNOTES

1   Flaws, Bob, *Nine Ounces, A Nine Part Program for the
         Prevention of AIDS in HIV Positive Persons*, Blue Poppy Press,
         Boulder, CO, 1989

2   Long, James, W., *The Essential Guide to Prescription Drugs
         1990*, Harper & Row, NY, 1990, p. 978-981

3   Every TCM medicinal has within it a Yin Yang ratio of Qi to
         Wei. Qi is the aromatic, active, Yang energy of the medicinal.
         Wei is its dense, heavy, Yin, nourishing energy. *Wei* literally
         means flavor in Chinese. Qi is aroma and *Wei* is flavor.

4   Vicariation is a term coined by Dr. Hans-Hinrich Reckeweg,
         an MD homeopath active in Germany during the mid century.
         Vicariation can be either progressive/pathologic or
         regressive/healing. According to Reckeweg's school of
         Homotoxicology, disease progresses sequentially through
         various embryonic tissues and to various organs in a more or
         less predictable way. Such progression tracks the
         transformation of a single disease process manifesting as
         various symptoms and disease categories.

5   Bensky, Dan & Barolet, Randall, *Chinese Herbal Medicine:
         Formulas & Strategies*, Eastland Press, Seattle, 1990, p. 47-48

6   Zhang, Qing-cai & Hsu, Hong-yen, *AIDS And Chinese
         Medicine* OHAI, LA, 1990, p. 143-144

7   Ibid., p. 143-144

8   Hsu, Hong-yen & Hsu, Chau-shin, *Commonly Used Chinese
         Herb Formulas with Illustrations*, OHAI, LA, 1980, p. 591

9   Bensky & Barolet, op.cit., p. 48

10   Zhang & Hsu, op.cit., p. 143

11   Tsung, Pi-kwang, *Immune System and Chinese Herbs,* Institute
          of Chinese Herbs, Irvine, CA, 1989, p. 84

12   Zhang & Hsu, op.cit., p. 152-155

13   Zhang, Dai-zhao, *The Treatment of Cancer of Integrated
          Chinese-Western Medicine,* trans. by Zhang Ting-liang & Bob
          Flaws, Blue Poppy Press, Boulder, 1989

KEEPING UP WITH THE JONES'

A PRELIMINARY DISCUSSION OF
THE IMPORTANCE & EXPANSION OF THE *BU NEI*
BU WAI YIN CATEGORY OF ETIOLOGY
TO BETTER MEET THE EXIGENICIES OF OUR TIME

Contemporary TCM discussion of etiological factors is based on Chen Yen's *San Yin Ji Yi Bing Zheng Fang Lun (Treatise on the 3 Categories of Pathogenic Factors and Symptoms)* published in 1174 CE during the Jin Dynasty. In this work, Chen Yen divides etiological factors or *Bing Yin* into three categories. These are *Wai Yin* or External factors, *Nei Yin* or Internal factors, and *Bu Nei Bu Wai Yin* or Neither External nor Internal factors. *Wai Yin* refer to the *Liu Xie* or Six (External) Evils. These are cosmopathogenic energies existing outside the individual which may, under certain circumstances, invade the organism and cause disease. They are Wind, Cold, Heat, Dampness, Dryness, and Summer Heat. In the mid-seventeenth century, Wu You-ke added to this list *Li Qi* or Pestilential Qi. *Li Qi* causes epidemic diseases and is not linked to the *Wu Yun Liu Qi* or Five Transports/Six Qi the way the *Liu Xie* are. *Nei Yin* or the Internal causes of disease specifically refer to the Seven Passions. These encompass *all* emotional causes of disease. TCM calls these Internal since they are generated internally and since they directly affect the internal Organs.

The *Bu Nei Bu Wai Yin* category of pathogenic factors is often translated as Miscellaneous causes in the Western TCM literature. I believe this is an erroneous translation and has led to an underestimation of this category of disease factors in the Western practice of TCM. To say miscellaneous in English connotes something left over, of little consequence, something relatively superfluous. However, I do not believe the Chinese *Bu Nei Bu Wai Yin* has such a pejorative connotation. I believe the *Bu Nei Bu Wai Yin* category of disease causation is co-equally as important as either the Internal or External categories.

That this is so is evidenced by the list of factors subcategorized under *Bu Nei Bu Wai Yin*. These classically include:

1) Diet
2) Activity
3) Rest
4) Sex
5) Trauma
6) Poison
7) Parasites
8) Iatrogenesis
9) Demonic affliction

This is no minor list of etiological factors. Looking at only the first three, I consider these co-equal with External and Internal causes in the production of most patients' disease. By translating this category as miscellaneous it tends to shift emphasis away from these factors and this, I believe, is a great mistake. Patients have relatively little control over the Six External Evils. Patients may also find it not so easy to modify their emotional life. But diet, rest, activity, and sex are activities subject to much easier and greater control through conscious endeavor. By de-emphasizing this category as a whole, TCM has tended to downplay the instructional role which the authors of the *Nei Jing* and Sun Si-miao saw as the true profession of the Chinese medical practitioner.

The early classics of Chinese medicine stressed prevention over remedial therapy. The *Nei Jing Su Wen* implies in its opening chapter that the true basis of health and longevity is proper regulation of one's diet and lifestyle. In addition, Sun Si-miao of the Tang stated that Chinese doctors should first attempt to treat patients through modifications in their diet and lifestyle and only if these are not enough should they prescribe medicines and professionally administered therapies. As Chinese medicine has become more and more of a technical profession, the tendency as in all contemporary professional medicines has been to emphasize internal medicines and professionally administered therapies such as acupuncture.

I see this as a great mistake. It mimics the mistake modern Western medicine has so glaringly made in this direction. Westerners turning to Chinese medicine are, in part, seeking the wisdom of the East in understanding and regulating their lives. If we confine ourselves to simply dispensing pills and sticking in needles, eventually patients will recognize that, though the medicinals we use are different, our *modus operandi* is essentially the same as Western allopathy. If the public comes to perceive us as a self-seeking, self-perpetuating, special interest group, there is no reason to believe that we will be held in any higher esteem than Western MDs today.

Such an emphasis on professionally dispensed medicines denies or at least obscures the most important gift Chinese medicine has to offer -- the gift of knowledge. Chinese medicine is a rational system of medicine by which a patient can regulate their life's activities thus gaining a large degree of control over their own health and well being. Confining our practice to prescribing pills and potions does not necessarily enlighten our patients on how to care for themselves. Lest we forget, professional practitioners of medicine should always be attempting to put ourselves out of business. Unfortunately, by emphasizing semantically Chen Yen's first two categories of etiological factors, we foster the dependence of our patients on our professionally dispensed nostrums.

In addition, the *Bu Nei Bu Wai Yin* category is a place where TCM can and, in my opinion, should undergo further theoretical development. TCM as a medical system is the product of a pre-modern, pre-industrial culture. There are a number of disease factors which either were not known at the time this schema was first advanced or were understood in a limited way. I believe that a number of modern etiological factors can be included under the *Bu Nei Bu Wai Yin* category. Some of these may be simply further elucidation of already existing subcategories mentioned above. Others may be entirely new subcategories added to this list.

For instance, it is now well known that electromagnetic, cosmic, nuclear, and microwave radiations can cause disease. The most glaring example of this is the higher incidence in pediatric cancer in neighborhoods under high voltage power lines. We are literally awash in all sorts of human generated electromagnetic and microwave radiation. We have opened a Pandora's box of nuclear radiation due to reactor malfunctions, nuclear warhead testing, and faulty nuclear waste disposal. Through CFCs' degradation of the ozone layer, we have increased the amount of cosmic radiation striking the surface of our planet. And by building our homes as airtight as possible and with deepset cellars, many of us are exposed to radon gasses seeping up out of the ground. Chen Yen in the Jin Dynasty never knew nor had to think about such pathogenic factors. We, on the other hand, must take these into account since they are real disease causing factors for us.

I believe it is axiomatic that until TCM consciously addresses electromagnetism, nuclear, cosmic, and microwave radiation as etiological factors we cannot rationally develop diagnostic methods and parameters nor effective therapies for diseases caused by these. Other medical systems, such as homeopathy and homotoxicology have addressed these issues, have developed diagnostic parameters, and have created therapies for the disease conditions caused by these various types of radiation. I believe electromagnetic, nuclear, cosmic, and microwave radiation should be added as a new subcategory under *Bu Nei Bu Wai Yin.*

Having added such a category, we must then develop TCM diagnostic parameters for identifying disease states due to these and effective therapies. It is possible that we may simply choose to adopt such diagnostic procedures as electronic and kinesiological testing using resonance filters as is done in EAV (Electroacupuncture According to Voll), Vegatesting, and Vega biokinesiology. We may also decide to adopt homeopathic and homotoxicological remedies for these disease conditions. Be that as it may, the first step in rationally addressing such disease states is to add such etiological factors to our present system.

Then there is environmental pollution. We have succeeded in polluting our water, our air, our soil, and our food. We are constantly ingesting all sorts of toxic chemicals the human organism never has had to contend with before: PCBs, CFCs, dioxin, fluoride, chlorine, BHT, BHA, MSG, DDT, etc., etc. There is even the whole issue of mercury poisoning from our dental amalgams. Although TCM has not previously had to grapple with such pollutants, I think they can be easily included under the general subcategory of poisons. Again, TCM practitioners will have to develop diagnostic parameters and treatments for diseases caused by such pollutants and toxins, but at least there is a theoretic niche waiting for them.

Modern practitioners are also recognizing the effect time and place have on the health of the human organism. The Chinese science of *Feng Shui* or geomancy has always posited the importance of time and place on human health. Traditionally, not a few Chinese doctors have also been students and practitioners of *Feng Shui*. In *Feng Shui* it is believed that disease can be caused by geopathic stresses of one sort or another or, at the very least, that such geopathic stresses can predispose a person towards a particular disease. In such cases, until such a *Feng Shui* factor has been identified and corrected, other medical intervention may not be successful.

Unfortunately, *Feng Shui* was outlawed as a feudal superstition in New China and all mention of *Feng Shui* has been expunged from contemporary TCM. However, because of our modern ability to gouge and shape the earth in almost any way we want, to build buildings in any shape and any place, and because cars and planes allow us to change times zones and even seasons in a matter of hours, geopathic and biorhythmic stress as a disease factor is becoming more and more apparent. Any practitioner who has ever had a flight attendant for a patient does not need to be reminded of the deleterious effects of scrambling one's biological clock and geomagnetic alignment.

Therefore, I believe that *Feng Shui* should be consciously included as an etiological subcategory under *Bu Nei Bu Wai Yin*, remembering that Chinese *Feng Shui* is actually a combination of both astrology and geomancy and, therefore, can serve as the heading for both geopathic and biorhythmic stress. Once such a subcategory of etiology is included in TCM, we can begin identifying Patterns of disharmony due to such factors and begin designing effective treatments. Steven Morrissey, a TCM practitioner and faculty member at the John Bastyr College of Naturopathy in Seattle has already developed a Chinese herbal decoction called *Feng Shui* Tea specifically to treat geopathic stress.

TCM has always recognized the potential for iatrogenesis.

Unfortunately today, because of the myopic methodology of modern Western medicine, iatrogenesis has become a major etiological factor. All Western TCM practitioners are well aware of the extent of Western medical iatrogenesis. Almost every patient history reveals at least some iatrogenesis, be that due to unnecessary surgery, over or inappropriate use of antibiotics, or the unavoidable side effects of so many Western pharmaceuticals. Therefore, a more conscious and deliberate assessment of iatrogenesis seems to be a necessary part of doing Chinese medicine in the post-modern West. As I have written in previous essays appearing in this volume, this means developing descriptions of the TCM functions and properties of Western pharmaceuticals. Already in the PRC, there is the deliberate use of TCM medicinals to offset or negate the iatrogenic side effects of chemotherapeutic agents. I believe such a use of TCM is extremely important and that the development of this approach would be facilitated by a more deliberate inclusion of iatrogenesis in our etiological literature.

I have also written elsewhere that I believe the subcategory *Chong* or parasites should be expanded.[1] In contemporary TCM, the definition of *Chong* is fairly narrow and is mostly confined to worms of one sort or another. However, *Chong*, although it does mean worms, also means all sorts of other small, creepy crawler vermin. I believe that broadening this category to specifically include various types of protozoa, bacteria, yeast, and fungi would allow greater specificity in TCM treatment of a number of disorders and could provide the rationale for incorporating Western microbial research into the treatment methodology of TCM.

Gui or ghosts have been a subcategory of Chinese etiology under *Bu Nei Bu Wai Yin* up until only the last forty or so years. It refers to the possibility of disease being due to demonic affliction or possession. This is a very ancient idea in Chinese medicine derived from shamanism. It is an idea that has been entertained seriously by many famous Chinese doctors from Sun Si-miao in the Tang to Xu Chun-fu in the Ming and Xu Da-chun in the Qing. When I first heard the teachings on Chinese etiology from Dr. (Eric) Tao Xi-yu in 1979, he included ghosts in his exposition, although somewhat embarrassedly. Dr. Tao learned Chinese medicine before the advent of modern TCM as a child from his uncle in Beijing. After the revolution, Dr. Tao practiced acupuncture in Taiwan and thus did not experience the TCM purges on the mainland.

The expurgation of ghosts as an etiological factor is part and parcel of modern TCM's attempt to conform to Western materialist science and the Chinese Communist regime's rejection of anything spiritual. Many Western practitioners of TCM, having gone through such a materialist phase themselves, have found such an outright denial of the spiritual dimension of human existence a serious deficiency in contemporary TCM. Personally, I have seen and treated American patients in the United States who have been possessed and who did not recover until after the afflicting spirits had been exorcised. Therefore, I believe that we should retain this subcategory of *Bu Nei Bu Wai Yin* and, perhaps, even expand and refine it in terms of our own Western experience. It is a fact that a disproportionately large number of Western practitioners of TCM are also practitioners of Asian religions who do believe in the possibility of demonic affliction and have personal experience of the reality of this dimension in the same way as did Ge Hung and Sun Si-miao.

A final subcategory which I think should be added under *Bu Nei Bu Wai Yin* is what is called *Pi Shi* in Chinese. This means disease due to addiction. Addiction to one substance or another is a growing concern in the world today. Many Westerners are addicted to alcohol, nicotine, cocaine, heroin, and other so-called recreational drugs. Due to the pioneering work of Dr. Michael Smith at Lincoln Hospital in the Bronx, acupuncture is more and more being recognized as an effective therapy for substance abuse and addiction. Although Chinese medicine has traditionally recognized addition as an etiology, I believe addiction should be consciously added to the list of *Bu Nei Bu Wai Yin*.

Based on the above additions to the Neither Internal nor External causes of disease, I suggest this list should now read:

1) Diet
2) Activity
3) Rest
4) Sex
5) Trauma
6) Poisons
7) Parasites
8) Iatrogenesis
9) Electromagnetic, nuclear, cosmic, & microwave radiation
10) Geopathic & biorhythmic stress
11) Substance abuse & addictions
12) Demonic affliction

This adds three subcategories to the nine above and also deliberately expands the understanding of at least two of the others. The world in which we live today is not the same world in which Chen Yen lived. Just as Zhang Yuan-su said in the Song Dynasty that new diseases need new treatments, modern patients today get sick for different reasons than ancient Chinese. If TCM is to keep pace with these modern diseases and offer treatments which are relevant to all modern patients, it must, in my opinion, continue to evolve its theory and practice. In particular, I believe that the *Bu Nei Bu Wai Yin* category of etiological factors is an area where such evolution can and should take place.

However, in expanding TCM, it is important that we do not completely lose touch with the tradition upon which our practice is based. This tradition has been honed over a period of not less than two thousand years and such a long tradition does provide the framework for well vetted experience. On the other hand, there is also no reason to believe that this system cannot be improved as the exigencies of our experience require. Chinese medicine as a system of thought has constantly reflected back upon itself and then modified its practices and theories to better meet the pragmatic necessities of the time. I believe it is time TCM addressed pollution, radiation, electromagnetism, iatrogenesis, geopathic stress, biorhythmic disturbances, and addiction better than it has so far. The first step in this process is recognizing these factors as the pathogens they are.

ENDNOTES

1   Flaws, Bob, *Cervical Dysplasia & Prostate Cancer: HPV, The Hidden Link?*, Blue Poppy Press, Boulder, CO, 1990

Flaws, Bob, *Scatology & The Gate of Life: The Role of the Large Intestine In Immunity, An Integrated Chinese-Western Approach*, Blue Poppy Press, Boulder, CO, 1990

OTHER BOOKS ON CHINESE MEDICINE
AVAILABLE FROM
BLUE POPPY PRESS
1775 Linden Ave
Boulder, CO 80304
303\442-0796

SOMETHING OLD, SOMETHING NEW: Essays on the TCM
Description of Western Herbs, Pharmaceuticals, Vitamins & Minerals
by Bob Flaws ISBN #0-936185-21-X $19.95

SCATOLOGY & THE GATE OF LIFE: The Role Of The Large
Intestine In Immunity, An Integrated Chinesse-Western Approach by
Bob Flaws ISBN #0-936185-20-1 $12.95

**CERVICAL DYSPLASIA & PROSTATE CANCER: HPV, A HIDDEN
LINK?** The Diagnosis & Treatment of Cervical Intraepithelial
Neoplasia & Prostate Problems Based On Traditional Chinese
Medical Theory & A Rational, Multimodal Approach to Therapy
Utilizing A Combination of TCM, Western Naturopathy, & Clinical
Ecology by Bob Flaws ISBN #0-936185-19-8 $23.95

**SECOND SPRING: A Guide To Healthy Menopause Through
Traditional Chinese Medicine** by Honora Lee Wolfe ISBN 0-936185-
18-X $12.95

**STICKING TO THE POINT: A Rational Methodology for the Step by
Step Formulation & Administration of an Acupuncture Treatment** by
Bob Flaws ISBN 0-936185-17-1 $14.95

**MIGRAINES & TRADITIONAL CHINESE MEDICINE: A
Layperson's Guide** by Bob Flaws ISBN 0-936185-15-5 $11.95

**ENDOMETRIOSIS & INFERTILITY AND TRADITIONAL CHINESE
MEDICINE: A Laywoman's Guide** by Bob Flaws ISBN 0-936185-14-7
$9.95

**CLASSICAL MOXIBUSTION SKILLS IN CONTEMPORARY
CLINICAL PRACTICE** by Sung Baek ISBN 0-936185-16-3 $10.95

THE BREAST CONNECTION: A Laywoman's Guide to the Treatment of Breast Disease by Chinese Medicine by Honora Lee Wolfe ISBN 0-936185-13-9 $8.95

NINE OUNCES: A Nine Part Program For The Prevention of AIDS in HIV Positive Persons by Bob Flaws ISBN 0-936185-12-0 $8.95

THE TREATMENT OF CANCER BY INTEGRATED CHINESE-WESTERN MEDICINE by Zhang Dai-zhao, trans. by Zhang Ting-liang & Bob Flaws, ISBN 0-936185-11-2 $16.95

BLUE POPPY ESSAYS: 1988 Translations and Ruminations on Chinese Medicine by Bob Flaws, et al, ISBN 0-936185-10-4 $18.95

A HANDBOOK OF TRADITIONAL CHINESE DERMATOLOGY by Liang Jian-hui, trans. by Zhang Ting-liang & Bob Flaws, ISBN 0-936185-07-4 $14.95

SECRET SHAOLIN FORMULAE FOR THE TREATMENT OF EXTERNAL INJURY by Patriarch De Chan, trans. by Zhang Ting-liang & Bob Flaws, ISBN 0-936185-08-2 $12.95

A HANDBOOK OF TRADITIONAL CHINESE GYNECOLOGY by Zhejiang College of TCM, trans. by Zhang Ting-liang, ISBN 0-936185-06-6 $17.95

FREE & EASY: Traditional Chinese Gynecology for American Women 2nd Edition, by Bob Flaws, ISBN 0-936185-05-8 $15.95

PRINCE WEN HUI'S COOK: Chinese Dietary Therapy by Bob Flaws & Honora Lee Wolfe, ISBN 0-912111-05-4, $12.95 (Published by Paradigm Press, Brookline, MA)

TURTLE TAIL & OTHER TENDER MERCIES: Traditional Chinese Pediatrics by Bob Flaws ISBN 0-936185-00-7 $14.95

ABOUT THE AUTHOR

Bob Flaws, DOM, CMT, Dipl.Ac., is an internationally known practitioner of and author on traditional Chinese medicine. He has written, translated, and edited over a dozen books on various aspects of Oriental medicine and numerous articles by Dr. Flaws have appeared in professional journals both in America and abroad. In addition, Dr. Flaws regularly lectures at many of the major American colleges of acupuncture and Oriental medicine and has been an invited speaker at several national and international medical conferences. His other credits include founding Blue Poppy Press.

Dr. Flaws originally studied acupuncture with Dr. Tao Xi-yu and at the Shanghai College of Traditional Chinese Medicine where he also studied Chinese herbal medicine and Tuina Chinese remedial massage. He is a founding member and past member of the Board of Directors of the Acupuncture Association of Colorado, a member of the American Association of Acupuncture and Oriental Medicine, was appointed a Research Associate of the Tibetan Medical Society, and is a graduate of the Boulder School of Massage Therapy. Since 1980, Dr. Flaws has conducted a private practice in traditional Chinese medicine in Boulder, CO.